China's Crisis of Success

China's Crisis of Success provides new perspectives on China's rise to superpower status, showing that China has reached a threshold where success has eliminated the conditions that enabled miraculous growth. Continued success requires reinvention of its economy and politics. The old economic strategy based on exports and infrastructure now piles up debt without producing sustainable economic growth, and Chinese society now resists the disruptive change that enabled earlier reforms. While China's leadership has produced a strategy for successful economic transition, it is struggling to manage the politics of implementing that strategy. After analyzing the economics of growth, William H. Overholt explores critical social issues of the transition, notably inequality, corruption, environmental degradation, and globalization. He argues that Xi Jinping is pursuing the riskiest political strategy of any important national leader. Alternative outcomes include continued impressive growth and political stability, Japanese-style stagnation, and a major political–economic crisis.

WILLIAM H. OVERHOLT is a Senior Fellow at Harvard University. He is the author of a number of books including, most notably, *Asia, America, and the Transformation of Geopolitics* (2008) and *The Rise of China* (1993).

China's Crisis of Success

WILLIAM H. OVERHOLT
Harvard University, Massachusetts

CAMBRIDGE
UNIVERSITY PRESS

CAMBRIDGE
UNIVERSITY PRESS

University Printing House, Cambridge CB2 8BS, United Kingdom

One Liberty Plaza, 20th Floor, New York, NY 10006, USA

477 Williamstown Road, Port Melbourne, VIC 3207, Australia

314-321, 3rd Floor, Plot 3, Splendor Forum, Jasola District Centre, New Delhi - 110025, India

79 Anson Road, #06-04/06, Singapore 079906

Cambridge University Press is part of the University of Cambridge.

It furthers the University's mission by disseminating knowledge in the pursuit of
education, learning and research at the highest international levels of excellence.

www.cambridge.org
Information on this title: www.cambridge.org/9781108431996
DOI: 10.1017/9781108368407

First published 2018

A catalogue record for this publication is available from the British Library

ISBN 978-1-108-42169-0 Hardback
ISBN 978-1-108-43199-6 Paperback

To every thing there is a season, and a time to every purpose under the heaven

Ecclesiastes 3, King James Bible

When you are studying any matter, or considering any philosophy, ask yourself only what are the facts. Never let yourself be diverted either by what you wish to believe, or by what you think would have beneficent social effects if it were believed.

Bertrand Russell, interview about what message he would leave to future generations

Contents

Foreword

China is in a crisis of success. Big success. Big crisis. Like an infant that has outgrown its baby shoes, China must refit itself to its new circumstances. Its old model of growth through exports and infrastructure investment now piles up debt without proportionately valuable economic development. The old model of governance, running the country for growth in the manner of a business in single-minded pursuit of profit, produces side effects for the environment and for people's lives that are no longer acceptable. While China's leadership has produced a wise and open strategy for what they need to do to fix a difficult but manageable economic transition, it is struggling to manage the politics of implementing that strategy and it has not produced a comparably insightful strategy for addressing political issues that are as formidable as the economic challenges.

Western nostrums, which assert a priori that China would have done better if it had been governed more like India or the Philippines, are unpersuasive to anyone who knows the region. But China's successes cannot persist if it continues to be managed the same way it has been – or, worse, if it reverts to some of the bad habits of the Mao Zedong era.

This book analyzes China's current crisis and seeks to illuminate the enduring elements that have shaped China's reform successes and determine China's future options. I detail the crisis, but always in the context of a larger framework: the model of development. The key questions we need to answer about China are as follows.

Why has China been so successful?
Why is it now facing a political–economic crisis?
What are the key issues and non-issues?
What are the principal alternative outcomes?

My answers to these questions vary considerably from what most readers are likely to read elsewhere; of course, the range of views about China is very diverse. Most discussions of China either extoll the country's strengths and project those into the future or focus on its vulnerabilities. This book tries to explore both the strengths and the vulnerabilities – across the economy, the society, and the politics.

Throughout the 1980s I wrote that Deng Xiaoping's reforms would make China a great power again and that Mikhail Gorbachev's reform strategy would destroy the Soviet Union. The basis for that argument was that Deng was emulating strategies that had succeeded in South Korea and Taiwan, and to a lesser extent in Japan and Singapore. Gorbachev was following priorities exactly opposite to those that led to Asian successes. In my mind the only question about Chinese success was whether the strategies of comparatively tiny South Korea and Taiwan could be scaled up. It turns out they can. In 1992 I traveled the length and breadth of China and compiled the main points from a decade of arguments into a book, *The Rise of China: How Economic Reform Is Creating a New Superpower*, published in 1993.

At the time those arguments were the opposite of Western conventional wisdom. The leading review in London said that my bank must have paid me a lot of money to write such nonsense. (Actually, my boss banned me three times from writing the book before finally acquiescing.) The **New York Review of Books** expressed contempt for my assertion that China's superior growth derived from Deng Xiaoping's reforms. The local head of Reuters banned its reporters from interviewing me because I was "too optimistic." (They interviewed me anyway, and told me about the ban, but stopped quoting me.) Gorbachev and his immediate successors, after all, were following a strategy recommended by Americans and Europeans. Deng was doing the opposite, and right-thinking Westerners ridiculed and denounced him, as they had done with Park Chung Hee in South Korea and Jiang Jingguo in Taiwan. It was common to believe, even at the top of the US government, that China was on the verge of collapse.

From the early 1980s these bullish arguments had a good run of nearly three decades. As the end of the third decade approached, I became convinced that the model was diverging from the earlier success stories and that the future was becoming much more uncertain. I assembled early thoughts in "Reassessing China," published in the *Washington Quarterly* in 2012. The time for totally confident predictions was past. Now we need scenarios. That is what this book is all about. The current economic and political turning point could lead to renewed vigor and stability. There is a very serious risk that it will not, at least with the current structure; if not, the ensuing crisis could become very big indeed. Where the Chinese administrations of 1979–2002 tracked the earlier Asian economic takeoffs, the administration of 2003–2012 took a pause for breath, and now the administration of Xi Jinping could, depending on the outcome of a titanic power struggle, be in the process of largely rejecting key lessons of the Asia Model.

The core conviction of *The Rise of China* and the core conviction of this book is that the best way to understand China's past success and future risks is to put it in the context of the other Asian successes. Doing this is remarkably rare both in popular writing and in the academic literature.

My respect for Asian nation-building and economy-building developed the hard way. In my first job, I wrote a draft contribution to a 1973 conference and book arguing that Park Chung Hee's lack of democracy and human rights would lead to instability and thereby hamper economic growth. That's what all right-thinking Americans knew then. My boss at the time, Herman Kahn, with whom I argued about everything, told me he was going to take me to South Korea and rub my nose in it. He did. He also took to introducing me to important people all over the world by saying "This is Bill Overholt. He spent seven years at Harvard and Yale and it just about ruined him. But we're trying to salvage him." On many issues I never agreed with him. As an illustration of our differences, I ran Asia policy and some aspects of human rights and nuclear policy for Jimmy Carter's 1976 campaign (Carter had 19 principal foreign-policy advisors leading task forces in the campaign, under Zbigniew Brzezinski's leadership, and I was one of the 19), while Herman Kahn flirted with Pat Buchanan, whom I viewed as dangerous. But, after Herman had introduced me to South Korea, I wandered all over that country on various occasions, and the ongoing improvement of people's lives, particularly in the rural areas and mountain villages, was so impressive that I sometimes became emotional when lecturing about it. Rarely in human history have people's lives improved so rapidly. I had the opportunity to do the same kinds of studies in Taiwan and found equally moving results.

At the time it was popular among many US scholars to argue that the economic growth rates in these two economies must be falsified; it couldn't possibly be true that these authoritarian states, constantly abusing human rights, were growing 10 percent annually. Decades later, in the 1980s and 1990s, it was similarly common to argue that China must have falsified its growth numbers.[1] Countries run by these authoritarian abusers of human rights just couldn't possibly do so well – according to our Western preconceptions. The preconceptions are exceedingly durable. So has been my curiosity about the contrast between preconceptions and performance.

From the early 1970s to the present I have been writing and speaking about the Asian miracle economies, several near-miracles, and about the implications of these takeoffs for geopolitics and the world economy. The resulting publications are mostly available on my website, www.theoverholtgroup.com.

Traveling to these countries, living in Hong Kong (18 years), the Philippines and Singapore, and trying to understand their successes and failures have led me to shape my work according to certain strong beliefs.

One, the core contribution of this book, is that, to understand any country, you must constantly compare it with other countries. Japan specialists, China specialists, Korea specialists provide indispensable insights. The deep digging that they do is the foundation of everything else we know about their countries. But then we must take our understanding to the next level, the level of comparison. The reason I was able to write *The Rise of China* was that I had spent a quarter century studying the neighbors – Japan, South Korea, Taiwan, Singapore – so I could see that Deng Xiaoping was mostly emulating models that worked extraordinarily well elsewhere. And I could see that Gorbachev's politics-first emphasis, so lauded at the time by US experts, would be a catastrophe because it ignored the Asian lessons.

---

[1] Chinese statistics in the early days were rough guides to the rate of growth. Statistics collection was erratic. There was much adjustment and smoothing at the National Statistics Bureau, most notably because most localities exaggerated their growth in order for the officials to earn promotions. On the other side, most businesses reported much lower growth than reality because they didn't want to pay taxes. Moreover, nearly everyone had an official job, generating income that was in the statistics, and a sideline, typically not in the statistics. For a long time the services economy was drastically underestimated. But anyone with experience in a variety of countries could see by walking around that the growth was roughly proportional to the claims. The independence of the statistics system was strengthened in 2015.

Second, really understanding a country requires demolishing disciplinary boundaries, which are quite arbitrary. The work of political scientists, economists, sociologists, historians in their individual disciplines is of course as indispensable as the work of country specialists. Focusing just on the economy or just on the politics simplifies issues so that one can build theories. But the economy functions within a framework established by politics, and the substance of political action is heavily a struggle over economic resources. The great political scientist Harold Lasswell communicated the intersection best with his book title *Politics: Who Gets What, When, How.* Asian countries stabilized their countries politically by giving their people a rapidly growing economic pie, and they consolidated their domestic and international security through growth that gave them desperately needed resources. There is no economy separate from politics, and no politics separate from the economy, but we mostly have to make up the discipline of political economy as we go along. (Some universities do actually grant degrees in political economy, but there's very little coherent substance to the field.)

Third, scholarly understanding comes best when it is grounded in real problem-solving for specific situations. In all disciplines, academic theorizing can become a cloud floating out of sight of the ground. Economics has benefited from, among many things, intense practical arguments over whether one should raise interest rates a quarter of a percent. Keynes wanted to get the world out of a depression. Good theories grow out of real problems. Political science is at its most valid trying to figure out how to get another 1 percent of the voters to vote for a candidate. Things go wrong when we fetishize a method rather than focusing on specific issues. For instance, teaching graduate students that their job is to find things to run regressions on can impede a discipline for half a century – which is exactly what has happened.

With grounded thinking, one goes and sees. One believes first in the evidence of the eyeballs. Economists are correct that anecdotes are not evidence, but when everything you see during a systematic personal investigation contradicts the literature, then the eyeballs must dominate. As a young bank risk analyst in the early 1980s I was sent to do a country risk study of Indonesia. The most influential literature said Indonesia was in terrible shape and getting worse. I visited many areas. Everywhere I went the women had decent clothes, the children no longer had the big bellies of kwashiorkor, men were going to work

on motorcycles rather than on bicycle or foot. It turned out the literature was driven by a Cornell professor who had studied declining
employment in the villages and deduced dire consequences and by an
Australian economist. The Cornell professor later recanted; he had
neglected to look at the towns, where burgeoning employment was
creating higher incomes. The Australian turned out to be a member of
the Indonesian Communist Party who was spreading disinformation.
Some disaffected political science professors had spread the erroneous
economic news widely.

Wandering around China in the 1990s provided a direct analogue of
that Indonesian experience. There has always been a debate about
whether Chinese statistics underestimate or overestimate the size of
China's economy. As noted in a footnote above, on the one hand, we
know that the performance incentive system leads almost every locality
to overestimate its growth. On the other hand, services are under-
counted and businesses underreport their performance to evade taxes.
Almost everyone one meets, from ministers to bottom-level factory
managers, has an official job, whose salary is in the statistics, and a
sideline, which typically isn't, and often the substantial income comes
from the sideline. The statistics bureau makes mighty efforts to correct
for localities' exaggerated growth reports; that is why the sum of
reported provincial GDPs has always been so much greater than the
reported national GDP. Wandering around China and other countries
at similar levels of development, seeing how people lived, it was
obvious the people were living much better than the statistics indicated.

A particularly vivid contrast between grounded and non-grounded
research can be found in the chapter on Chinese politics below. I lived
in Hong Kong for 18 years and had many opportunities to explore
China and speak, sometimes negotiate, sometimes argue with Chinese
officials. The subjects ranged from agriculture development to cleaning
up the water supply to business arbitration mechanisms to trade negotiations with the United States to internationalizing the renminbi
(RMB) to governance at the Asian Infrastructure Investment Bank to
correcting oversupply in cotton spinning and a list of other topics that
would fill a chapter of this book. I can't think of one official who
wasn't worried about meeting his or her official performance goals.
That goes for Zhu Rongji, for Bo Xilai (who was desperate in
2010 about a financial shortfall), and everyone right down to local
mayors and university Party Secretaries. I wandered around much of

China and even in the poorest provinces the roads, airports, and wireless communications infrastructure were superior to their US counterparts. What then does one make of a political science literature that claims to prove that officials are promoted without regard to competence or performance? Are Chinese officials all afflicted by a false consciousness that leads them to think their performance matters when it actually doesn't? Can China's extraordinary infrastructure and growth all be the product of 70 million utterly incompetent corrupt louts? Of course, having noticed that the grass is green, one has to figure out how "sophisticated" statistical methodologies have led to the conclusion that it is orange, but the important part is to keep one's eyes open.

Ideology is the great enemy of grounded thinking. At Columbia University Zbigniew Brzezinski ran a Wednesday lunch seminar for leading thinkers. In a not-unusual example, a noted East German professor explained to us that, because East Germany and other East European countries were run for the whole people, the environment in East Germany was treated with far greater care than in blighted West Germany. His theoretical presentation was coherent and passionately argued. The problem with his theory, as all were able to see when the wall came down, was that in actuality the East German environment was devastated compared with democratic West Germany. If you went and looked, you could cut through all the theoretical nonsense.

That's hilarious and seemingly incomprehensible when it's someone else's ideology. But throughout the West professors teach, and students diligently memorize, that democracy in very poor countries will, through electoral competition and free media, solve or reduce corruption. When one actually functions in politics in Thailand or the Philippines, as I have, one learns that very poor people can't organize themselves to defend their interests and can't contribute to political campaigns, so the only political contributions are bribes plus a few personal investments in future office intended to earn a return. Democratic elections in such places are not a cure for corruption but rather a particular form of corruption. Misguided ideological preconceptions like these have consequences, sometimes fatal ones. It is worth recalling the sense of victory of Bush and Cheney when finally an election was held in Afghanistan or Iraq, or of Hillary Clinton when the Arab Spring led to elections. Finally, all will be well! Peace and prosperity are imminent! If neurosis is doing the same thing over and over and expecting it to have different consequences, then ideology – including our ideology – is often a form of neurosis.

Closely related to this, a fourth lesson is always to look for, and explore, anomalies. Anomalies are weird things that don't work out the way normal things do, or that work very differently from what our preconceptions say should happen. When I found that South Korea was working so differently from everything I'd been taught, I became obsessed with understanding why. Similarly, my first exposure to Asia was in the Philippines in the early 1960s, when the Philippines was not only the perfect third-world democracy but also superior to all other developing countries on every economic index but one (railroads). As a graduate student I wrote a book about that, and got it accepted for publication by Yale University Press, then became uneasy about it and shelved it. When I lived in the Philippines in 1963, every family of substance had an *amah* from impoverished Hong Kong to cook, clean, and watch over their children. By the time I lived in Hong Kong (1985–2001 and 2013–2015), even the secretaries had a *filipina* from the now relatively impoverished Philippines to cook and clean. From such anomalies one learns.

Or one doesn't. Writers who want to preserve their ideological preconceptions resort to characteristic modes of thought. If the nearly perfect Philippine democracy produced bad results, it must have been that bad guys messed it up. The problem was Ferdinand Marcos, who appears in such thinking as a deus ex machina. Certainly Marcos was a bad guy; I nearly lost my life fighting him, and my two best Philippine friends did lose their lives. But why did Filipinos rally around him at first? And why, after the best corruption-fighting democratic President with the highest economic growth rates (Benigno Aquino III, President 2010–2016), did a cruder version of Marcos, a homicidal rogue named Rodrigo Duterte who became president just as I was finishing this book, gain similar adulation? Why, given the wonderful qualities of a system designed to be of the people, by the people, for the people, do the actual people – of the Philippines, of Thailand, of many other places – so consistently feel themselves ignored and abused that they turn to dictators or homicidal rogues who promise to rescue them? I provide some answers in the politics chapter below.

Above all, my most important lesson from decades of wandering in Asia has been to focus on what happens to real people not the GDP; not the rich people but the farmers, workers, and middle class. This is not just about theory. It is about fundamental values. Are people living longer? Are they healthy? Do the mothers die in childbirth and the children succumb to diarrhea? Are they safe? Do they have good food? Do they have a place to live? Can they read? Do they have wide access to ideas and information? Are they free to choose their job, their location, their spouse? Are men and women treated with comparable respect? Are they free to move around? Does everyone have a reasonable chance to become prosperous or influential? Do they feel their life chances are fair? Can people speak their minds? Can they promote their interests? These are the ends. Everything else is instrumental. Communism, democracy, parties, unions, NGOs, parliaments, GDP growth, GDP per capita, indices of inequality, movements ... are means to an end. But the means are often fetishized in our thinking and we come to regard them as the ends. Unions are a perfect example; in some contexts they are essential to both income and worker safety but in others they inhibit growth and create a worker elite at the expense of mass unemployment and impoverishment. When one insistently digs beneath the means, and focuses on the fundamental conditions of life, no system is perfect and *all* ideologies are embarrassed, including our own. No system works the same way, or has the same consequences, in all social contexts.

A lifetime of studying and working in these countries has convinced me that the Asian miracle model works only under very limited conditions. There is no Beijing Consensus that is widely applicable. Likewise, transplanting Western electoral and judicial systems into the poorest countries often just legitimizes social oppression. The Washington Consensus often leads to mass misery and political instability. If some of the analysis that leads to such conclusions puts heavy demands on the reader, I hope that the importance of the conclusions justifies the effort. The illusions about a nonexistent Beijing Consensus and a practicable Washington Consensus form the basis of a remarkable amount of high-level foreign-policy thinking; if these are wrong, we need to know it. They are wrong.

In addition to the highly focused specialists, and in addition to those who do global statistical studies, we need synthesis, trying to weave the specialist studies into patterns. That is what I do. The task requires both hubris and humility. Nobody can master all that is known in several disciplines and about several countries. A historian of the economy of Ming China can master virtually everything that has been written about his or her subject. I can't master all the economics and politics and social and military issues of China and its neighbors. I am always conscious of, and anxious about, all the things I haven't read yet. But somebody has to cross the boundaries. The weakness of the specialist is that he or she lacks context. The weakness of the synthesizer is that he or she may miss important details or perspectives. We need both. I am encouraged by the fact that some of my controversial predictions have come true and some of my practical work, based on my understandings, has borne fruit. I am humble in awareness of how much I don't know and can only hope my work will provoke more refined studies that will move us forward.

There are peculiarities of each discipline that one can overcome by looking through the eyes of multiple disciplines. To take just one example, political scientists are under enormous pressure to use regression analysis, a technique for showing how one thing (e.g., education levels) is related to another (e.g., economic growth). To get promoted, you have to publish in leading journals; and to get published in leading journals, you have to do some regression analyses. In the hands of economists, regressions are enormously fruitful, because economists have refined their concepts and persuaded governments to spend tens of billions of dollars cumulatively creating valid databases. For political scientists they are also very useful in studies of voting behavior in Western elections, because there is an existing and natural database (votes, polls, ethnic groups, income levels, education levels, employment status . . .). In analyzing emerging countries' politics, there are few issues that satisfy the assumptions underlying regression analysis and there are hardly any valid databases for the concepts. So we get regression studies that use whatever data happen to be available, with little thought to validity, and this leads to results that can be the exact opposite of the truth. Some US academicians' studies of the Chinese government promotion system, addressed in the chapter on the Chinese governance model, are the perfect example.

There is in fact an amusing analogy between the problems of Chinese officials and problems in some academic disciplines. When a Chinese mayor is pressured to produce growth through investment after most fruitful construction investment opportunities have been exhausted, he or she may build a giant hotel in a small town, spending four dollars to produce one dollar of growth – thereby subtracting from the economy's future prospects. When political scientists are published and promoted for doing regressions where no valid regressions are possible, their regressions may subtract from the sum of human knowledge.

Modern political science has been more successful at characterizing the qualitative evolution of institutions and of relations among them. For China, political scientists and economists have steadily increased clarity about the Party, the state, the military, the state-owned enterprises (SOEs) and relations among them.[2] Likewise we have learned a good deal about social stresses and how the regime manages them[3] and how the regime responds to particular social challenges like rapid urbanization.[4]

Specializing in a single country has created knowledge of enormous depth, particularly for China studies. But it sometimes leaves specialists vulnerable. As I note in the discussion of corruption, Western political experts on China frequently believe that its corruption problems are so severe because of its communist system and that they would improve if China became more democratic. But these analysts seem never to reflect on the fact that such evolution would make China more like India and the Philippines, where corruption has far more destructive consequences. Likewise with much of Western thinking about environmental issues in China; as soon as one puts the issues in comparative perspective (India's pollution is more damaging to human health) everything looks different.

On issues like corruption, the environment, and the Chinese government promotion system, there are schools of scholars who have reached something like a workable consensus. After I did a blog post that became the first draft of the corruption section of this book, one senior scholar, for whom I have the greatest respect, publicly rebuked me for not understanding that there is a professional consensus that the seriousness of China's corruption problems results from its communist

---

[2] An outstanding example is Zheng Yongnian and Weng Cuipen, "The Development of China's Formal Political Structures," in Robert Ross and Jo Ing Beekevold, eds., *China in the Era of Xi Jinping: Domestic and Foreign Policy Challenges* (Washington, DC: Georgetown University Press, 2016), pp. 32–65.

[3] See Joseph Fewsmith, "The Challenges of Stability and Legitimacy," in Robert Ross and Jo Ing Beekevold, eds., *China in the Era of Xi Jinping: Domestic and Foreign Policy Challenges* (Washington, DC: Georgetown University Press, 2016), pp. 92–113.

[4] Shahid Yusuf and Anthony Saich, *China Urbanizes: Consequences, Strategies and Policies* (Washington, DC: World Bank, 2008).

system. I do understand this consensus and others. I think – emphatically – that they are wrong. The strategy of this book is to take the consensus, subtract the ideological bias, ignore the methodological fetishes, and add systematic comparisons with neighboring countries. The result is quite different, sometimes opposite. I ask readers to keep this formula in mind; they can then judge its value.

The difference between what I am trying to accomplish and what many good academic scholars do is typified by the section on corruption. I published a summary of my overview of corruption issues, later incorporated in this book, in 2015. In early 2016, Hualing Fu's superb essay, which I have cited in the corruption section below, became available. To understand how corruption is fought in China his work is absolutely indispensable. The accumulation of scholarship like his is what makes broader views possible and also what makes it possible to test views like mine. But these days we are short of analyses that cut across disciplines and across countries, so I make an effort to fill that gap. Likewise, Minxin Pei's analysis of the special way that corruption works in China (a book that also came out in 2016) will long be essential reading for anyone who wants to understand China, but its lack of comparative perspective can lead to facile generalizations about democracies and autocracies.

Since I cannot know everything, this book does not try to cover everything important about Chinese development. I have tried to focus on what is decisive for the present and crucial for the future – and particularly on issues where I think I have some value to add. I have deliberately neglected issues, including important issues, that I have written about elsewhere and those that I judge will not be decisive for China's future.

I have chosen to write with a voice that I hope speaks to a broad audience. In physics and biology there is sound reason to write about quarks and mitochondria, terms that are incomprehensible to the general public. Although there is plenty of jargon in academic writing about China, no such excuse is valid for any of the subjects addressed here. One leading scholar cringed at my labeling of the Chinese administrative system as the "GE Model." Well, I could have used or invented some polysyllable that readers would have had to look up in a thesaurus, but I think the phrase communicates what needs to be communicated and the metaphor's limitations are obvious.

Chinese, Japanese, and Korean names follow their national custom in having the family name first, e.g., Mao Zedong, Abe Shinzō, and Park Chung Hee. Chinese names are transcribed in pinyin (e.g., Jiang Jingguo), except where most potential readers are more likely to be familiar with a traditional spelling (e.g., Chiang Kai-shek, father of Jiang Jingguo) or where an author or other person uses a preferred transliteration.

I write as an American who is proud of US democracy and strength. But I try very hard to be objective and balanced, and some of my conclusions will upset fellow Westerners. I listen very closely when I speak with Japanese, Chinese, Korean, and Filipino thinkers. This leads to different angles on US policy – as well as on Japan and China. One of the incalculable benefits of being an American is that one is free to criticize one's own country's ideology and policies. Proper patriots of all major countries will be offended by some of the views in this book. If so, maybe I've got it about right.

Most Western media commentary on Asia, and much scholarly analysis, is ultimately rooted in images of good guys fighting bad guys. Park Chung Hee, ruthless authoritarian, was seen in the United States as a bad guy, a really really bad guy. Read the **New York Times** of 1976. But he saved his country, made his people prosperous, and created the social foundations for what later became one of the emerging world's two most successful democracies. Wandering around rural Korea and seeing people lifted from sub-human poverty and illiteracy into decent lives, I came to revere Park Chung Hee (President of South Korea, 1961–1979), but I visited Kim Dae Jung (Korea's leading dissident during Park's presidency and later President) every time I could when I was in Korea, notwithstanding severe Korean CIA efforts to intimidate me; eventually I risked my career to save him from execution. They were both good guys, but their country needed different skills at different times. The quote from Ecclesiastes that I have placed at the beginning of this book is an invocation to ideological humility.

Theologians call this division into good guys and bad guys Manicheanism. The Manicheans saw everything as starkly divided into good and evil. Americans tend to see the world that way. China is bad because its government is authoritarian. India is good because it elects its leaders. But the justification for democracy is a conception of human dignity, and human conditions in India are so much worse than in China that there can be no serious argument for Indian superiority based on human dignity. Yes, that malnourished, illiterate, 12-year-old girl, whose mother died in childbirth because Indian healthcare for the poor is so much worse, and whose father is crippled by air pollution far more debilitating than China's, who has never seen a toilet, and who was forcibly married to an old man, will have the right to vote, but is that really what is most important to her human dignity? The number of Chinese who own homes is almost twice the number of Indians who have access to a toilet. To feel the difference, go to Mumbai and walk through the slums, then visit Shanghai. Or read Katherine Boo.

Conversely, it is inappropriate to judge India by Asian miracle standards. As this book will emphasize time and again, the system that has led to such wonderful growth in South Korea, Taiwan, Singapore, and China could not possibly work in most countries, including India. This book will have numerous comparisons between China and India. The point is not to disparage India, which is growing well by historical standards, indeed a multiple of the 2 percent that Britain achieved in the industrial revolution and ever since, but rather to highlight the hypocrisy of those who claim to advocate a philosophy based on human dignity but in fact denounce the countries that are doing the most wonderful things for human dignity (South Korea, Taiwan, and Singapore in 1970, China in 2000), while praising countries that condemn most of their people to short, brutal, abused lives but go through the rituals of Western-style elections (India, the Philippines, Thailand, and Cambodia during their democratic periods).

Similarly, in the current popular US view Japan is a good democracy and China is an evil dictatorship. In the American conception, the conception on which policy is based, the difference between the two is night and day. Of course, Japan is indeed much freer and much more democratic. But both are dominant-party systems, created – in Japan's case with CIA help – to ensure that the opposition parties are hapless. (China has eight very tame opposition parties.) Japan's polity, like its economy, is of course far more developed and subtle. The opposition parties in Japan even have had two chances to briefly gain the prime ministership, but during such evanescent interludes they quickly trip and fall while real power over both the economy and national security continues to reside with the deep LDP government. Few Americans know that 99.8 percent of those arrested in Japan are found guilty – a slightly higher percentage than in China – and fewer still, including many professional Japan specialists, know how those convictions are obtained. The way the United States and the Japanese right collaborated to create and institutionalize a system with an overwhelmingly dominant party that could ram through economic reforms and consolidate the United States–Japan alliance does not feature in most studies of Japanese politics. One of my early assignments as a consultant was to analyze whether there was any residual risk that the opposition might win – and implicitly whether there was any need for the United States to provide some additional weight on the conservative side of the scales. In the common Manichean view, such things are conveniently forgotten.

As I write, senior advisors to the Chinese leadership, who recognize that Japan's polity is one potential ideal for China, are in Japan studying ways to import some of the sophistication of Japan's dominant-party system. We need to think in terms of spectra. On the spectrum from totalitarianism (0) to full competitive democracy (100), one might rate Khmer Rouge Cambodia as 0, Mao's China 10, today's China 50, Japan 75, Hungary and Poland 80, India 80, South Korea and Taiwan 95. Intriguingly, Western media are very hard on the leaders of Hungary and Poland, who are pushing their countries to be more like Japan, but they are much softer on Japan's Prime Minister Abe Shinzō, whose country is more authoritarian than Hungary and Poland and is openly determined to make it substantially more authoritarian. We Westerners are quicker to apply caricatures to Asian countries.

Americans' perceptions of who is good and who is evil periodically reverse.[5] For some periods of history Japan was the bad guy and China was the good guy. During the period before and during World War II Americans believed that Chiang Kai-shek stood for democracy, and they read uncritically the most influential US anthropologist of that time, Ruth Benedict, who taught that authoritarianism and other evil traits were inherent in Japanese culture because of Japanese child-rearing practices. Now Japan is the good guy and China evil. Scholars

---

[5] For deep insights into the peculiarities of mutual perceptions, see Akira Iriye, *Across the Pacific* (Chicago, IL: Harcourt Brace, 1967). More recently, James Bradley has taken up some of these themes in *The China Mirage: The Hidden History of American Disaster in Asia* (New York: Little Brown, 2016).

with distinguished titles tell us that the only thing that holds China's Communist Party together and generates Chinese growth is corruption. The US national security elite particularly embraces strong ties to Prime Minister Abe and his deputy (and former Prime Minister) Asō Tarō, who lead a movement that blames the United States for World War II, seek to move their country away from democratic ideals, and seek eventually to free Japan from dependence on the United States. Caricatured images distort our perception and lead to policy errors that waste resources and create gratuitous conflict.

Black and white make for easy, bad policy decisions. It is embarrassing to read about the old caricatures; how could anybody have taken seriously the view of Chiang Kai-shek, a proud Leninist, as standing for democracy? It would be convenient to believe that our predecessors were just dumber than ourselves, but I haven't found any evidence of that. It will be embarrassing for future generations to read about our caricatures, particularly if those caricatures prove fatal for some of our military-age children.

Manicheanism particularly affects swaths of contemporary political science, and particularly some studies of China. There is now a whole literature that contrasts democracies with authoritarian countries, in other words good guys and bad guys. Almost the entire literature is nonsense. Democracies include Philippine extractive peasant democracy, Japanese dominant-party rule and the UK middle-class multi-party system; their dynamics are utterly different. Lumping theocracies (Iran), ethnic dictatorships, Latin American caudillos, African tribal kleptocracies, totalitarian systems (North Korea), disintegrating empires (Soviet Union), Asian economic mobilization systems, and others together in a single category of "authoritarian countries" makes no analytic sense. It leads to all sorts of false conclusions, including for instance articles in leading policy journals (**Foreign Affairs, The National Interest**) asserting that democracies consistently outperform non-democracies in economic growth (conclusions authoritatively refuted by more careful analyses, usually done by economists). It leads inter alia to the false generalization, addressed in this book's chapter on the Chinese political system, that authoritarian systems like China generally appoint less competent people because of insecurity at the top – a description that is the exact opposite of what happens in China and a perfect description of Japan (particularly in the first decade of this century) and other democracies. In fact, Trump's cabinet and

Obama's choice of ambassadors (to Japan, the most important US ally, and many other places) are the perfect counterexamples. This reflects a more general problem: much of Western social science has become profoundly ideological and this ideological thinking is now so deeply entrenched that it is largely unconscious.

Because the Asian miracle political economies don't work the way Western ideology says they are supposed to work, they attract extreme positions, playing into the Manichean mentality. Gordon Chang, long a favorite of Congressional China haters, predicted in *The Coming Collapse of China* (2001) that the Chinese regime would collapse within five to ten years. Each year he updates the prediction to give it a little more time. At the opposite extreme, journalist James Mann tells us that anyone who emphasizes developmental pressures for liberalizing change in Chinese politics has sold out for Chinese lucre. We heard the same things a generation ago about South Korea and Taiwan. Those who pointed out the positive transformations of people's lives in Taiwan and South Korea during the 1970s were frequently called fascist militarists. Those who pointed out the similar positive transformations in China in the early days were called panda huggers. I have been called both, repeatedly and loudly. I may well be called worse after people read this book. What I care about is people living longer, being fed and clothed, getting educated, and (albeit from a low base) eventually living freer personal lives.

So far, none of the Asian miracle societies has ever collapsed, despite predictions at the time that each would. However, all have had major bumps in the road, and all have had to continuously transform their economic, social and political structures. China is unlikely to collapse, but it is undergoing the latest stressful structural transformation and is at increasing risk of a severe bump in the road. The regime in 2017 is fearfully, frenetically combating the liberalizing pressures of feminists, environmentalists, NGOs, religious groups, students who want full internet access, human rights lawyers, professors, publishers, farmers who want to be compensated for their land, entrepreneurs who resent Party exactions and unfair constraints on their access to resources, and many others. At the same time, it is trying to implement an economic reform that will damage the interests of every powerful group in China. In the spirit of the Chinese curse "May you live in interesting times," this has put China's leadership in an interesting position, which the leaders have made even more interesting by simultaneously alienating the foreign business community and challenging China's maritime neighbors and the US Navy.

As China seeks to cope with its crisis of success, it has tremendous strengths and tremendous weaknesses. That makes for a complicated book. I want the reader to comprehend these weaknesses and strengths fully, so I have to lead the reader through the evidence on a myriad points. *We must understand why China has been successful. We must also understand why its current crisis could prove ominous if mishandled.* To gain such understanding, we have to explore contradictory economic, social, and political trends and we need to dig deep. This is complicated. The benefit of working through the complications is that we can eliminate the caricatures and equip the reader to make her own judgments while the news is moving fast.

Successful economic modernization eliminates the kind of fear that once energized the economic miracle economies. It replaces relatively simple economies and polities with immensely complex ones. Economic and political complexity are two sides of the same coin; the rise of large, rich, efficiently organized economic sectors is the same as the rise of large, rich, powerful interest groups with conflicting interests of immense complexity. Chinese leaders have recognized, albeit sometimes more in theory than action, that the only effective, efficient response to economic complexity is to delegate from the state to the market a dominant role over resource allocation. What is the best way to manage political complexity? Successful leaders, faced with an incoming tide, seek to channel it rather than to push it back.

In William Makepeace Thackeray's famous poem about King Canute, the king orders the incoming tide to retreat:

From the sacred shore I stand on, I command thee to retreat; Venture not, thou stormy rebel, to approach thy master's seat: Ocean, be thou still! I bid thee come not nearer to my feet!

Perhaps Thackeray was a closet political economist.

Acknowledgments

A volume like this owes so much to so many that no acknowledgments could ever be adequate.

This research was supported by a generous grant from the Smith Richardson Foundation, to which I am extraordinarily grateful. I also have to give special thanks for their patience because at the beginning of the grant I was suddenly offered an opportunity to help manage a think tank in Hong Kong; that two-year hiatus aided my research but hindered my writing timetable.

My deepest debts are to participants in dozens of conferences, mostly in China, mostly held under Chatham House rules. I am likewise indebted to an ongoing series of presentations at Harvard University, sponsored by various institutes, but most notably the Critical Choices for Contemporary China weekly series that has been managed chiefly by Ezra Vogel, with support from William Hsiao and myself.

I am grateful to Harvard University, particularly the Ash Center of the Kennedy School under Anthony Saich, and the Asia Center under Arthur Kleinman, for their willingness to harbor an unconventional thinker. In a busy and risk-filled life, the gift of time to reflect and to systematize is a luxury beyond price. I owe more to Harvard, and in particular to Ezra Vogel, than I know how to express.

I also have debts to colleagues at the Fung Global Institute, where I was honored to serve as president, particularly to Victor Fung, Andrew Sheng, and Patrick Low but also to other researchers, as well as to the research teams at Li and Fung.

Cui Cui Chen provided valuable research assistance, as did Paris Sanders and Jenny Wang. Chen Yang, a Chinese sociologist based in Hong Kong, provided research on Chinese housing. Merrick (Lex) Berman kindly created a map of provincial economic weights (Figure 3.2), a task more technically complex to do precisely than I would previously have imagined.

I am grateful for detailed comments by Ezra Vogel, William Ascher, Pieter Bottelier, David Dapice, Susan Shirk, Roderick Mac-Farquhar, Tony Saich, Michael Szonyi and others. They provided me with many insights and saved me from many errors. Their comments totally reshaped the book; having said that, they do not all agree with everything said in this book. Whatever foolishness remains is mine alone.

I have drawn parts of this book from the following previously published articles.

"Japan's Inexorable Decline," *The International Economy*, Autumn 2010, pp. 26–29.

"The China Model," **Fudan Journal of Humanities and Social Sciences**, June 2011, pp. 1–18.

"Reassessing China: Awaiting Xi Jinping," **The Washington Quarterly** 35(2), Spring 2012, pp. 121–137.

"The Battle for China's Soul: The New Politics of Rock, Paper, Scissors," *The International Economy*, Spring 2012, pp. 46–47, www.international-economy.com/TIE_Sp12_Overholt.pdf.

"China's New Leaders: Conservative Immobility or Streamlined Decisions?," PacNet 78, November 28, 2012, http://csis.org/files/publication/121128_Pac1278_0.pdf.

"China's New Reforms in Theory and Practice," Project Syndicate, November 15, 2013, www.project-syndicate.org/commentary/william-h–overholt-examines-the-economic-and-political-implications-of-the-chinese-authorities–latest-market-oriented-changes.

"China's Xi Factor," Project Syndicate, December 16, 2013, www.project-syndicate.org/commentary/william-h–overholt-traces-thee-origins-of-xi-jinping-s-rise-to-power-in-china.

"Revive Multilateralism or Fail Global Development," East Asia Forum, February 19, 2014, www.eastasiaforum.org/2014/02/19/revive-multilateralism-or-fail-global-development/.

"The Four Arrows of Abenomics," *Nikkei Asian Review*, September 24, 2014, http://asia.nikkei.com/Viewpoints/Perspectives/William-Overholt-The-four-arrows-of-Abenomics.

"Policymakers Need to Recognize That the Clock Is Ticking," *Nikkei Asian Review*, November 27, 2014, http://overholtgroup.com/media/Articles-Japan/Clock-is-Ticking-NikkeiAsianReview-27NOV2014.pdf.

"Will the Dollar Remain the Reserve Currency?," *The International Economy*, Fall 2014, www.international-economy.com/TIE_F14_ReserveCurrencySymp.pdf.

"China's Corruption Problem," *East Asia Quarterly* 7(2), June 2015. Subsequently republished in condensed web form at www.eastasiaforum.org/2015/09/15/the-politics-of-chinas-anti-corruption-campaign/.

Duterte, Democracy, and Defense," Brookings Institution, January 2017, www.brookings.edu/research/duterte-democracy-and-defense/.

"Cartoonish Sketches of China As a Villain," book review of Stein Ringen, *A Perfect Dictatorship*, in *GlobalAsia*, March 2017, www.globalasia.org/bbs/board.php?bo_table=articles&wr_id=9188.

"The Great Betrayal: How U.S. Elites Are Failing to Confront the Realities of Trade Politics," *The International Economy*, Winter 2017, www.international-economy.com/TIE_W17_Overholt.pdf.

Introduction

China has reached another of the great turning points in its history. Because it constitutes such a large proportion of humanity this means that our world has reached a turning point.

We need to understand the Chinese regime as a system, a political–economic–social system or model. The "China Model" is a variation of the Asia Model, a collection of strategies pursued by the other Asian miracle economies. China[1] has succeeded by emulating its predecessors (Japan, South Korea, Taiwan, Singapore) and now faces similar challenges. The current leadership has cut loose from emulation of the predecessors, but we can triangulate China's choices by recalling how others faced the same challenges.

The Asia Model is a political–economic strategy for achieving rapid development, social stability and national security based on an initial obsessive priority for economic growth. It comprises tough imposition of radical economic and social changes by an authoritarian leadership, which is motivated by leaders fearful of catastrophic collapse and supported by a population fearful of catastrophic societal collapse. It entails an early decisive downgrading of emphasis on political ideology and geopolitical ambition in order to give overwhelming priority to economic growth. Its economic strategy involves strong central planning and control gradually giving way to a more open and market-oriented economy. As fear gives way to confidence and simplicity gives

---

[1] Throughout this book, I will frequently refer to "China" or "India," rather than "the current communist regime in China" or "the current electoral regime in India." This is a common ellipsis, although "China" can refer to the physical country, the Chinese people, or the current regime. In Western literature some writers insist on carefully differentiating every time between China the regime and China the people. The distinction is absolutely correct, but the intention is virtually always clear from context and the insistence on underlining the distinction in the case of China, but not in the cases of countries like India, is a subtle way of communicating that the Chinese system is less legitimate or less permanent. I reject that derogatory usage.

1

way to complexity, the model can remain successful only by evolving into a much more market-oriented economy and a much less centrally managed polity.

The Asia Model, which ignores the shibboleths of Western theories of economic and political development, provides the fastest way yet discovered to improve the livelihoods of a society's people, stabilize its domestic politics, and enhance its national security. Rather than acknowledge this, most Western writers have denounced the successive places – South Korea, Taiwan, and Singapore, now China, and even to a lesser extent Malaysia and Indonesia – that followed the early part of this path to development. Western scholars have mostly recommended giving politics priority over economics, administering economic and political shock therapy rather than incrementalism, copying Western-style elections and courts in the poorest societies, eschewing detailed economic planning, setting up Western-style unions everywhere, eschewing strongly egalitarian redistribution, and so forth. But the Asian miracle economies, which do the opposite of these things, grow faster, improve the lives of their citizens faster, stabilize their polities faster, and improve working conditions faster than the preferred Western alternatives. The rapid emergence of an educated middle-class society also creates superior foundations for stable democracy, if that alternative is tried as it was in South Korea and Taiwan, although it provides no assurance that it will be tried.

The lesson of the smaller Asian miracles is that the fastest path so far invented for a poor country to achieve a successful capitalist democracy begins with Leninism in politics and socialism in economics. The ironies of the real world confound all ideologies.

The Asia Model has numerous variations. South Korea used big, Japanese-style conglomerates, Taiwan a plethora of smaller, more specialized firms. Singapore is tiny, China huge, and social control techniques that work well in tiny Singapore (for instance detailed scrutiny to stop people from urinating in apartment elevators) often don't work in China – to the distress of Chinese leaders like Li Peng who have favored the Singaporean version. In Japan, the trust essential to successful business is based on corporate relations; in China it is based on family and personal connections. But just as the wide-ranging differences among capitalist countries do not obscure some common themes, and the variations among electoral democracies do not eliminate some common themes, Asia Model variations do not contradict the common themes mentioned above that give them common successes and shared problems.

At the same time, detailed scrutiny of the preconditions of the Asian miracle economies shows that the model is applicable only to a very limited group of countries and is viable only for a limited period of time in those countries. The fallacy that the Asia Model is inherently unstable because of lack of democracy in the early phases is mirrored by two other fallacies: that the methods of the early mobilization phase can be effective indefinitely; and also that there is a Beijing Consensus that is widely applicable internationally. As we shall see, neither the nonexistent "Beijing Consensus"[2] nor the regrettably existent Washington Consensus works in most poor countries. China knows that its model is not universally applicable and wisely refrains from proselytizing it. The West has not been so wise and therefore makes three errors: it is inordinately fearful that China's success might lead other countries to emulate China; it projects early Japanese or Chinese success into inevitable world domination; and it believes against all evidence that the Western-approved model can work everywhere.

In China's crisis of success, the intensity of the crisis is proportionate to the scale of the success. The Chinese economy must transition to a new model in more ways than have been widely understood – as will be elaborated on in the next chapter. The required transition may be the most complex in history. In response, Chinese leaders have formulated the most impressive economic plan in history. But the implementation of that brilliant plan depends on a successful political strategy. Xi Jinping's administration has chosen to take on every major power group in Chinese society simultaneously, at two levels. First, the economic reforms seriously damage the interests of every power group. Second, the anti-corruption campaign, which began as a lever to impose the reforms despite the implacable resistance of China's most powerful interest groups, frightens those who are needed to implement reform, often immobilizing them, and also damages the interests of every major power group. This is the polar opposite of the strategies of

---

[2] The term Beijing Consensus was popularized by Stefan Halper, *The Beijing Consensus: Legitimizing Authoritarianism in Our Time* (New York: Basic Books, 2010). Many writers use the term to signify proselytization in the manner that Western countries have proselytized electoral democracy and abrupt deregulation of economies. Under Mao Zedong China made the mistake of proselytizing a universal ideological nostrum and, at great cost, learned its lesson.

leaders like Deng Xiaoping and Mustafa Kemal Atatürk, who picked selective targets and then pivoted to other targets. Xi Jinping's political approach is the most risky political strategy being implemented by any leader of an important country anywhere in the world.

The political risks are compounded by a strategy of responding to social mobilization, a phenomenon that occurs in every successful economy, by suppressing it. So far, this has never worked anywhere else for a long period of time.

The possibility of China's responding to this new phase of development with forms of Western-style electoral democracy as the other Asian miracle countries did has diminished for both domestic and international reasons. Domestically, this is a period of hubris when much of the leadership thinks that everything is possible and that the Chinese system has demonstrated an ability to rise to the economic and corruption challenges without fundamental political reconsideration. The cosmopolitan leaders Deng Xiaoping and Zhu Rongji, who studied South Korea, Taiwan, and Singapore so carefully for clues to success, have given way to a top leadership that doesn't think it needs to undertake such study and probably hasn't done it (although scholars and officials a few tiers down have).

Internationally the Global Financial Crisis of 2008–2009 convinced many in China that the West provides a deeply flawed economic model, and the demagoguery of the 2016 US election campaign and the 2016 British Brexit campaign have devalued Western political models. Finally, the hostile, subversive US ideological posture toward China, and its confrontational military posture, have given political liberalization the color of national defeat and thereby made it less likely. All this is understandable, but there remains the fact – a hard fact – that the structure of Chinese society has changed in ways that are as challenging politically as they are economically and the leadership has not yet complemented brilliant economic plans with incisive political plans.

The current leadership's strategy carries two formidable risks. One is that massive resistance to economic reform could lead to an analogue of stagnation in Japan, where key interest groups effectively took ownership of the government and protected their interests against vitally needed structural reform.[3] This could occur even though China

[3] Throughout this book I shall make frequent reference to Japanese stagnation, loss of competitiveness and the roots in interest group politics. For my understanding

has a much more competitive economy and more cosmopolitan society than Japan.[4] Second, the leadership could split, reigniting the political instability that plagued China earlier. A split might create prolonged chaos or it might enable the emergence of a more sophisticated, more representative political strategy.

Aside from the economic reform itself, there are key social issues that are crucial for the stability of the society and the continuity of the regime: inequality or inclusiveness, environmental degradation, corruption, and globalization. On each of these, much of the conventional Western wisdom is wrong. On environmental degradation, China's priorities up to now have served the Chinese people well, and now China is turning the corner on environmental degradation as decisively as the earlier economic takeoffs such as Britain and Japan did. If the center holds in Chinese politics, China could become a leader in global environmental amelioration.

On corruption, if one understands the different forms corruption takes, then one can easily understand why the Chinese economy performs well, and why India doesn't, despite corruption on a scale that might otherwise seem similar. Nonetheless, China's leaders are right to believe that the current level of corruption threatens their legitimacy, and it remains to be seen whether their anti-corruption campaign can contain it and institutionalize the containment.

---

of this phenomenon, see William H. Overholt, "Japan's Inexorable Decline," *The International Economy*, Autumn 2010, pp. 26–29. For a very thorough analysis, see Richard Katz, *Japan, the System That Soured* (New York: Routledge, 1998). For a superb description of Japan's evolution from a dynamo into its current status, see R. Taggart Murphy, *Japan and the Shackles of the Past* (London: Oxford University Press, 2014), especially Chapters 8 and 9. Japan has high standards of living and has maintained or slightly improved them at the cost of staggering debt that, absent structural reforms, must eventually be repudiated, inflated away, or evaporate in a gigantic bond market crisis.

[4] As an island economy, Japan should have much higher ratios of foreign investment and trade to GDP than a continental economy, but in 2013 (the latest available Japanese data) FDI into China was 3.72% of GDP while Japan's was only 0.08% (source: World Bank). In 2014 China's trade equaled 42% of GDP while Japan's was only 33% (source: CEIC Data Company Ltd.). Particularly astounding as an indicator of relative openness, since China's modern banking system is so much younger than Japan's, is that foreign banks' loan market share in China (2.7% for 2013) is almost double their share in Japan (1.5%). China welcomes foreigners into senior roles and sends its students and officials abroad to an extent that is unimaginable for Japan.

China sees globalization as a source of ultimate economic and geo-political advantage, whereas Japan crippled its economy by turning away from globalization. But China's leaders have not yet convincingly addressed the tensions between globalization and domestic controls on information and other things.

The leading Western development economists of our day, Daron Acemoglu and James A. Robinson, have persuasively shown that economic inclusiveness is the key to long-run sustainable growth while its opposite, an extractive regime, tends to be unsustainable. But they follow the ideologically correct assumption that political democracy equates to economic inclusiveness at any level of development. On the contrary, the authoritarian Asian miracle economies have succeeded through social and economic inclusiveness of a kind unrecognized in the West; for instance, a far higher proportion of Chinese than Americans own their own homes. Conversely, at low levels of development (which China has only recently surpassed) Western-style electoral and judicial systems create extractive, unstable regimes. See the chapters on social issues (Chapter 3, first section on inequality) and politics (Chapter 4) below.

Will sophisticated economic plans carry China to a new level or will unsophisticated political strategies derail the economic growth? Anyone who can give a totally confident answer doesn't understand the complexity of the situation. But we can understand the moving parts and track the emergence of a clearer scenario. On the answer rests the prosperity of the Chinese people, the stability of the Chinese state, and much of the relationship of China to the rest of the world.

1 | China Model/Asia Model

In a famous comedy skit, Mel Brooks plays a 2000-year-old man. The interviewer asks, "What was the means of transportation [2000 years ago]?" His answer: "Mostly fear ... Fear would be the main propulsion."

Why has China succeeded?
What are the chances that it will continue to succeed?
What are the risks that it will not?

The Chinese Miracle succeeded by emulating the essential features of the other Asian miracle economies. Those essential features include strengths and achievements that Western commentators have been slow, even reluctant, to acknowledge. However, China now faces challenges that the other Asian miracle economies faced, with eventual success, but seems to be taking a different path from those that led to success in its predecessors. The current leadership is taking unprecedented risks.

In the course of examining the roots of the Asian miracle economies' success I argue that only a few countries can follow the Asian miracle model; hence Western fears of an imagined "Beijing Consensus" are entirely misplaced. The achievements of these countries – especially South Korea, Taiwan, Singapore, and China in their first-generation takeoffs – should be respected and celebrated rather than deplored and feared. Conversely, the imposition on very poor countries of institutions that work well for the advanced industrial democracies often leads to results that are the opposite of what was intended. If these findings are accepted, the foreign-policy implications are transformational. Western fears that countries in Africa and elsewhere might find ways to develop that do not utilize Western electoral institutions should be condemned; if you care about human dignity, the first task is for people to live long enough to have some human dignity, to have enough food and shelter and medical care to have some human dignity, and to have at least the rudimentary education that is the foundation of dignity in any modern society. If you are malnourished and ill and illiterate and your children are at risk, participating in an election doesn't help much.

We have long understood the economic details of how developing economies can achieve extraordinary growth. Among many others a voluminous 1993 World Bank report called *The East Asian Miracle*[1] collected the evidence of seven fast-growing economies along with the insights of some of the world's great economists. Few economies in world history have been more carefully studied for policy insights than the fast-growing Asian economies. More recently the Growth Commission[2] collected the wisdom of the world's leading growth economists. The foundations of economic growth are not particularly mysterious, although the ways of achieving them attract great controversy.

Fear and Simplicity

For all we have learned and widely publicized about promoting economic growth, fewer than 10 of the world's nearly 200 economies have been managed in the ways necessary for very rapid growth. Why? Isn't growth the main task of developing countries? The central insight is not that of the World Bank but rather the wisdom of the 2000-year-old man. The societies that have been able to implement the required policies are all ones that have experienced excruciating trauma and intense fear: Japan after losing World War II; South Korea after the Korean War; Taiwan after the Chinese Civil War; Singapore after its traumatic separation from Malaya (which meant facing two much larger powers, Indonesia and Malaysia); Vietnam after wars with France, the United States and China; and China after a century of foreign humiliation and tens of millions of deaths from domestic strife. The tier of societies that have sustained just slightly lower rates of progress shares

---

[1] World Bank, *The East Asian Miracle: Economic Growth and Public Policy* (Washington, DC: World Bank, 1993). For a more recent survey, see Dwight H. Perkins, *East Asian Development: Foundations and Strategies* (Cambridge, MA: Harvard University Press, 2013).

[2] Commission on Growth and Development, *The Growth Report: Strategies for Sustained Growth and Inclusive Development* (Washington, DC: World Bank, 2008).

some of the characteristics – Indonesia after the horrors of the Sukarno years and the bloody 1966 transition to Suharto, Malaysia after decolonization threatened by Indonesia's *Confrontasi* (confrontation), Thailand after the Vietnam War. The policies required for rapid growth entail enormous social dislocations, and political leaders who consider imposing such dislocations reasonably fear for their jobs. They only try when they are terrified of the alternative, and when a population fearful of collapse accepts otherwise unacceptable stresses. These are the political prerequisites of miracle-level growth.

The fear I am addressing here is broadly shared fear of societal collapse or destruction, such as occurs in a context of imminent, present or recent great war or ecological or other collapse. One of China's current problems is that shared national fear of collapse has given way to complacency and some hubris. There is lots of fear, to be sure, fear for top leaders' positions, fear for the Party, fear that the anti-corruption campaign will destroy one's family's wealth and safety. But this is not the shared fear that leads to near-universal willingness to accept shared sacrifice in order to save the society. These narrower fears often lead to opposite kinds of behavior, including inaction, neurotic reinforcement of obsolete norms, and personal selfishness or organizational suboptimization at the expense of any larger social goals.

Even though pervasive fear is not an important variable in modern political science or economics, it is true everywhere that a frightened society, with both a frightened leadership and a frightened populace, works differently from a "normal" political economy. Faced with World War II, the United States and United Kingdom chose exceptional leaders, Franklin D. Roosevelt, Harry S. Truman, and Winston Churchill. In normal times the United States chooses more comfortable, incrementalist leaders, like George W. Bush, who gained a decisive margin of support from being seen as a genial guy with whom to share a beer. Similarly, other peacetime leaders get elected for reasons other than extraordinary talent and experience; inexperienced Barack Obama and Donald Trump would never have been elected in the midst of a world war. The wartime leaders pursued grand visions and took great risks, and they were supported by their people because the world situation made people afraid and willing to accept enormous stresses and sacrifices. This phenomenon, married to modern learning about the process and benefits of rapid economic development, is the political key to the Asian miracle economies.

Pervasive societal fear stimulates leaders to take great risks and peoples to support leaders who take great risks and impose otherwise unacceptable social stresses. It does not ensure that those leaders get it right or that the people invariably follow wise leadership. Mao Zedong took great risks, and a hopeful populace followed him, but his mistakes led to the greatest losses of life in human history. What happened with the Asia Model was that Japan and then several smaller countries found a strategy for rapid, overwhelming success and others, including belatedly China, emulated earlier successes.

In several cases, the advantages of fear in unifying adequate support for stressful policies have been supplemented by the power of foreign imposition. Most notably, in Hong Kong the government was the colonial United Kingdom, imposing economic policies from London with only limited dependence on local Hong Kong interest groups – and managing a comfortably small place, unlike colonial India. (I have not included Hong Kong in most of my commentary on the miracle economies, despite its rapid growth, because, as a pure colony, its politics was different. Likewise I have not included Vietnam, because it follows after China rather than creating lessons for China to follow – and its reforms may be stalling earlier than China's.) In Japan, South Korea, and Taiwan, redistributionist policies, especially land reforms, were imposed or facilitated by a foreign power, the United States. Moreover, in Taiwan the government that imposed land reform came from the mainland and was not redistributing its own people's farms. This pattern of outsider-imposed policies emphasizes the political difficulty of implementing the economic policies, particularly the egalitarian policies, needed for rapid economic development.

Digging deeper, these few societies shared a temporary simplicity of the political–economic task they faced. Their economies, except Japan, were relatively simple – mostly basic agriculture, simple manufacturing, and infrastructure. Japan is a partial exception because it was rejuvenating a previously modern economy, not building one for the first time – only a partial exception because rejuvenation is much simpler than building from scratch.

Fear, properly managed, simplifies politics in these countries. It does so by engendering widespread popular willingness to accept social stresses that would normally be unacceptable. It also motivates leaders fearful of collapse to take risks that national leaders normally would not take. People are desperate; they fear total social collapse, and they often fear that their families will not have enough to eat.[3] Hence they are prepared to follow leadership that they find credible even at the cost of extraordinary social upheaval.

Populations were willing to accept, for instance, radical land reforms, loss of 45 million state enterprise jobs under Zhu Rongji, and many other things, because fear created wide agreement that the country's situation required radical measures and shared sacrifice. When China joined the World Trade Organization, its 128 small, inefficient car companies, its steel and other major industries, were forced into overnight transformations, each undergoing changes in a few years that would be considered intolerable over decades in the West.

Reformist China is the archetype of fear-driven leadership. Surveying the wreckage of China's government, Party and economy after Mao's Cultural Revolution, Deng Xiaoping decided to acquiesce in Anhui farmers' move to take back their farms, sacrificing the direct Party control over farmers' livelihoods that provides control in a socialist state – at the time a frightening risk for Deng to take. When the benefits became clear, acquiescence evolved into promulgation. Later the Party curtailed much of its direct management control of industry, again losing direct control over workers' lives. We now take it for granted that the ensuing economic improvements generated popular support, but at the time these were daunting risks.[4]

---

[3] Hunger was endemic in China in the first half of the twentieth century, and Mao's misguided policies led to the starvation of at least 30 million people in 1958–1961. Korea's last Japanese Governor General wrote that many Koreans spent the winters looking for grass and bark to eat; the Korean War then made things even worse. Before their great economic takeoffs, Taiwan and South Korea were among the world's most impoverished economies, well behind impoverished African economies at the time – a fact that has nearly vanished from memory. Following World War II, even the Japanese suffered from widespread hunger. Singapore at the time of independence was frequently characterized as just a malarial swamp.

[4] Encapsulating Deng's strategies, and the drama that surrounded them, in a few sentences is necessary but the compression is almost painful. For a thorough and compelling analysis of those times, see Ezra Vogel, *Deng Xiaoping and the Transformation of China* (Cambridge, MA: Harvard University Press, 2013). Vogel has also written extensively on the other Asian miracle economies that I frequently reference here. Part of Deng's pragmatic genius was to accept bottom-up movements, such as the ones for peasant control of farms and of local officials to found entrepreneurial town and village enterprises, that spread prosperity at great cost to ideological orthodoxy.

Fear of collapse lay behind the willingness of Deng, Jiang Zemin, and Zhu Rongji to risk loss of the Party's most important levers of social control. Fear of collapse led them to risk upheaval by imposing wrenching job changes on tens of millions of people. Zhu risked his job repeatedly to avert financial collapse. In 1998 China's most prestigious international trading company and its largest foreign borrower, Guangdong International Trust and Investment Company (GITIC), became insolvent through mismanagement and corruption. Guangdong is far from Beijing and traditionally resistant to rule from the center, and was China's best-performing province. Zhu decided to let GITIC go bankrupt. That precedent made furious foreign lenders more cautious; my estimate at the time was that it cost China at least US$50 billion of potential foreign loans, but it saved China from the risk of future Latin America-style financial collapse. I asked Zhu whether the political costs for him weren't pretty serious. He said, through a translator, "Yeah, they're trying to get rid of me again, but I think I'll be here a little longer."

Fear underpinned the courage of Deng and Zhu. Fear made China's vast population willing to accept their painful decisions. One of the problems of today's Chinese leaders is the difficulty of adapting to a new era where, in the absence of popular existential fear, people and interest groups do not easily acquiesce in demands for sacrifice, and, in the absence of leadership fear of collapse, leaders lack the motivation to take the reformist risks that early leaders took. This contextual change underlies China's loss of reform momentum under Hu Jintao and the great dilemmas of belated reform against resistance that Xi Jinping and his colleagues face today.

The Philippines, the most highly developed third-world country after World War II, both in institutional sophistication and in terms of all major indices of development, was not a candidate for an Asian miracle reform because US protection removed the potential reasons for fear by protecting it from foreign threats and intervening against domestic threats. In sum, a relatively simple economic problem, an existing sense of shared identity, and politics simplified by terrifying fear constitute the prerequisites of the great Asian economic miracles.

Simplified politics does not of course mean the absence of politics. Every society has factions. Every leadership has to ensure a certain amount of social support and must fear losing it. By 2003 the Chinese population was tired of Zhu Rongji's reforms and angry; it took years before appreciation for his heroic reforms revived. Moreover, China in the reform era has always had powerful factions. Deng Xiaoping's industrial reformism had to contend with Chen Yun's conservatism. Zhao Ziyang and Li Peng fought from opposite ends of the political spectrum. Jiang Zemin's exceptional political skill kept – with difficulty – Zhu Rongji's market reformism and Li Peng's favoritism toward state-owned enterprises (SOEs) working inside the same tent. But the leadership's search for big, sometimes iconoclastic strategies and willingness to incur huge risks, backed by the population's willingness to accept extraordinarily stressful changes, made the task of rapid transformation possible. Again, the same thing happens in Western democracies during world wars.

The Asian miracle developed from the example of Japan and from a dialogue shared among South Korea, Taiwan, and the ASEAN countries. Belatedly, China tapped into that shared experience under Deng Xiaoping's leadership after 1979. What they learned from each other was, first, to focus obsessively on economic development; and, second, some techniques for achieving that development.

Shared Identity

In addition to simplified economics and politics at the beginning of these Asian miracles, they are societies with some degree of shared identity and national cohesion, so they don't have to build a national identity first. Laos isn't a candidate for an economic miracle, and Indonesia had to build a national identity under a wild-eyed, confrontational, ideological post-independence leader, Sukarno, before it could embark on rapid growth under his successor, Suharto.

Emulation and Limits

Note how constraining these prerequisites are. The Asia Model is viable only in a very small number of developing countries. And the mobilization around economic growth at all costs is viable only as long as the fear lasts. I shall return repeatedly to this point, because it is crucial to an ongoing debate about the spread of the "Beijing Consensus."

The China model is a variation of an East Asia Model that has repeatedly proven successful in achieving domestic political stability, prosperity, international influence and domestic legitimacy but also has characteristic pitfalls. One of the original drivers of the China model was Deng Xiaoping's recognition that key Confucian neighbors were achieving these aspects of modernity with a speed and resilience that far outpaced what Maoist policies were accomplishing in China itself. After multiple conversations with Zhu Rongji (economic czar and prime minister under Deng's successor, Jiang Zemin[5]), I came away convinced that he had a better comprehension of South Korea's developmental structures and policies than any Western expert on South Korea. Li Peng and others sought to emulate aspects of Singapore's development, even to the point of giving Singapore control of an area the size of Singapore outside Suzhou. Study of the successes and failures of other Asian miracle countries, particularly the Confucian neighbors, has been a fundamental reason for China's success.

The China model, like its predecessors, is not just about economics, or just about economics and politics. It is an approach to the creation, out of poverty and chaos, of a society that achieves China's multi-generational goals of wealth and power,[6] along with the related goals of stability and legitimacy. It is, in short, a strategy for creating a modern society.

As a variation of the Asia Model, China has had the huge advantage of being able to build on the experience of the other Asian miracle economies, most notably South Korea, Taiwan, Singapore, and Japan – and even Hong Kong. To say this is not to imply that there is a single template that can be applied to all the great Asian economic successes; there are of course enormous variations among those earlier successes. For instance, as noted in the Introduction, South Korea has built its miracle with giant conglomerates while Taiwan's dynamism comes mainly from numerous smaller companies. Nor could China simply copy anyone else's experience; China's conditions, most

---

[5] Jiang was Deng's successor as "leader." They had different titles. Jiang was President, Communist Party Secretary and Chair of the Central Military Commission. Deng, with lesser titles, became the "paramount leader" even when his only title was honorary chairman of the Chinese bridge players' society.

[6] To understand China's multi-generational search for a path to wealth and power, through some combination of borrowed Western techniques and traditional Chinese institutions and values, see Orville Schell and John DeLury, **Wealth and Power: China's Long March to the Twenty-First Century** (New York: Random House, 2013). Their technique of mapping China's national journey through biographies of its most influential thinkers yields exceptional clarity.

notably its huge scale, multiple dialects, and different conditions in different regions, contrast strikingly with the smaller and generally more homogeneous earlier successes. I will address some of China's unique techniques below.

Some commentators have ascribed these countries' success to culture or to a tradition of hard work. Confucian culture does provide a boost, because the biggest success stories share a history of relatively merito-cratic bureaucracy and of reverence for education. But these do not explain most of their success. South Korea, Taiwan, Singapore, and China were among the world's poorest countries as late as 1960. Their success was because they implemented basic growth policies with an efficiency that was lacking elsewhere. Other countries, with different cultures, that followed a fairly high proportion of the same policies – Malaysia, Thailand, Indonesia – also achieved high rates of growth. (These countries do have substantial ethnic Chinese minorities that are the most dynamic part of the economy. But other countries, like the Philippines, which have the ethnic Chinese community but not the policies, lack the economic dynamism.) Likewise, when the policies change, as in Thailand, the economic performance declines even though the Confucian minority remains the same.

Without the policies, the labor force didn't work hard. Before Park Chung Hee took power in 1961, South Koreans were famous for the opposite; in making an appointment, South Koreans would specify the date and place but not the exact time. One person would just wait around until the other showed up. Market competition and Park's military-style discipline changed the mentality to one where it was an insult to show up a minute late. Likewise, when visiting Chinese factor-ies in 1982 I was amazed at the way so many workers just stood around smoking and chatting. Competition and incentives made the difference.

Despite the variations, there are vitally important resonances among the Asian success stories. Through most of the 1980s, after Deng Xiaoping and Gorbachev became leaders, at a time when the Western consensus was that Deng would fail and Gorbachev would succeed, I used Table 1.1 in explaining why the opposite would occur. (This table became the analytic core of my controversial book *The Rise of China*.[7])

[7] William H. Overholt, *The Rise of China: How Economic Reform Is Creating a New Superpower* (New York: W. W. Norton, 1993).

Table 1.1 *East Asian priorities versus Gorbachev's*

East Asian priorities	Gorbachev's priorities
1. Agriculture	1. International politics
2. Light industry	2. Domestic politics
3. Heavy industry	3. Heavy industry
4. Domestic politics	4. Light industry
5. International politics	5. Agriculture

These were not the only decisive differences, of course. Most notably, Chinese incrementalism enabled all social groups to gain continuously, albeit at different rates, whereas the shock therapy promoted by Western economists and accepted by Russian leaders created unconscionable human suffering. (Russia suffered a 40 percent decline in GDP and the losses of some social groups greatly exceeded that.) That suffering discredited Western capitalism and democracy, and led directly to Russia's reversion to authoritarian politics and crony economics. In contrast, the initially authoritarian East Asian model creates the potential, although no assurance, for prosperous democracy.

The Asian priorities typically produce rapid growth, domestic political stability based on the fruits of that growth, international prestige because of the rapid increase in prosperity and stability, and a solid educated middle-class foundation for potential political liberalization later on. The Gorbachev priorities, which are applauded by US and European elites, more often lead, especially when implemented in very poor countries, to weak economic performance, persistent political instability and international weakness. In the 1970s, when my career was beginning, there was a near-consensus that authoritarianism in South Korea and Taiwan would lead to political instability and economic failure while India's priority for Western-style political values would lead to superior performance. Jimmy Carter's Asia policies began with his determination to disconnect the United States from the horrors (as he and some advisors saw them) of South Korea and Taiwan. The same arguments that were applied to South Korea in 1976 were the source of consensus in the George H. W. Bush administration of the early 1990s that China would prove unstable and fail economically.

The consistent success of the Asia Model has been ideologically unacceptable to most of Western opinion most of the time, whether in South Korea and Taiwan in the 1970s or in China in more recent years. American political scientists wrote eloquently about how Gorbachev would succeed because he understood the need to achieve political legitimacy before focusing on economic reform. Leading US economists advocating shock therapy for Russia insisted that their approach was the only correct one, to the point of blocking publication of articles that contradicted their view. But the Asia Model has succeeded on such a scale that historians will write centuries from now about how it changed the world.

The Western world needs to accept two realities. One is that, in the limited situations where it is possible, the Asia Model is the most efficient path to improving human dignity. People's lifespan doubles in several decades. Illiteracy vanishes. Desperate hunger and malnourishment give way to modern diets; the next generation is inches taller. The emergence of an educated, middle-class society creates for the first time the potential, although not the certainty, of a more pluralistic political order consistent with high levels of economic development.

Conversely, and this is why I have emphasized the prerequisites of the Asia Model, this model works only under very constrained conditions – a relatively simple economy, intense fear, some minimal level of cohesion – that are present only in a small number of countries and that dissipate with success. While most societies' sense of common identity and cohesion tend to rise with economic success (see Indonesia), simplicity and fear dissipate with success. China is having a very difficult time coping with the transition from fear to confidence or hubris, because the politics of an era of confidence is radically different from the politics of an era of fear. Moreover, the side effects of obsessive priority for economic growth accumulate with success and force changes in the model.

With the transition from fear to hubris, and the transition from a relatively simple economy and social structure to a modern complex economy, the period of obsessive mobilization for economic growth ends and the period of relatively simplified politics ends too. Moreover, around this time the society discovers that the obsession with economic growth has had huge costs, for instance environmental degradation, that must be urgently addressed. The early period where resources are obsessively mobilized for economic growth can best be termed a mobilization system.

A Mobilization System

The core of the Asia Model is a mobilization of society's resources around a single goal, namely economic growth. The concept of the mobilization system comes from the military and can only be properly understood as an evolution from a military process. It is not only an analogue of military mobilization but also an evolution of military mobilization systems. Napoleon learned to mobilize a mass army, drawing more of society's resources into battle and thereby winning great victories. In World War I, more extensive mobilization occurred and was defined as a specific preparation for imminent war. We say that Serbia, Austria, and then successively Germany and Russia mobilized in July 1914. Although the same word is used, this is different from Mao's idea of mobilization (riling up riotous masses) or from the social scientists' use of the word to describe the precipitation of social interest groups that occurs when societies modernize.

As the world moved toward World War II, modern military–economic mobilization began. Japan adapted from Hitler and Stalin key aspects of a modern system of mobilizing for war. The government asserts extensive control over the economy. Because the banks are susceptible to direct control, finance is organized around banks rather than stock and bond markets. Companies are subordinated to administrative guidance (or direct government ownership elsewhere). Since one can't afford to let a crucial military supplier go bankrupt, the survival of all important companies is guaranteed by embedding them in a giant conglomerate (pre-war zaibatsu or postwar keiretsu). Employees are subject to ruthless discipline, including demands for total loyalty, but are promised continuity of employment. Egalitarian policies reduce the risk of revolt from below and enhance the military-like sense of camaraderie.

These policies, or structures, passed from Germany and the Soviet Union to Japan and onward to South Korea, China, Taiwan, and Singapore. There were important variations. State control was exercised through administrative guidance and control of credit in Japan; through detailed guidance of privately owned chaebol from the president's office in South Korea; through state ownership in China; through Guomindang Party ownership of the crucial

40 conglomerates in Taiwan. For central control of national resources, socialism or its analogues and Leninism or its analogues are optimal. During wartime governments employed these resources to direct maximum devastation against the enemy and to shift deployments decisively when needed. The genius of the East Asian miracles lay in the discovery that the same mobilization resources could be employed to foster the most rapid economic development in world history. They built roads and bridges and telecommunications; imposed order on strife-torn societies; imposed the social changes attendant upon wildly rapid economic change; and planned for the economy and society the way a good military commander would plan, with intricately detailed models but with enough flexibility to cope with unplanned changes.

The relative simplicity of the impoverished economies, and the relative simplicity of rejuvenating modern industry in Japan, along with the relative simplicity of leading a population whose fears made them malleable, made the success of this economic mobilization system possible.

Conversely, the evanescence of those conditions, which economic success transforms within a generation, limits how long governments can succeed with mobilization policies. To understand those limits one need only imagine the US military leadership put in charge of managing the economy and social policies. Those military leaders are probably among history's most talented, but they would make a mess of Silicon Valley. Equally, of course, one would not want Silicon Valley's brilliant disrupters running the military. The tasks of managing a modern military and managing a modern economy require different skills and different organization structures. But there is a sweet spot of overlap, a very limited sweet spot in geography and time, where structures invented for military mobilization can succeed at economic mobilization.

Priority for Economics

As noted, the single most important policy aspect of the mobilization period of the Asia Model is an obsessive priority for economic growth. "Priority" means that economic growth receives attention and resources at the expense of other national concerns, most notably the military and the political process.

Economics over Geopolitical/Military Goals

The Asian miracle economies have been particularly noteworthy for their downgrading of military priorities in favor of investment in economic growth. Before 1945 Japan destroyed itself by emphasis on military and geopolitical ambitions. After 1945 it never spent more than 1 percent of GDP on the military but rapidly became recognized as one of the world's preeminent powers because of the rapid growth and size of its economy, along with the domestic stability and prestige that resulted from its economic success. It lost that preeminence when, in a gradual shift after 1975, it downgraded its priority for sound economic management. The devastating consequences of Japan's shift from economic priorities to a priority for patronage politics remind us that Asian miracles can go backward, not just forward, if the priority for economic efficiency is completely abandoned.

South Korea failed to achieve growth, domestic political stability, or even minimal international security under the Rhee Syngman regime of the 1950s, which emphasized military priorities, or the brief, unstable, hapless Chang Myon regime of 1960–1961, which emphasized democratic political processes. But when, in 1961 under General Park Chung Hee, it shifted to an overriding priority for economic development at the cost of greatly reducing the military's share of the national budget and greatly deemphasizing democratic political values, growth rapidly rose to over 10 percent annually, domestic politics gradually stabilized, and the balance of power between South and North Korea gradually shifted from one that greatly favored North Korea in 1961 to one that greatly favors South Korea at present. Today the South Korean economy is between 20 and 30 times the size of North Korea's, and the balance of domestic stability, diplomatic recognition and international prestige, not to mention the difference between the human dignity of South Koreans and the malnutrition of North Korea's people, has shifted overwhelmingly in South Korea's favor. See Table 1.2.

In Southeast Asia, the transformation of Indonesia, from a society on the brink of civil war and riven by some of the world's most dangerous ideological and religious divisions, to a stable country widely recognized as the leader of ASEAN, resulted from a shift after 1966 not only to better economic policies but also, crucially, to priority for economic development at the expense of downgrading ideology

Table 1.2 *Asia Model priority for economics*

Priority for economics	Priority for military or politics
• Park Chung Hee's South Korea, 1961–1979	• Rhee Syngman's South Korea, 1950–1960 (military) • Chang Myon's South Korea, 1960–1961 (politics) • North Korea (military)
• Suharto's Indonesia (1966–1998) • Japan, 1955–1975 • Deng Xiaoping's China	• Sukarno's Indonesia (geopolitics, ideology) • Japan, 1975–present • Mao Zedong's China

and of quietly abandoning territorial claims that had previously covered much of Southeast Asia.

Likewise, the beginning of China's rise coincided with a similar shift of priorities. Military analysts in the United States estimate that in 1976, at the end of the Cultural Revolution, 16 percent of China's GDP was going to the military. Deng Xiaoping reduced that to around 3 percent. The theory of peaceful rise – a rise emphasizing economic development in a context of peace – articulated by Chinese foreign affairs expert Zheng Bijian summarized not just a Chinese concept but the broader experience of the most successful Asian societies.[8] Focus

---

[8] Zheng Bijian's arguments about China's peaceful rise, modified to more politically correct form in others' discussions of "China's peaceful development," have appeared in many forms, in diverse publications and in many languages. (Zheng served in a number of positions as a foreign-policy thinker and spokesman, including Executive Vice President of the Central Party School.) In English, his best-known publication is "China's 'Peaceful Rise' to Great-Power Status," *Foreign Affairs* 84(5), 2005, pp. 18–24. Western security specialists usually treat this thesis just as a propaganda point, but it is central to the course Deng Xiaoping actually set for China. Deng learned the lesson from neighbors. I first noted the tendency for economic priorities to displace military ones in the Asian miracle economies in publications like William H. Overholt, "International Violence in Asia," in Tunde Adeniran and Yonah Alexander, eds., *International Violence* (New York: Praeger, 1983), pp. 116–129; "Progress and Politics in Pacific Asia," *International Security*, Spring 1983, pp. 180–194; and "The Pacific Basin Model: The Moderation of Politics," in James Morley, ed., *The Pacific Basin* (Washington, DC; Academy of Political Science, 1986), pp. 35–45. None of these focused on China, but rather they focused on the models that China subsequently emulated. Chinese thought leaders developed the "peaceful rise" concept a decade

on these priorities kept the big-power peace in Asia for half a century. (More recently, the United States, Japan, and China have all shifted toward traditional geopolitical competition.)

While militaries always protest that these cuts leave their nations vulnerable, in practice the result of a focus on economic growth has been a great improvement in national security – because of greater domestic stability, because of the prestige that comes from demonstrated success and decisiveness, and because an economy growing 10 percent annually supports very rapid growth of the military even if its percentage of GDP is relatively small. In most years, China has kept the growth of the military budget at or below the growth of government revenues (which have grown much faster than the overall economy), so that the military share of government spending has over time generally declined even though actual spending has been able to increase very rapidly.[9]

In most of these cases, including China during its 1980s fear of the Soviet Union, US protection facilitated the decision to give priority to economic growth. That does not make their decision less important. It is difficult for extremely threatened countries to curtail their own military expenditures. In most cases, most notably China and Indonesia but including all of the great economic takeoffs, the shift to economic priorities entailed abandoning major territorial claims or geopolitical ambitions or both. North Korea could have relied on its allies for protection and chosen to emphasize economic development, but its failure to do so has left it a basket case.

Economics over Politics

Similarly, a priority for economics means that political values often take a subordinate position, whether "political values" mean political

---

later and many believed it to be uniquely Chinese. Deng Xiaoping and Zhu Rongji knew better.

[9] As growth slows, military spending growth necessarily slows. See Andrew S. Erickson and Adam P. Liff, "The Limits of Growth: Economic Headwinds Inform China's Latest Military Budget," *Wall Street Journal*, March 5, 2016, http://blogs.wsj.com/chinarealtime/2016/03/05/the-limits-of-growth-economic-headwinds-inform-chinas-latest-military-budget/. It is worth noting, in reading all US articles about Chinese military spending, that the Western media always – without any exception that I have ever seen over a period of decades – report economic growth in real terms (i.e., with the inflation taken out), but military budget growth in nominal terms (i.e., with the inflation left in).

opening or democratization or creating Mao's new socialist man. National unity and order are of course always a top priority, but even these are often optimized by a shift of leadership attention and resources in favor of economic progress. Just as South Korea did not fare well in the 1950s with a priority for the military, it also fared so poorly in its brief experiment with political democracy in 1960–1961 that the population broadly supported a coup by General Park Chung Hee that promised strength through a focus on economics. Democratization at an extremely low level of economic development has often fared poorly, as happened in South Korea, the Philippines, Thailand, and until recently India. (More on this can be found in Chapter 4.) After the development of an educated middle-class society, the outcomes of democracy have typically been much better. South Korea and Taiwan not only found that the emergence of an educated middle-class society enhanced pressures for political democratization; they found that it made stable, prosperous democracy possible.

Likewise, China remained backward and weak when national priorities were defined by "Politics in Command" and by an emphasis on red (loyalty to communism and Mao) over expert. Deng Xiaoping's slogan "It doesn't matter whether a cat is black or white so long as it catches mice" is just a colorful way of expressing his successful decision to replace Mao's "Politics in Command" with economics in command.

The decision to put economics in command comes to pervade national life. In China, South Korea, Taiwan, and Singapore, allocation of infrastructure investments is determined primarily by a national plan based on efficiency. In the Philippines and India, allocation is determined principally by patronage political decisions. In China, a mayor seeking promotion will be judged by whether he has met specific goals such as increasing his city's GDP, investment, foreign investment, educational performance, and employment. In the Philippines, he will succeed or fail depending on whether he has cobbled together enough support from local elite interest groups. A Chinese mayor who succeeds will typically be assigned a different kind of challenge in a different part of China and continue working up by confronting diverse challenges in diverse areas, whereas in the Philippines or India most politicians succeed by consolidating and enhancing a certain collection of elite interest groups in a particular geographic area. China, South Korea, Taiwan, and Singapore achieved their economic takeoffs by running their economies like businesses. (See the detailed discussion in Chapter 4.)

This distinction is not a black and white one. Every governance system involves patronage. In every governance system, personal loyalties matter. In every governance system, factions form. What is distinctive about China and the other Asian miracle economies is the emphasis on achievement of specific goals as a prerequisite of promotion or job retention. In the Asian miracle economies everything is framed by an economic plan and an organizational structure designed to implement that plan. China operates more like a modern business than an entourage. Even in GE or in an investment bank, there are factions, patronage, and personal loyalties, but if an executive can't meet his or her assigned objectives that executive will fail. There is intense competition over objectively defined performance, and those who outperform generally succeed (notwithstanding the controversies about this in the Western political science literature reviewed in Chapter 4).

As noted earlier, the period where obsession with economic growth overrides every other priority is a form of *mobilization system*.[10] In Japan the postwar mobilization system lasted from 1955 to 1975; in China it lasted from 1980 to 2002. Most mobilization systems are created for war or the prospect of war. The original modern Asian mobilization system was instituted in Japan as it prepared for what became World War II, and its essential features were copied from Hitler's Germany and Stalin's Soviet Union: centralized, authoritarian politics; a financial system dominated by banks rather than stock and bond markets since governments can control banks; government guarantees that no essential firm will go bankrupt in order to ensure continuous supplies; assured employment to avoid unrest; and government guidance of banks and big firms. The Japanese system emphasized

---

[10] In China the term mobilization usually refers to Maoist mobilization of the masses into great social campaigns. I am using the term in its more universal sense. Mobilization systems are social systems where the resources of society are mobilized toward a single overarching goal. The principal examples of mobilization systems are Hitler's Germany, the wartime Soviet Union, Japan's prewar mobilization that copied Hitler's and Stalin's techniques in preparation for war, postwar Japan that used many of the same techniques for economic growth, the Guomindang and Communist Party systems during war and civil war, and the obsessive concentration of national resources on economic growth by South Korea, Taiwan, Singapore, and, later, China.

lifetime employment, seniority pay, company unions, priority for employees over shareholders, a financial system organized around main banks, and administrative guidance as key features of the new system created to support the war.[11] The South Korean, Guomindang Chinese, Communist Chinese, and early Singaporean systems in turn emulated key mobilization features of wartime Japan, often with an ideological overlay of socialism. All of these systems had their origins in war, civil war, or the preparation for war. They were, in other words, designed for specific situations of great stress and danger. They require drastic modification in order to function well in other environments.

When the mobilization system has run its course, other priorities begin to compete and the prerequisites of this kind of mobilization system – scared leaders, scared people, relatively simple economy – fade, growth rates gradually decline but comparatively rapid growth can continue if meritocratic, performance-based governance systems persist. They have persisted well in South Korea, Taiwan, and Singapore. They became involuted and structurally corrupt in Japan, Malaysia, and late-Suharto Indonesia.

Second-Order Consequences

Although the Asia Model gives overwhelming priority to economics at the expense of military and political goals, as noted above rapid economic growth typically supports rapidly increasing military power even if the military share of GDP is small. Park Chung Hee's decision in 1961 to cut South Korea's military budget in order to focus on economic development led to today's military superiority over North Korea. Suharto's abandonment of vast geopolitical claims in favor of economic priorities made it possible for Indonesia to become maritime Southeast Asia's military leader. Deng Xiaoping's cuts of the military share of GDP made possible the increasingly powerful Chinese military of today.

---

[11] For a detailed account, see Tetsuji Okazaki and Masahiro Okuno-Fujiwara, eds., *The Japanese Economic System and Its Historical Origins*, translated by Susan Herbert (New York: Oxford University Press, 1993), especially pp. vii–viii. Japanese politicians and others often characterize these as aspects of traditional Japanese culture. They are not. They were transplanted from totalitarian systems for use in wartime.

Likewise for politics. Domestic stability comes much quicker when economic growth is benefiting everyone and creating a shared sense of benefit from a growing economic pie. Social pressures for political liberalization (which the leadership can accommodate to facilitate further growth as in Taiwan and South Korea or can resist at great risk) emerge much faster in a successful economy. Technological progress turns out to require considerable freedom of discussion. Foreign and domestic investors alike press for rule according to law, transparency, freer flow of information, and accountability; to list a company on a major stock exchange, or to issue a bond to international investors requires an extraordinary level of information and when that information turns out to be wrong the consequences are often quite severe. In an educated society people are better able to make informed political decisions, as a democracy requires. In a middle-class society, as opposed to one divided into landlords and peasants, citizens are debating how to achieve shared interests rather than engaging primarily in class conflict.

China has achieved the benefits of the stability that comes from growth and a sense that everyone is sharing a growing pie. It has a mixed record, in some periods quite positive, recently quite negative, in responding to the pressures for liberalization, but the pressures created by a more pluralistic society exist. For more than a decade protests of various kinds have multiplied; whether the leadership can respond creatively will determine China's stability as economic modernization creates new kinds of challenges. I shall elaborate on this in the politics chapter below.

Priorities within Economics

Within the overall priority for economics, the most successful Asian economic takeoffs have begun with land reform – termination of feudal landholding systems that previously reduced vast parts of the population to virtual serfdom and put farms into the hands of a few elite families – combined with infrastructure and other support to help small farmers succeed. In China, which inserted a costly intermediate misstep into industrial-style communes, this was a more complicated process than in Japan, South Korea, and Taiwan, but the eventual result was the same: an entrepreneurial burst of rural production that lifted the economy, together with a sense by rural people, who comprised the overwhelming majority of the population, that the government cared about and promoted their interests.

After agriculture, the Asia Model economies have tended to emphasize labor-intensive industry, supported by an infrastructure program that provides roads, railroads, airlines, ports, airports, and telecommunications. An emphasis on production of inexpensive consumer goods, both for domestic consumption and for export, has the benefit of creating the maximum number of jobs. This is politically stabilizing. Nothing is more destabilizing than mass unemployment, and conversely nothing is more stabilizing than a process that gives people a stake in society: land for farmers, jobs for workers, eventually housing for families. Chinese leaders have been extremely sensitive to the risks of mass unemployment and, so far, extremely successful at maintaining jobs in the face of disruptive structural change. When 45 million state enterprise workers had to change jobs under Zhu Rongji, most workers were absorbed into the service economy and the remainder were retired on unusually generous terms. China now faces a challenge of comparable social change as it seeks to eliminate industrial overcapacity.

Crucially, the labor-intensive industry that drives early industrialization in these economies employs mainly women. Confucian societies have been particularly patriarchal. Pre-revolutionary China had a very high rate of female suicide, and the communists gained strength in the villages from organizing women, along with tenants and youth, into groups that held "speak bitterness" sessions which channeled them into Party-supportive organizations. Mao Zedong's ideological declarations that "women hold up half the sky" translated into very limited improvements in the roles of women in Chinese society of his day, but Deng Xiaoping's reforms led to an economy of factories that were staffed mainly by women. The bosses were primarily men, but the textile factories, computer assembly factories, and most of the other light industry hired mainly women, not men. Along with high rates of female education, the employment of women, often far from the misogynistic constraints of their traditional villages, explains why Chinese women are so much more confident and empowered than Indian women, whose government has not fostered light industry to anything like the same extent. Chapter 3 on vital social issues addresses this in detail.

While the early phases of development, focusing on agriculture and labor-intensive industry, require the building of infrastructure – a form of heavy industry – the most successful Asian economies have typically focused on building capital-intensive industries such as steel, aluminum, concrete, shipbuilding, and automobiles only after a period when growth came predominantly from the labor-intensive sectors.

Strategies of Economic Development

Of course, it is possible to prioritize economics but get the strategy wrong. Early post-independence Burmese leaders believed that economic development would best be achieved by cutting their economy off from a world dominated by predatory colonial powers. Indonesia's first post-independence leader, the fiery, charismatic Sukarno, had a parallel belief that the key to national success lay with confronting, and severing ties to, the old colonial powers. Dependency theorists argued that engagement with the world economy automatically brings further subordination of developing economies to the wealthy countries. (It was amazing that dependency theory, still taught with a straight face in many universities, persisted so long in the face of the rapid rise of the Asian economies. Self-justifying nonsense is highly resilient to facts.) Early Latin American and Filipino leaders promoted an emphasis on building domestic industry behind high protectionist walls in order to substitute domestic production for imports (a strategy called import substitution industrialization) and a priority for heavy industry. These perspectives and strategies lead consistently to failure.

The China Model has followed the Asia Model in making gradual opening of the national market and marketization of the economy the core strategies. Opening means the encouragement of international trade and investment and the acceptance of international market practices. Marketization means the replacement of many forms of state-imposed pricing and economic decisions by market mechanisms, along with development of a regulatory infrastructure that enables markets to function. So many volumes have been written about reform and opening that I shall not repeat the details here.

In the Asia Model these reform processes are achieved by rapid incrementalism rather than shock therapy. "Gradualism" is not the right word to describe, for instance, the dismantling within just a few years of China's communes in favor of family farms. Given the size of China's population, its vast geography, and its social diversity, reforms have in fact occurred at extraordinary speed. The difference between the Asia Model and the shock therapy model is not speed so much as careful attention to sequencing and field testing so that reforms achieve maximum effectiveness with minimum social disruption. This is also the way most successful Western societies developed, both economically and politically, although Western societies reformed far more slowly.

During the latter part of the twentieth century it became fashionable in the West to recommend shock therapy to others and to deride incrementalism. This was a recommendation to do what we (the West) say, not what we do. Western advocates of shock therapy ignore the lessons of virtually all successful economies, including Western Europe, North America, and East and Southeast Asia. The shock therapy strategy led to unspeakable suffering and economic decline. With GDP falling 40 percent, in the former Soviet Union, suffering and decline discredited Western-style capitalism and democracy in Russian eyes and led to the rise of Vladimir Putin.[12] The same approach, shock therapy rather than the kinds of incremental development congruent with social development that made Western democracy viable, is almost always advocated today regarding political development. In one country after another, this approach leads to division, violence, and decline, but a majority of respectable Western theorists and officials refuse to draw the conclusions.

Certain other characteristics of the Asia Model deserve highlighting. First, competition. The Asian miracle economies achieve efficiency through competition. In textiles, consumer electronics, and cars, Japan's and South Korea's economies have been marked by extreme competition – twice as many car companies, for instance, as in the giant US market. The China Model follows this. Starting in the last few years of the 1990s, China broke up many sector monopolies, for instance in telecommunications, and replaced them with frenetic competition. That has driven costs down and productivity up. Within the Asia Model it is noteworthy that sectors have succeeded to the extent that there was open competition. Japan is most successful in its truly internationalized and competitive sectors – for instance, cars and video games – and is relatively backward in protected sectors such as

[12] Because the Soviet Union, like China, did not properly measure services, average incomes fell less than 40 percent, but the shock was still far more traumatizing than the Great Depression in the United States. Some groups lost almost everything – income, homes, pensions.

agriculture, finance, cell phones, and many more protected industries. In rural Japan, notwithstanding the very high average incomes of the country, many housewives still launder the family clothes by hand. In China, open competition has led to the emergence of world-class companies like Lenovo precisely because they had to survive fierce competition rather than benefiting from state pampering. (Lenovo, the world's largest laptop computer company, started with a grant of US$25,000 to an employee of the Chinese Academy of Sciences whose bosses were paying him off to get rid of him.)

Importantly, the extent to which Chinese leaders will continue to accept this lesson of competitive success remains to be seen; some decisions in the Xi Jinping years seem to be going in the opposite direction as inefficient SOEs are consolidated into large-scale "national champions." In this and other areas the Xi administration expresses determination to reform, but it has sought to have its cake and eat it too.

More broadly, the core feature of the Asia Model is the systematic search for, and adoption of, international best practice – in a word, globalization. Early in its development, both in the early Meiji era of the mid nineteenth century and in the early postwar era of the mid twentieth Century, Japan sent teams all over the world to discern best practice (German education, the British navy in the nineteenth century, underutilized US quality-control methods and labor-management tech-niques in the twentieth, and much else) and help the mother country adopt such practices. The most important secret of the Asia Model's success is this globalization by adoption of best practice. China has carried this aspect to its highest level, sending not just its best students, not just the children of its political and business elite, but also current leaders abroad to ensure that China understands best practice. At Harvard's Kennedy School, we have a succession of Chinese vice ministers who are there to ensure that their country understands best practice of every kind. This does not mean that Chinese leaders blindly copy foreign practice, any more than early Meiji Japanese leaders did. It does mean that, more than any other world leaders, they understand a variety of management practices other than their own and therefore can systematically choose what seems to them to be best practice for China.

Here, too, contemporary China is deeply conflicted. In some ways the Xi Jinping administration continues the policies of sending large numbers of students and officials abroad, and importing large numbers of foreign counterparts, but it is also waging a campaign against officials sending their families abroad and it is severely constraining the ability of officials and even scholars to attend conferences abroad. More on this will be given in Chapter 5 below.

The Vital Role of Policies

There is a strain in Western commentary, from a minority of political scientists and humanists, that the Chinese regime should get no credit for its achievements. In this view, all the reformists did was to remove the constraints the communists had imposed on growth and let the hardworking Chinese people achieve what they would have without the communists. I address elsewhere the essentially racist cultural myth that Chinese and Koreans are naturally hardworking; like other people they become hardworking when they face starvation or the right market incentives or military discipline. In works that I cite elsewhere, Stein Ringen asserts without evidence that China would have grown just as fast without the regime. Kate Xiao Zhou ascribes all the success to local entrepreneurship. Her emphasis on the importance of local entrepreneurship was a major contribution to scholarship, but that entrepreneurship was enabled by government policies such as road building and education. Perry Link's review of my book *The Rise of China*, in the prestigious *New York Review of Books*, asserted that the reason for China's rapid growth was not Deng's policies but rather Mao's previous suppression of Chinese wages; on the contrary, places with much lower wages often stagnate, and China continued to grow fast long after its wages had far surpassed those of previously more prosperous neighboring countries. A great deal of internet blog chat maintains the theme that reforms just removed obstacles to the country's natural growth.

If this were true, then the default growth rate of humanity would be 10 percent and countries would achieve less only if they had interfering communist governments. Obviously that is the opposite of the history of mankind; it took millennia before parts of mankind learned to grow 2 percent annually in what we call the industrial revolution. Japan and the United States managed 3 to 4 percent as they ascended to dominance in their regions during the late nineteenth and early twentieth centuries. Only after World War II did a tiny number of countries manage 10 percent for two or three decades. The thesis that China, or the other Asian miracles, just had governments that got out of the way of natural growth ignores what no economist would ever ignore, namely the crucial roles of high-quality roads, airlines, ports, telecommunications, and power systems; of mass education of the right kinds; of competent administrative institutions; of thoughtful plans that prepare areas for industry and cities for urbanization; of help to farmers displaced by industrialization and to factory workers displaced by the transition to a service economy; of egalitarian efforts to ensure that most or all groups acquire a stake in society.

Layered over all of these arguments is a kind of magical thinking that efficient markets emerge automatically if people are just left alone. Similar magical thinking affects many right-wing Republicans in the United States, who think that if you just eliminate government the economy will grow. Likewise it was a crucial reason why shock therapy, implemented on the advice of liberal Democrats, was such a catastrophe in the Soviet Union. On the contrary, efficient markets require good infrastructure and finely honed legal, accounting, and supervision structures and need constant, and constantly evolving, maintenance by properly structured organizations of skilled professionals. The transition to such markets is often catastrophic if not carefully planned and implemented.

Political Reform

If the essence of the Asia Model is a priority for economic development, the corollary is that the country is managed for economic efficiency. It is, in short, managed in many ways as if it were a business. I shall speak later of the GE Model of governance. As in the economic sphere, political reform in the Asia Model is a process of rapid incremental progress.

The Asia Model presupposes a certain kind of leadership motivation. In the Philippines, most of Latin America, and most of Africa for much of the modern period, politicians have wanted to become leaders of their countries because it was the most effective path to become rich. The Asia Model works only where the country has found a way of selecting top leaders who focus instead on what future historians will say about them. Ferdinand Marcos wanted to be President of the Philippines so that he could become rich. Park Chung Hee of South Korea, Jiang Jingguo of Taiwan, Lee Kwan Yew of Singapore, and the early contemporary Chinese leaders such as Deng Xiaoping and Zhu Rongji have been motivated primarily by wanting to ensure that future historians will say they did great things for their country. In the new century some Chinese leaders, most notably Prime Minister Wen Jiabao, who served under a more circumspect Party Secretary Hu Jintao, have muddied this pattern, becoming fabulously rich at the expense of serving their country's future. Generals pondering how to make their next million – or hundred million – dollars are probably not focused on teaching their troops how to shoot straight; China's leadership is currently engaged in a great struggle over whether the Asian miracle model or the get-rich-quick model will predominate. Chapter 3 on social issues will examine corruption and the anti-corruption campaign.

The foundation of political reform in the China Model, as elsewhere, is the transition from governance based on charisma to governance based on institutionalized rules. The transition from government by Mao's whim to governance by contemporary China's institutionalized management is itself a revolutionary change. China started by stabilizing the leadership in key areas so that people, including foreign investors, could rely on continuity. The emergence of a rules-based system began with rules on retirement of officials and proceeded to things like (incompletely) separating regulatory functions from ownership and operation of the SOEs. Stable governance across a vast territory requires rules-based governance. Markets can develop only on the basis of a vast infrastructure of widely understood rules. Competition-based efficiency can emerge only if competition is based on clear rules of the game. Domestic investors will have the confidence to invest on a large scale only if the rules are relatively clear. Foreign investors are even more insistent on clear rules, implemented by a system that does not depend on political whim.[13] Hence a gradual transition to the rule of law becomes imperative.[14]

---

[13] Contrary to common assumption, moving to the market, or "deregulating" the market part of an economy, requires an enormous network of new rules and institutions to enforce them. See Steven K. Vogel, *Freer Markets, More Rules* (Ithaca, NY: Cornell University Press, 1996). This makes incrementalism essential and is one of the reasons why Soviet shock therapy privatization was a catastrophe. (Vogel's book focuses on developed economies, but the core point is even more important for developing ones.)

[14] On the strengths and weaknesses of China's movement toward a law-based system, the decades of works of Jerome Cohen and Randall Peerenbohm are

China has made enormous progress in creating a rules-based system, but it has a long way to go. The government has, for instance, sought to eliminate irregular local taxes and fees on rural people and to constrain irregular takings of land for development, but ownership rights in a large proportion of local companies with partial government sponsorship remain unclear, and farmers' rights in their land remain somewhat ambiguous. A Party Commission can determine the outcome of any legal case. Here again China has reached a point where fundamental choices need to be made and the direction of those choices is currently unclear. See the further discussion in the chapters on politics.

Other forms of political development are driven by the requirements of science and the market. Scientific progress requires disagreement and debate, so a degree of freedom of speech comes to physics and chemistry departments. Then it turns out that finding the optimal economic policies requires disagreement and debate and broad freedom to conduct that debate, and so do decisions about the balance between the needs for urban redevelopment and the interests of people who live in the area to be redeveloped. A successful market requires that people be free to choose their jobs and hence to choose the location where they will live. The result is a broad increase in personal freedoms. In this area as in others, China's experience in the first three decades of reform tracks that of the other successful economies, in this case most notably Taiwan, but the future in China is less clear.

As the economy modernizes, transparency becomes an imperative. Taxation requires accounting transparency. Investment requires transparency, whether that investment is in a joint venture or in stocks and bonds. In the political arena, even a tough authoritarian state finds it difficult to get people to pay their taxes and to comply with policies, and in larger societies this problem becomes exponentially more difficult. Hence, increasing transparency becomes imperative for both economic and governance reasons.

Likewise, accountability becomes ever more complex and difficult as the economy and society become more complex. How are top leaders

particularly valuable. For running commentary, see www.jeromecohen.net/jerrys-blog. Current developments are somewhat schizoid, making progress in some areas and retreating drastically in others. For a revealing debate see "The Future of China's Legal System," www.chinafile.com/viewpoint/future-of-chinas-legal-system.

to know what is really happening in the towns and villages? A vast network of communications and bureaucratic checks certainly helps. But increasingly top leaders need feedback from the public. Hence increasing use of polls, of monitoring internet opinion, of allowing the press some freedom to criticize, of tolerating protests within limits, of listening more to the views of legislators and others who represent diverse groups, of permitting (constrained) village elections.

While fear drives the "miracle" phase of development, the phase properly called an economic mobilization system, success eventually dissipates fear. As fear segues into confidence, the willingness of the population to endure terrible stresses dissipates and so does the motivation of the leaders to take great risks. Relatively rapid development can continue if the government has been organized in a highly meritocratic way, what I later call the "GE Model of development." But even a highly meritocratic system more focused on growth than most other countries has to evolve quickly away from an exclusive focus on GDP growth to a broader set of environmental and social welfare goals.

One driver of this political evolution arises from the changing needs and values of the citizenry. When people are scared and hungry, they yearn for stability and food above all else. The citizens of Japan in 1950, South Korea and Singapore in 1960, and China for much of its modern history have been driven by fear of disorder, war, and hunger. Whoever seemed able to bring order, unity, food, and shelter received their support. But success brings with it new issues. When people live to 75 years rather than 40, when their children virtually all survive and virtually all get an education, when they have a home and a car, they become both more rooted in their society and more demanding.[15] China is in the early stages of this, but the signs of transition are everywhere. People care about the environment and speak out. They care about how urban development is managed and they organize in support of their views. Society supported the vast social stresses that occurred under Zhu Rongji, whose term ended in early 2003, because they saw most of the change as necessary, but attitudes turned negative in his last 18 months and people began to express a

---

[15] The standard reference on people's hierarchy of needs, which I have interpreted to mean changing values as life improves, is Abraham Maslow, "A Theory of Human Motivation," *Psychological Review*, 50(4), 1943, pp. 370–396.

yearning for a more harmonious society. Willingness to accept a society run like a business, with the overriding goal of economic efficiency, was beginning slowly to fade. In all the Asia Model modernizations, success eventually puts limits on the extent to which society can be run as a business. These economies are still managed more like businesses than most others, but social pressures diminish the ruthlessness of change.

Before moving on to more detailed discussion in subsequent chapters, key points stand out. First, for the Western audience: the image of the China Model as politically unchanging and brittle has no basis in reality. Given its scale as one-sixth of the human population, China's political evolution has been extraordinarily rapid. In its first three decades the China Model was fully consistent with the successful evolution of the other Asia Model economies, which has been stressful but largely peaceful. Despite the consensus Western views of the 1970s, South Korea and Taiwan were not candidates for revolutionary upheaval. But, as with the economic part of the China Model, politics evolves through rapid incrementalism, not through shock therapy. That is to say, it evolves the way most of Western politics evolved, just faster, not the way much current Western thought approves of other societies' evolution.

The message for Chinese scholars and leaders is one that they mostly understand very well: the success of the China Model has depended upon very rapid evolution in governance as well as in economics. Continued success will require continued evolution. That does not necessarily imply that politics in Beijing will end up looking like politics in Washington, DC, but it does mean that China faces social imperatives, arising from the complexity of modern society and the evolving values of citizens when they become more economically secure, that parallel the imperatives faced earlier by other exemplars of the Asia Model. The chapter on domestic politics below looks at this imperative. Whether Western or anti-Western, it is not at all clear that the Xi Jinping administration has a coherent political approach to the era of complexity in social structure and complexity in values. While there have been improvements in administration under Hu, and some recent backsliding under Xi, overall measures of governance have changed remarkably little in the new century – a sharp difference from rapid political reform under Deng Xiaoping and Jiang Zemin.

Distinctive Aspects of the China Model

While the China Model is a variant of the Asia Model, building on the experience of its predecessors, it obviously has distinctive characteristics. The sheer scale of China's geography and population entails important differences.

The most noteworthy aspect differentiating the China Model is its creative use of "One country, two systems" (for Hong Kong and Macau and originally intended for Taiwan), "One sector, two systems" (for transitions away from state enterprises and the planned economy), "One city, two systems," and even "One company, two systems" to minimize social stress in the process of potentially stressful transitions. Professor Lawrence Lau has elucidated how this "One, two" system leads to remarkably efficient transitions[16] that allow almost everyone to keep moving forward.[17] The transition to mostly market prices in agriculture exemplifies the "One, two" model. In early socialism, the peasants had to turn over their grain to the state and there were quotas for how much they had to produce and turn over. In the transition, they still had to produce and turn over the quotas, but they were encouraged to sell any additional production on the market. Gradually the "additional production" overwhelmed the quota production and the system transitioned to a largely market basis.

Also distinctive is China's use of large-scale field tests for new policies. The early Special Economic Zones (mainly for processing);

---

[16] Lawrence Lau, "Gain without Pain: Why Economic Reform in China Worked," in Gung-Wu Wang and John Wong, eds., *China's Political Economy* (Singapore: Singapore University Press, 1998), pp. 43–70.

[17] Most readers will be familiar only with the "One country, two systems" model developed for Taiwan and applied to Hong Kong. Taiwan rejected the model and Hong Kong recently hit serious bumps in the road as China cracked down on controversial booksellers and others. But even with the bumps the model avoided a great historical crisis between China and Britain, sustained Hong Kong's prosperity, maintained Hong Kong's British-style economic and legal systems, and maintained free speech and much (not all) of the legacy of critical media. The domestic Chinese economic aspects – one sector, two systems; one company two systems ... – have worked very smoothly indeed. Both in the agricultural transition and in the industrial transition, the transition to the market occurred without depriving those dependent on traditional state quotas and subsidies. *Contrary to Western preconceptions about heartless authoritarianism, this care for what happened to families is the most important distinguishing factor between Asian incrementalism and Western-sponsored shock therapy.*

the observation of the effects of dissolving the communes prior to encouraging such dissolution throughout the country; the employment of special development zones in Shenzhen, Pudong, Tianjin Binhai, and Chongqing; the testing of new political ideas in Shenzhen; the experiments with three (mis-named) Free Trade Zones under Xi Jinping; and many other field tests too numerous to mention all demonstrate a pragmatic, careful, scientific approach to modernization. China's leaders "cross the river by feeling the stones," in the famous phrasing that Deng Xiaoping appropriated from Chen Yun. They think very carefully before stepping, and they test their balance on each stone before moving forward. But they often move through this process quickly and decisively.

If the priority for economics leads Asia Model countries to manage themselves on the analogy of business management, China has refined the art of managing a country as a business to a distinctive level. Infrastructure development, indicative planning for the growth of different sectors, seed investments in Tianjin Binhai and Chongqing, and many aspects of development are handled the way they would be handled by a large-scale business. This reaches its most characteristic form in government personnel management. More on this can be found in the politics chapter below.

China has also been distinctive among the larger societies in the degree to which it has pursued what one might call social globalization. Chinese students go abroad in greater numbers than those of any other country (although South Korea sends proportionately more). China welcomes foreign experts and workers with needed skills to an exceptional degree. More than any other country, it sends its senior government officials abroad to acquire knowledge of what other countries believe to be best practice. As noted earlier, perhaps the single most important determinant of success of the Asia Model is a reaching out for global best practice. In Japan, this search for global practice was particularly vivid in the early Meiji period and in the three decades after World War II, but then Japan turned inward.

Both Japan and Korea, as relatively homogeneous, insular societies, have had difficulty accepting many aspects of social globalization. One South Korean president after another battles against the social barriers to globalization, from belligerent xenophobic unions to riots against any imports of US beef, with sporadic but cumulative success. South Korea, amazingly for the former Hermit Kingdom, now defines itself as a multicultural society. Proportionately South Korea sends more of its students abroad than any other society. As the South Korean example shows, Japan's introversion cannot be explained by invoking an aging society, a trend Japan and South Korea share, but rather resulted from a decision by the governing elite. As a consequence, South Korean per capita incomes, once among the world's poorest, are on the way to equaling or surpassing Japan's, something nobody would have imagined possible even a few years ago.

Japanese politicians have been less interested in overcoming the barriers. They turned inward after 1975, falsely attributed Japan's early success to "unique Japanese cultural characteristics," and created layers and layers of protectionism, and stopped sending their people overseas for experience.[18] Japan still has some very impressive global companies, but they are in limited sectors. Japan now sends fewer students abroad than South Korea or tiny Taiwan. (It does, however, send more students to neighboring China than the United States sends.) Some leaders, most notably recent Prime Minister Hatoyama Yukio, have actively denounced globalization. The consequences for Japan's economy have been tragic. At the other end of the globalization scale have been the city-states Singapore and Hong Kong, which, partly by virtue of their size, have been very open to global best practice and competition. China falls at the enthusiastic end of the spectrum of social globalization, although of course, given its huge population, it cannot match the proportions that South Korea, Taiwan, and Singapore send abroad.

While demographically China cannot match Singapore's globalization, the thrust of its policies has been more like Singapore than like Japan. Chinese students learn English; Japanese students study English but do not learn it. The children and grandchildren of China's leaders go abroad for education. Japan's stay home and those few who do go abroad are usually penalized with less successful careers. For many years, a Japanese student who attended Harvard would stunt his (or her, but almost always his) career. The number of Chinese students in the United States now exceeds that of any other nationality; the number of Japanese students in the United States has declined precipitously and now is less than that of Taiwanese or South Koreans. Senior

[18] See R. Taggart Murphy, *Japan and the Shackles of the Past* (London: Oxford University Press, 2014).

Chinese officials often spend a semester or more studying in the United States or elsewhere. Such practices, even more than the details of economic opening and marketization, are the ultimate key to China's current success and its prospects for continuing that success.

China does not only send its best people abroad; it also imports talent enthusiastically. Its electronics factories and sports teams pay Western-level salaries to import top international talent. Because Shanghai's extraordinary collection of modern buildings strained the available construction talent, Shanghai imported not only the architects but also substantial numbers of plumbers and construction workers. There is now a little colony of Chicago plumbers and construction workers in Shanghai, happily earning more than they could at home in Chicago.

China is distinctive in the diversity of its social progress. Shanghai is part of the modern world. Qinghai is still an impoverished, backward economy and society. This unavoidable diversity worsens the inevitable income and social disparities between rural and urban areas, between coast and interior. Those disparities are difficult enough to manage economically. But they create even more serious challenges for political development. Political progress tends to be accompanied by strong waves of feeling across a nation, but Shanghai is ready for things that Qinghai is not.

Risks of the Asia Model

The Asia Model is always implemented by a dominant party, or a coalition with a dominant core as in Malaysia or Japan. A dominant party has many advantages for stability, for continuity, and for implementing socially stressful policies in the face of opposition. But it also carries the risks of ossification and debilitating corruption. Indonesia's Golkar and Mexico's Institutional Revolutionary Party (PRI) succumbed to these risks. Japan and Malaysia have more quietly lost their dynamism because of these risks. Hubris and interest group subversion of the national interest lead to decay, loss of productivity growth, economic stagnation, and political alienation. The China Model incurs such risks but faces them with superior economic openness, superior domestic economic competition, and superior social globalization. Hence China's chances are socially better, but can be fulfilled only with wise leadership. Bureaucratic metastasis under Hu Jintao

(2002–2012) and nationalistic assertion under Xi Jinping (2013–present) could jeopardize China's advantages.

The speed of development of the Asia Model means that the parts can easily get out of sync. For continued success, the economy must continually upgrade at the expense of obsolete sectors. Political reform must keep up with economic reform. The state-enterprise-based economy must give way to an economy where growth, jobs, and innovation come heavily from small and medium-size firms of which a large proportion are private. So far, China's ability to keep the different parts in sync, for a vast population of very diverse circumstances, has been remarkable, but the challenge arises anew every year. Later chapters will focus on these challenges.

Geopolitically, a large country that grows rapidly into a major modern economy with great military power requires an evolution from one that takes the international system for granted to one whose own success entails taking responsibility for maintaining the system. Japan had great difficulty with this. By maintaining a relatively protectionist economy that is totally dependent on exports for growth, Japan seriously harmed the improvement of the world trade system and has suffered humiliating, gratuitous stagnation at home. Japan, which needed to change back in the late 1970s, never made the transition that China is now attempting from an export-led economy to one driven by domestic demand.

In contrast, so far China has forthrightly faced the imperative to change, whereas Japan's ruling party has refused to pay the interest group price for such a transition and under Abe has gone backward.[19] Nonetheless, China is in a phase where it wants to celebrate its status as a great power but resents being told that it has some responsibility for limiting nuclear proliferation in the Middle East and for avoiding the aggravation of global trade imbalances. Here too China has reached a turning point, and here the trends seem auspicious in some areas, especially on global warming, Iranian nuclear proliferation, and

---

[19] I addressed this in William H. Overholt, "Policymakers Need to Recognize That the Clock Is Ticking," *Nikkei Asian Review*, November 27, 2014, http://overholtgroup.com/media/Articles-Japan/Clock-is-Ticking-NikkeiAsianReview-27NOV2014.pdf. Japanese domestic and international protectionism raises prices and transfers money from consumers to corporations, creating a shortage of final demand. Abe cut taxes on corporations and raised them on consumers – the kind of decision that for decades has ensured continued stagnation. Likewise, the drastic devaluations that Abe has promoted raise the cost of imported goods and therefore reduce people's purchasing power.

global trade imbalances, but quite inauspicious in others, most notably creating a peaceful rules-based or consensus-based maritime regime.

The Inexorable Crisis

Always the Asian miracle economies approach a point of crisis. A crisis does not mean inevitable collapse. In medicine, when a patient has severe pneumonia, the crisis is when the patient gets to the point of resolution; he will either live or die. In political economy, the choices are more diverse: the patient will prosper, stagnate, or decline. South Korea and Taiwan have prospered. Japan has stagnated, fortunately at a very high level.

The Asian miracle economies eventually come to a point where fear no longer simplifies politics, where society has reached a level of development where the economy is just too complex to be managed from the top leader's office, and where the polity comprises a myriad conflicting interest groups that likewise cannot be managed in detail by a small central leadership. At that point transformative economic and political changes are required.

How does one know when the point of crisis has come? After all, fear dissipates gradually and economic and political complexity increase gradually. At any particular point it appears that this process might go on forever. But when one knows what to look for the signs are clear. In South Korea, by 1978–1979 Park Chung Hee faced a combination of escalating financial squeeze and escalating political demonstrations. The old model had the president's office deciding major loans, production quotas, export quotas, and much else. Over-investment in heavy industry was creating a financial squeeze. People's economic and military fears no longer led them to accept increasingly dictatorial rule. Resolution of the political crisis took more than a decade, and economic transformation sufficient to take things to a new and stable level took until after the Asian Crisis of 1997–1998.

In Taiwan a similar dynamic occurred. An economy dominated by 40 Guomindang conglomerates was becoming inefficient and overindebted, and suffered a financial collapse in 1990. The polity was increasingly unwilling to accept harsh rule by a mainland elite, so the leadership moved toward a high level of Taiwanization and democratization by the late 1980s. As in South Korea, the political issue and the economic issue are two sides of the same coin. The economic interest groups whose power and complex interactions force a change of economic structure are largely the same as the political interest groups that contend in radically more complex ways and with fast-changing values.

Once one looks for the pattern, its emergence in China is unmistakable. The mood of the Chinese population has evolved from fear of collapse to hubris. China faces a financial squeeze and possibly world history's most complex economic transition. China's leaders have responded by proclaiming a fundamental shift to market allocation of resources and hundreds of detailed policy changes that follow from that imperative. Simultaneously Xi Jinping and his colleagues have argued successfully that corruption and interest group resistance to reform risk both the legitimacy and the effectiveness of Communist Party rule, and they have responded by restructuring the leadership and drastically changing the norms of Chinese politics. The economic transition to greater acceptance of market forces is precisely analogous to what happened in South Korea and Taiwan as the government roles diminished and the chaebol and the Guomindang companies were forced into acceptance of market pressures. But it remains to be seen how effectively China will implement the proclaimed economic transition, and it has chosen a radically different approach to the political transition.[20]

Geopolitics of the China Model

The core of the Asia Model's geopolitics is that Japan, South Korea, Indonesia, Singapore, and China have all enhanced their geopolitical stature when they reduced their military and geopolitical assertiveness in order to concentrate their resources and management attention on economic growth. As already noted, rapid economic growth provides superior political stability, and a military budget that is a small share of GDP grows so fast under the Asia Model that it becomes very impressive even while remaining a small share. Just as Indonesia became the leader of Southeast Asia in part by giving up claims to sovereignty over

---

[20] One of the problems of writing about China is that the flood of new studies is hard to keep up with. Here as elsewhere I will try to acknowledge important work that came out after my own book was submitted for review. David Shambaugh is one of the great contributors to our understanding of China. His *China's Future* (Boston, MA: Polity Press, 2016) provides important insights into the set of transitional crisis issues discussed in this section. My angle of approach is different, my balance is different, and my sense of some of the economic issues is quite different, but the work is broadly complementary.

much of the rest of Southeast Asia, so also China achieved its great stature of today in part by resolving 12 out of 14 of its land border disputes peacefully to the satisfaction of the other parties. Compromise on land borders has, however, now given way to domineering assertion on maritime borders, creating risks both for foreign countries and for China's continued progress.

A corollary of the downgrading of geopolitical assertiveness has been the cessation of revolutionary subversion and ideological proselytization. Mao's China tried to subvert governments all over the world and to promote Maoist ideology everywhere. The result was conflict with the majority of the world's governments. Reformist China does not try to subvert any government and does not try to change the ideology of other countries. This has allowed China to focus on economic progress.

The key geopolitical fact about the China Model is that China is not promoting a China Model, notwithstanding a whole Western literature about a (nonexistent) Beijing Consensus. Beijing is simply refusing to go along with the idea that one model of Western democracy should be imposed everywhere, rather than trying to replicate its own structure around the world. Paradoxically this has greatly strengthened China's global influence; African countries in particular prefer to be told to find their own path rather than being told by Washington and Brussels that their diverse circumstances should all be subordinated to a US or UK model.

Many in the West are upset that China does not join in promoting the Democratic Model in Africa, Latin America, and parts of Asia. Those who are committed to the universality of the Democratic Model feel threatened by the fact that China's success lights a path to development that does not depend on democracy. This writer's view is that, if there are other paths out of human misery, then we Westerners have no right to object and in fact should applaud. It is also true that the most robust democracies in the emerging countries are those where Asia Model development rapidly created the educated, middle-class societies within which democracy most easily flourishes. No democracies in the emerging world compare with the vitality of South Korea and Taiwan, which build upon social structures created by particularly dictatorial predecessors. As long as China merely creates a model of success, without imposing it on anyone else, nobody has the right to object if other countries choose to emulate some aspects of China. I have argued above that most countries lack the omnipresent fear and sense of national identity that are prerequisites of following the Asia/China Model in full.

China's trade, aid, and investment policies in Africa do sometimes undercut Western efforts to impose certain governance criteria on aid programs. If there were any evidence that Western aid has actually led to superior performance, then the objections would be valid. I will leave it to proponents of different approaches to demonstrate empirically what actually works. At the time of writing this book, the fastest-growing economy in the world seems to be Ethiopia, which has followed more advice from the Chinese chief economist of the World Bank, Justin Lin, than from the West. Washington and Brussels are arguing that there should be only one basic governance path to development. The Chinese view is that different circumstances may justify different paths and that countries should be left to decide for themselves. In most cases, given the demonstrated validity of the Asia Model as a path to economic development and political stability, and given the possibility that the Asia Model is the most reliable path to stable democracy, Western defensiveness is unjustified. It is also based on completely misplaced apprehensions, since, as noted earlier, the conditions of fear and cohesiveness that enable the Asian miracles are quite scarce.

Of course, if political laissez-faire is taken to the extreme of willingness to rationalize military sales to genocidal tyrants, then genuine moral issues do arise.

As in domestic economics and domestic politics, China has reached a point in its development where it faces fundamental geopolitical choices. The Washington view that China has turned decisively toward expansionism is a caricature, but Chinese behavior regarding maritime disputes is the polar opposite of how it handled land disputes and that raises the most fundamental questions about the future.

The following chapters tackle in sequence the following issues: the great economic transition China faces; vital social issues affecting China's future; the prospects of the political model; and alternative choices.

Again, the questions this book tries to answer are as follows. Why has China succeeded? Why does it now face a crisis? How might the crisis work out?

2 | *The Economic Crisis of Success*

In 1982, when I first traveled around China, Northeast China still had one-pants families, families so poor that the man wore the family's one pair of pants to work in the field and the wife, who stayed home naked during the day, got to wear them for her errands after he had returned home. Two decades earlier, nationwide, at least 30 million Chinese people had starved to death. Today the average *rural* family, with only one-third the income of the typical urban family, nevertheless has 1.2 television sets and fractionally more than two cell phones. A quarter have computers, three-quarters have washing machines and refrigerators, 11 percent own automobiles, and two-thirds own motorcycles.[1] Much more prosperous urban people make China the world's largest market for luxury goods and for more cars than are sold anywhere else.

As noted earlier, fear – fear of social collapse, fear of invasion, fear of war, fear of starvation – led people to accept ruthless leadership that promised national salvation. They initially followed Mao Zedong, whose ideas were "Politics in Command," "Red over Expert," and "Political power emerges from the barrel of a gun," in other words a priority for politics over other values, for ideology over technical expertise, and for a predominant military role. He advocated replacing material incentives with social prestige and safeguarding China's economy by walling it off from the rest of the world. He had an agrarian hatred of bureaucracy, expressed in the chaos of the Cultural Revolution. By the time people had experienced the Great Leap Forward (1958–1961), with tens of millions of deaths due to crazy development policies and unwillingness to acknowledge the disaster, and the Cultural Revolution (1966–1976), which decimated the Party, the government, and the military and caused social chaos for everyone, every major group of the population had had

---

[1] *China Statistical Yearbook 2015*, p. 193.

enough.[2] That universal disgust opened the door for Deng Xiaoping to offer a new path to salvation – Economics in Command, experts in command, military expenditures drastically reduced, gradual market-ization, and opening the economy to foreign trade and investment.

Recent History

Under Jiang Zemin and Zhu Rongji, Deng's successors, whose terms ended in 2003, China introduced crucial market reforms, centralized administration, continued to upgrade the bureaucracy, capped corruption, and saved the country from an imminent banking system collapse.

At the beginning of their administration, the government could not manage the budget or control inflation, nor could a top leader easily fire a provincial governor. A budget reform in 1994 channeled most tax revenues to the central government, which then doled funds out to the provinces. By the end of their term, inflation was consistently under control because of a drastically improved banking system, a highly competent central bank, and Zhu Rongji's successful assertion of authority over provincial governments. He had a lever for controlling the money supply that most central banks lack – the ability to threaten execution of bankers and officials who didn't respect the limits. By the end of his term that lever was no longer necessary.

Likewise the central government successfully asserted control over local officials. The problem of officials who made decisions on the basis of the Guangdong saying, "The mountains are high and the emperor is far away," pervades Chinese history. At the beginning of the Cultural Revolution, the leading official in Guangdong, Tao Zhu, lived luxuriously in a castle and required aspiring young actresses to sleep with him. Powerful as Mao seemed, he could not dismiss Tao Zhu. So he offered him the number four leadership position in Beijing and then, as soon as Tao Zhu had arrived in the capital, arrested him. In contrast, to take one famous example, after Jiang Zemin and Zhu Rongji had ruled China for a few years, the prime minister could look across the

---

[2] The authoritative work on the Cultural Revolution is Roderick MacFarquhar, *Mao's Last Revolution* (Cambridge, MA: Belknap Press, 2006). My favorite brief summary of the devastation of China's elite is Charles Neuhauser, "The Impact of the Cultural Revolution on the Chinese Communist Party Machine," *Asian Survey* 50(4), 1968, pp. 465–468. The reader will instantly understand why the entire elite was ready to take a new direction.

table during a meeting and say to a provincial governor, "That's a really nice watch you're wearing. It cost more than my annual salary. You're fired."

Zhu Rongji fixed the banks' crisis by first reforming their customers – the state-owned enterprises (SOEs). At the time, the SOEs as a group were losing so much money that they threatened to take China's finances down in the manner that happened in the Soviet Union. Later he recapitalized and reformed the banks themselves. Zhu, expanding on earlier policies of Deng Xiaoping, chose a limited number of large SOEs as essential and let the others go. Tens of thousands were devolved to local government ownership. Local governments picked the ones they wanted and sold off the rest. It was forbidden to call this process privatization, but a large number were in fact sold to private owners, including foreigners, who sometimes bought over 100 at a time.

In addition, the leadership became devotees of competition. By the late 1990s the *Wall Street Journal* and the media organs of the Chinese Communist Party were the world's greatest cheerleaders for competition. China's phone companies, for instance, competed as if they were private companies in a fully marketized economy; that led to huge efficiency gains. By the end of this process, the remaining central government SOEs were highly profitable as a group and the government was able to fix the banking system by recapitalizing it, moving the bad loans to bad banks (called asset management companies), reforming the management and accounting, appointing foreign directors and senior executives, taking on foreign minority partners to learn best practice, and listing the banks on stock exchanges outside the mainland.

Zhu also reformed the government. He set a goal of cutting the government and Party bureaucracies in half – more Reagan than Reagan by miles. At the top levels he approached his goal; the use of consultancies and other devices to ease the transition for displaced officials does not diminish his achievement. And he gave every bureau a quota of regulations to cut, to make government more efficient and to reduce the opportunities for graft. When I visited Laura Cha, a senior Hong Kong regulator hired as deputy head of the China Securities Commission, she was urgently looking for regulations to cut so as to meet her quota. In the meantime Zhu quadrupled salaries so officials would not need graft in order to live.

These reforms were successful at the cost of social stress that would have been intolerable in most countries. They reduced SOE employ- ment by about 45 million in 10 years. For comparison, the loss of 3 million US manufacturing jobs in a decade caused a serious political reaction in the United States.

By the end of the Zhu Rongji era (late 2002/early 2003), China's people were exhausted by the strain of constant reforms. For the last 18 months of his term anger was widespread and intense. People blamed him for causing so much upheaval without definitively solving all of China's major problems. (One frequent comment was "Look at the problems in the rural areas. What has he done about that?") Today he is again regarded as a hero, but when he left office people were demanding a different approach – like Latin Americans denouncing neoliberal reforms.

Jiang Zemin and Zhu Rongji had been cosmopolitan marketizers, both having served as mayors of leading coastal city Shanghai, who were determined to repair China's economy whatever it took. It took as much as people could stand. In reaction, China turned to provincial officials whose ideal and slogan was a "harmonious society," a phrase with many layers of meaning but with a core of "No more Zhu Rongji market reforms causing social upheaval." The new top leader, Hu Jintao, was a hydropower engineer whose high-level experience was focused on the backward interior provinces of Guizhou and Tibet. The new prime minister, Wen Jiabao, was a geological engineer whose primary leadership experience was in the backward interior province of Gansu. Neither had any experience of coastal, not to mention international, markets. Their provinces were way behind the coastal provinces in both reforms and mentality. It was as if the United States had got new leadership by stolid bureaucrats from Arizona and Wyo- ming. They were the opposite of cosmopolitan, marketizing reformers. Market reforms largely ended. Political reforms largely ended.[3]

---

[3] Before Hu Jintao became the top leader, he was, inter alia, President of the Central Party School. During those years, the Central Party School elaborated scenarios for alternative courses to democratization. Three alternative paths were publicly debated, basically a Japan model, a Taiwan model, and a more conservative model, even on television. Therefore the early Hu years brought expectations, at least among foreign observers, including this one, of major political reforms. The hopes were disappointed and the debates faded.

Nonetheless President Hu Jintao and Prime Minister Wen Jiabao addressed key forms of inequality, reduced unfair local exactions from rural people, reformed the personnel system, and got China through the Global Financial Crisis. Whereas coastal growth had previously far outpaced the interior, they poured resources and political talent into the core interior provinces, Sichuan and Chongqing, where growth rates soared to 15 percent. Think of two Germanies growing at 15 percent annually, faster even than China's coastal exporting provinces had grown. Xinjiang, in the far northwest, had already been growing nicely, although the benefits of growth went disproportionately to Han Chinese migrants from other provinces. The other provinces in the interior/far west had little population, so this constituted a major success against regional inequality. Likewise, they acted to relieve farmers and other rural people of an intolerable burden of local fees and other exactions. Above all, they got China through the Global Financial Crisis by empowering local officials on a spending binge that dwarfed what any other country did. The crisis had a terrible impact on local communities, particularly along the coast. Even in a single city, millions of people had to move back from the coastal city to the rural countryside. But Beijing's spending binge ensured quick recovery.

After the binge comes the hangover. And after the vacation from reform comes the need to catch up with work left undone. In an essay for *Harvard China Review* at the beginning of Hu Jintao's administration,[4] I compared China to a man being chased by a tiger. If you focus your camera on the man, you say, "Wow, this man must be the world's fastest runner." If you focus on the tiger – that is, on the problems of urbanization, demography, employment, corruption, and so forth – you say, "Wow, that's a really big tiger that will eat anything in its path." By the end of the Hu–Wen administration, the tiger was gaining fast.

In addition, Hu and Wen allowed some of the great successes of Jiang and Zhu to unravel. Where Zhu had tried to halve the bureaucracy, under the Hu–Wen administration the government and Party bureaucracies metastasized from 40 million to 70 million officials. Corruption ballooned, and even the prime minister's family leveraged

---

[4] William H. Overholt, "China's Economy, Resilience and Challenge," *Harvard China Review*, Spring 2004, pp. 47–52, available at www.theoverholtgroup.com/publications/asia/china/index.html.

his influence into billions of dollars of wealth. The amounts involved in corruption started to be one or two orders of magnitude larger. The administration's coddling of the SOEs allowed them to become uncompetitive. Whereas Jiang and Zhu had centralized administrative power, by 2005, only two years into the new administration, leading scholars were expressing concern that centrifugal forces – the rising power of individual bureaucracies, local government, SOEs, and the military – were leading China back in the direction of long-term administrative and political disintegration. When Prime Minister Wen announced curbs on the housing industry, one ministry publicly disregarded him, and leading property executives, with whom I was having a series of dinners at the time, laughed derisively at what they believed to be his inability to enforce them. (Wen eventually won that battle, but the interest group attitude was telling.) Likewise, countless Chinese remarked bluntly that they saw Hu as a spineless bureaucrat, expressing neither respect nor fear of retribution.[5] Many ended up dismissing his tenure in office as a "lost decade."

The Crisis of Success

This left the next administration with extraordinarily complex tasks. Xi Jinping's new administration had to cope with all of the following: a crisis of success caused by the exhaustion of the old drivers of growth; a crisis of obsolete priorities; the inevitability of slower growth; and a serious financial squeeze.

When an entrepreneur invents a new product and markets it successfully, the company can grow very fast under his ad hoc leadership, but one day it reaches a scale where a new structure is required. It needs professional accountants, professional human resources people, professional financial managers, professional marketers and communicators, and a rule book. That is a crisis of success. The success is real, but the crisis is real too, and many companies fail to survive the transition to a more mature structure. China hit a crisis of success at the end of the first decade of the new century.

[5] Some Chinese scholars report that Hu was crippled by severe diabetes to an extent that changed his personality from relatively lighthearted to rigid, humorless, even robotic. But the system could not replace him without upsetting the equilibrium among factions. If true, this inability to make changes is a very fundamental problem of the political structure.

The old drivers of growth had been net exports and investment in heavy industry and infrastructure. When, in the early days, the reform administration built a first-class highway from Beijing to Shanghai, the resulting efficiencies quickly paid for the investment and much more. Construction of roads, railroads, airline systems, ports, and telecommunications knit China together and created a far more efficient economy that, as a consequence, grew fast. Ultimately the core of success was the gradual creation of a national economy out of what had been many largely separate economies. By the end of the Hu Jintao era, the easy efficiencies had been exhausted. A lot of the new construction comprised things like building very big shopping malls and huge city halls in small cities. Efficiency gains were often between zero and negative. Greatly worsening this, the spending binge to get through the Global Financial Crisis had authorized extraordinary amounts of construction that would never have been approved except as a response to crisis. The hangover of debt was quite severe.

Simultaneously the exclusive priority for economic growth had become an obsolete strategy. Going obsessively for GDP growth was the secret of all the Asian miracle economies. But there is always a price for emphasizing one thing over everything else. In the Soviet Union the saying was that, if you paid a nail factory for the pounds of nails it produced, you got one big nail. If you paid for the number of nails, you got millions of tiny nails. Similarly, in investment banks we learned that we had to change the bonus formulae every couple of years because smart people learn how to game the system.

After 30 years of reform obsession with GDP growth in China, everyone had learned how to game the system. You could get local or corporate growth by borrowing large amounts of money and investing it, even if the investments were inefficient. You could get outsize local or corporate growth by allowing companies to pour all their waste into the rivers, air, and soil. You could get growth by exploiting people who had moved from other areas, failing to provide them with education, medical care, and pensions. You could get GDP growth by taking farmers' land for industrial development and not paying them appropriately for it. In broad social terms, you could get GDP growth by ruthlessly jerking people around the way investment banks hire and fire people ruthlessly as the market changes – for instance forcing 45 million SOE workers to find new jobs – but investment bankers get paid well enough to tolerate the jerking around whereas peasants and elderly SOE workers don't.

Underlying all this was an even more fundamental problem. The economy had moved from the era of simplicity to an era of complexity. Imagine an economy that is just peasants growing rice, landlords (individual or governmental), road construction, and textiles. That is an economy simple enough for even a government to understand. You build good roads in the right places, give the peasants their land, allow workers to sell their labor inexpensively to foreigners, and you sell a lot of cheap socks to the foreigners. The economy grows like a weed. That model works for several succeeding layers of complexity, but then you find that the economy has semiconductors, hundreds of competing apparel and shoe brands, dozens of kinds of steel, computers, pads, cell phones, cars, half a dozen competing kinds of power-producing companies (coal, gas, wind, hydro, nuclear), power transmission companies whose interests compete with those of the power producers, a panoply of ever-changing software companies, hundreds of kinds of services companies ... and orders of magnitude more, many with competing interests. Making detailed central government decisions and trying to implement them the old way just doesn't work anymore.

Finally, when a company has decided to move to a new product line, say from textiles to semiconductors (a transition some Chinese companies actually made),[6] it is very important to do it at a time of booming demand. That way, during the transfer of resources from the old line to the new, the new line has a good chance of ramping up production before the old line goes bust. For a society changing its economic model, if growth is generous then the stress imposed on society can be cushioned by new opportunities. That was the story of the first three decades of growth, but not from 2010 onward.

As the transition to what became the Xi Jinping administration loomed, that is the set of challenges China faced. The new administration would have to create a new model of development, managing 1.4 billion people through six levels of government,[7] under extremely inauspicious financial conditions.

As they worked on the transitional issues, there was a crucial development in the background. By the Hu Jintao era, the fear of social,

---

[6] Bankers at HSBC described to me being asked by long-term Hong Kong-based customers to finance just such a transition. It seemed impossible, but they backed their long-term customer in the interest of the relationship and it worked.

[7] The levels of government are central, provincial, county, municipal, town, and (unofficial but important) village.

economic, or financial collapse had given way to hubris. As noted earlier, in the era of overwhelming fear, Deng Xiaoping had allowed the farm families to take back control (although not ownership) of their land, giving up government control of their lives, and subsequently Jiang Zemin and Zhu Rongji took similar risks in industry. As it turned out, the surrender of direct control was more than compensated by popular loyalty due to the resulting economic growth, but for the leaders making the decisions these were enormous gambles. Dry economic texts cannot possibly communicate the scale of the political risks they took.

By the Hu Jintao era the fear was gone. There were no overwhelming incentives to take the risks of stepping back from direct control of the banks, from direct control of the stock market, from direct control of the courts. Although Hu Jintao remained very concerned about the stability of Party rule, he did not have to fear economic collapse or national fragmentation, so he had little incentive to take big risks. The population was exhausted by the disruptive reforms of Deng and Zhu. Hu had been chosen for stability and harmony. His leadership team was not configured for disruptive decisions entailing great risks. His team – the Politburo Standing Committee of nine men – operated somewhat like the US Supreme Court. Hu had one vote of nine. He was not even in the decisive position of Ben Bernanke or Janet Yellen in the governance of the US Federal Reserve Bank. His concern was to maintain his political base, not to take great entrepreneurial decisions in order to avoid economic collapse.[8]

Meanwhile, the Global Financial Crisis (GFC) disillusioned Chinese leaders, who had previously seen the US and EU economies as nearly ideal models for China to emulate, but now believed that China needed a more state-driven system. The other Asia Model economies had evolved toward variants of the US model. There were big variations, of course. South Korea was dominated by a few big firms, and Singapore had far more government planning and management than the United States, but they fit roughly into US-style laws, US-style capital markets, US-style competition, and acceptance of the Bretton Woods institutions and the US dollar as the foundations of the global

---

[8] The main change under Hu was the dissipation of social fear. As noted, this change was accompanied by a change in the leadership structure, with leadership dispersed among nine members of the Politburo Standing Committee.

economy. China had accepted that it was on a similar path and was explicitly copying a wide range of US institutions, from capital markets to aviation regulation. Now it seemed that acceptance of the US model, and the reigning economic order, meant being vulnerable to sudden, shattering global crisis even if one had managed one's own economy quite well. The GFC changed China's worldview, empowering those who said that China needed to find its own way, a way that would minimize the risks exposed by the GFC. This book will repeatedly return to this point.

The Plan

Long before the transition to the new team under Xi Jinping in 2013, China's leadership focused on how to get through this new economic transition.

Working with the World Bank, they prepared a broad, candid look at the issues China had to face, published by the World Bank as *China 2030*. They reached around the world to consult leading experts, such as Western Nobel Prize winners. They articulated each problem forthrightly and debated solutions. By the time the new administration had taken power in early 2013, the plans were quite advanced. Before the new leaders were chosen, one of the leading planners had the office across the hall from me at Harvard's Kennedy School. I made a list of the candidates for the top positions in the new administration and said to him, "Okay, you have brilliant plans, but the candidates for the new leadership have very different views of how China should proceed. What makes you think your plans will ever be implemented?" He said, "Mr. Overholt, yes, our potential new leaders are very diverse. But we have a great advantage. They all understand numbers."

In other words, they all understood that building infrastructure and pushing exports were providing severely diminishing returns. They knew decisive action was imperative. And they knew their regime depended on coming up with an answer that would work. This was very different from Washington, DC during Obama's second term, when differing viewpoints, incomprehension of important numbers, and sheer partisanship led the Congressional leadership to impede almost every kind of executive initiative. However, getting top leadership assent has so far proved different from getting the machinery of Chinese government to implement the strategy decisively.

Their new plan, announced at the Third Plenum (the annual plenary meeting of the Central Committee) in 2013, organized the planned reforms around the core theme of moving to market allocation of resources.[9] Although they did not announce it this way, or necessarily think of it this way, that is the key to solving the problem of complexity: decision makers sitting in offices in Beijing can't possibly master the complexity, so the market has to make the decisions. That in turn entailed moving to market interest rates, a largely market foreign exchange rate, a level playing field between SOEs and private enterprises, a market rather than political approach to listing on stock exchanges and issuing bonds, gradual lifting of controls on movement of capital in and out of China, a gradual opening of stock and bond markets to foreigners, giving rural migrants the same access to social services that urban residents get, strengthening farmers' property rights, allowing farmers to rent out their land and borrow against it, giving fairer compensation to farmers whose land is taken for development, letting the market set natural resource prices, forcing companies to internalize the cost of environmental pollution, licensing more banks, including internet banks, and much else. It also acknowledges the need to address key problems like inequality, urbanization, local government debt, the need for budget reforms, and the necessity for changing the promotion and compensation systems for officials away from an exclusive focus on economic growth.

This plan is arguably the most sophisticated reform plan in world history. Certainly no other plan known to this author has engaged such a broad spectrum of global expertise. Contrary to a laissez-faire ideology common among US rightwingers, a society changing so fast needs a plan. Otherwise, there will be no roads or ports for the emerging manufacturers and no houses for the rural–urban migrants. China's plan is a good balance of preparing for major changes, but not imposing the kinds of rigidities that made Soviet plans counterproductive. The trick is in the implementation, which is complex economically and extraordinarily difficult politically. (See the chapter on politics below.)

There is also a catch in the way the plan is interpreted. The overall theme of market allocation of resources implies a broad displacement

---

[9] For a superb overview in English of the Third Plenum plan, see Daniel H. Rosen, "Avoiding the Blind Alley: China's Economic Overhaul and Its Implications," Asia Society Policy Institute Report, October 2014, http://asiasociety.org/files/pdf/AvoidingtheBlindAlley_FullReport.pdf.

of political decision-making at the sector, industry, and company levels, with the government just setting broad guidelines and regulations. But each part is subject to interpretation on the balance between state and market. For an analogy it is useful to go back to the 1990s phrase "socialist market economy." Hostile Western critics treated that phrase as an oxymoron. It could have been a cover for retaining most traditional political controls. But at the time Chinese planners patiently explained that it meant a decisive shift in favor of the market, while trying to retain socialist values. That interpretation proved to be accurate. The current, Third Plenum plan promises a move to market allocation of resources while retaining Party controls. Several years into that plan there are prominent moves toward the market, notably on interest rates and the currency, but elsewhere, particularly with regard to state enterprises and the legal system, bureaucratic resistance and Xi Jinping's concern for political control have seemed predominant. China's future hangs on that balance.

The Transition

China's economic transition actually comprises multiple economic and social transitions. Most of these are easy to list but difficult to achieve.

From Exports and Investment to Domestic Consumption

China must move from growth driven by exports and investment to growth driven by domestic consumption. This is a transition Japan should have made in the late 1970s and early 1980s but failed to implement in several decades because of domestic interest group pressures. As noted, China's growth of net exports is declining, even negative in some years, and the efficiency of infrastructure investment has declined so much that it threatens to become negligible. The obvious solution is to boost domestic consumption, which seems to have been suppressed since, at a little over one-third of the economy, it has only half the share of its US counterpart.

The problem with this solution is that consumption has been growing at a rate that could not imaginably be decisively accelerated. As shown in Figure 2.1, over a 20-year period what Chinese consume has grown almost 9 percent per year, a higher rate than in any other significant country. Only Saudi Arabia and Qatar come close; the

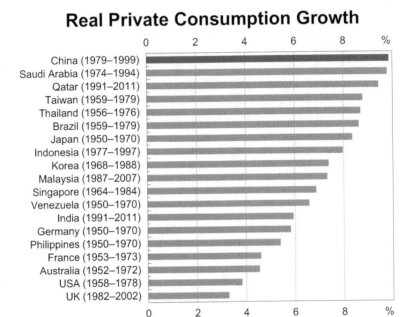

Figure 2.1 Real private consumption growth, fastest 20 years.

corresponding consumption growth rate for the United States and United Kingdom is under 4 percent.[10]

These findings about consumption have implications that go far beyond technical economics. On the evidence of internet blogs, Western political scientists are almost universally convinced that consumption in China has been unreasonably suppressed, potentially resulting in discontent. The statistics show that the opposite is the case. Moreover, the statistics almost certainly understate both the level of consumption and its growth. When one travels in China, one of the most obvious things nearly everywhere is that living standards are much higher than the statistics imply. Moreover, the way the statistics are constructed

[10] The cited figures are published in Guonan Ma, Ivan Roberts, and Gerard Kelly, "A Rebalancing Chinese Economy: Challenges and International Implications," in *Structural Change in China: Implications for Australia and the World* (Reserve Bank of Australia, 2016), pp. 177–237, www.rba.gov.au/publications/ confs/2016/pdf/rba-conference-volume-2016-ma-roberts-kelly.pdf. This paper shatters much of the global conventional wisdom about the Chinese economy and it vividly demonstrates the difficulty of the transition China faces.

understates family consumption. What most Chinese families want to buy is a better home and a car. Home purchases are accounted as investment. For tax reasons most people buy their cars through their companies, so their purchases are accounted as business investment. But the most important point is that the consumption numbers look low mainly because they are overshadowed by ridiculously high investment. Indeed, the consumption statistics may be so miscalculated that Chinese consumption is actually on a par (60–65 percent of GDP) with other successful Asian economies.[11] China's governance system incentivized officials to achieve growth and employment. If they invested they got growth and created jobs, leading to likely promotion even if the investment produced unprofitable hotels or poor-quality goods, so investment soared beyond any reasonable level.

While the consumption story is a lot better for families than the Western conventional wisdom, nonetheless the statistics show that the transition must come mainly from investment rates declining rather than from consumption rising faster. That means lower growth and a difficult transition.

Given that the country cannot simply jack up consumption sufficiently through subsidies for cars and appliances, better mortgage rates, and the like, the leadership has shifted to a focus on what it is calling supply-side reforms: moving industries up-market, encouraging entrepreneurship and innovation (discussed later in this chapter), facilitating urbanization, cutting taxes, and reducing red tape. The problem of red tape became a particular focus when leadership discussions at Beidahe in the autumn of 2014 focused on the calculation that most manufacturing had become cheaper in California than in China – because US energy was cheaper, Mexican immigrant workers were cheaper than Chinese workers, and the US regulatory system was so much more transparent and efficient. Of these three factors, the one the leadership can change significantly is the regulatory system. Entrenched interests are, however, fighting back hard against loss of their (sometimes arbitrary) regulatory power. See the next chapter's discussion of the anti-corruption campaign for a characteristic example of pushback in education.

---

[11] This is the argument of Jun Zhang and Tian Zhu, "Poor Economic Statistics Fuel China's Low Consumption Myth," *World Economics* 14(2), 2013, pp. 13–18.

Upgrading Manufacturing

China's early takeoff was based on simple, labor-intensive manufacturing of things like clothing and shoes and on assembly of electronics and other things, largely for foreign brands. But China's wages have risen so fast that these functions are increasingly moving to Vietnam, Bangladesh, and Africa, among other places. Now China must do higher value-added manufacturing and create its own brands. This upgrading process is something that China excels at. As with the other Asian miracle economies, China has a planning system that foresees these changes and helps industry adjust. It has welcomed rising wages, for instance telling the provinces that each area should increase its minimum wage at least 13.5 percent annually during the most recently completed five-year plan, and it has further accelerated the process by letting its currency rise. Through training, fiscal incentives and technological assistance, it facilitates the shift.

In creating its own brands China has done particularly well. In 2003, Asia experts Tarun Khanna and Yasheng Huang predicted that India would outperform China on the basis of the fact that India had three times as many globally recognized brands as China.[12] Thirteen years later, China has 11 of the top 100 global brands and India has none.[13] In this part of the transition, China will undoubtedly succeed.

Indeed, tracking sector by sector, China's shift up-market is proceeding remarkably well. A decade hence, if Xi Jinping's reforms are judged a success, it will probably be mainly because China's semi-private firms have responded so well to the need to move their products upward. If, on the other hand, Xi Jinping's reforms are ultimately judged a failure, it will likely be because state enterprise reforms moved too slowly and because subsidized SOEs were allowed to bulldoze their way into dominance of otherwise dynamic new sectors. Western analysts tend to obsess too much about reforms of the big state enterprises and underestimate the importance of structural shifts that involve many thousands of companies making market-based decisions with encouragement from the state.

---

[12] Yasheng Huang and Tarun Khanna, "Can India Overtake China?," *Foreign Policy*, July 1, 2003, http://foreignpolicy.com/2003/07/01/can-india-overtake-china/. At the editors' request I wrote a rebuttal that was published afterward.

[13] Scheherazade Daneshkhu, "Tech Groups Lead Game of Snakes and Ladders," *Financial Times*, June 8, 2016, p. 3, citing the leading authority, BrandZ rankings.

At the upper end of China's upgrading ambitions, however, it may well probably encounter difficulty. In its efforts to break into biotech and other areas of high technology, the administration has been repeating mistakes from the Mao and early reform era. It is buying the latest equipment but lacks the management experience and supportive systems to use much of the equipment efficiently. The management experience and supportive systems (including financial, legal, and intellectual property systems) normally come from working closely with foreign investors in these areas and emulating their management and systems, but currently the Chinese government is alienating exactly the partners it needs by trying to strip them of their technology and giving preferential treatment to domestic companies. (For example, the current administration cracks down hard on foreign companies for alleged infringements of the anti-monopoly law, but exempts domestic SOEs from that law.)

From Manufacturing to Services

The economy must also shift from manufacturing to services. A good deal of this transition has already occurred, since China's economy in 2015 was 50.5 percent services. But moving to an efficient, competitive services economy entails a difficult social transition. In a manufacturing company, say a garment factory, the typical structure is extremely hierarchical, with orders coming from the top down. The boss decrees what each worker is supposed to do at exactly which time; the most efficient assembly plant is one where the workers do exactly, rigidly what they are told. In a typical service establishment, say a restaurant, the boss trains the workers very well but then must give them considerable autonomy in deciding how to handle each situation. Chinese society, from its politics to its education system, is congruent with the textile factory structure but less so with the bottom-up requirements of the service sector. While the way I have stated the contrast is somewhat more black and white than reality, the adjustment can be difficult and can take time.[14]

---

[14] I am indebted to Po Chung, the founder of DHL International, for colorful descriptions of the complexity of building a flexible service operation in a culture almost entirely informed by hierarchical mindsets.

While China's service sector is now more than half of the economy, it remains largely unreformed. Reformist attentions focus on the manufacturing sector, but the services sector – the core of China's economic future – remains highly protected and inefficient. Banking, capital markets, insurance, accounting, law, and education, among others, remain backward compared with manufacturing and compared with their international peers. Rapid progress will require a rapid opening to the outside world. In some areas of finance, this has been planned but has not yet made much progress. In other areas, plans are at best thin. In law and education, new political controls will reinforce the most prominent problems.

From Engineering to Markets

The reformist leadership of modern China has been dominated by engineers and by an engineering mentality. Almost all the members of Jiang Zemin's Politburo Standing Committee were trained engineers, although they typically spent most of their careers in administration. This has served China well in an era where the country desperately needed roads, railroads, ports, airports, telecommunications, and power. As China moves into an era where expanding services, creating sophisticated markets, and refining a legal system are the key issues, an excess of the engineering mentality can become a problem. At the simplest level, engineers tend to keep on building the things they are comfortable building, and some aspects of contemporary China seem to be a story of engineers gone wild. Big shopping malls, huge dams, luxurious mega-hotels in small cities, the world's greatest railroads, and much else now include both much that impresses and substantial unproductive excess. China's railroad to Tibet is a truly extraordinary engineering feat and one of great beauty. But it conveys the same feeling as wild valuations at the height of a stock market bubble.

More subtly, and perhaps more importantly, a lifetime of seeking the single solution by decomposing a problem into its constituent parts makes it very difficult to think in terms of market equilibria, alternative scenarios, and strategic synthesis. For part of my career I made a good living helping CEOs who had risen through their firms as engineers to think about broad strategies. The backgrounds of China's top leaders are becoming more diverse, including one Politburo Standing

Committee member with a degree in economics (albeit from North Korea) and a prime minister with advanced degrees in law and economics. But the engineering mentality remains pervasive and, in addition to being very helpful in many ways, shows its limitations in such things as fumbling management of stock market crashes. The transition is happening, but it will take time.

From Property-Based Finance to Credit-Based Finance

In the process, the economy must shift from property as the basis of virtually all finance to a more credit-based system. In the existing system, when the government wants to undertake a new development, it buys land from farmers or others at a very low price, then announces that it is going to build infrastructure and universities on the land, and it is able to sell some of the land at ten times the original price, in order to pay for the roads and the universities. (Universities are particularly prestigious, so announcing plans to build them is a particularly effective way to drive up the land price. Announcing a mine or a subway can accomplish the same thing.) Likewise, a company wanting to borrow needs to put up property as collateral unless it has an explicit or implicit government guarantee; SOEs typically have implicit guarantees. Going forward, more and more credit will have to be based on assessments of business creditworthiness – a severe challenge in an economy where most business accounts other than for the big SOEs contain a considerable proportion of fiction and where local credit agencies assign almost all big companies the same very high credit rating.[15]

From Simple Priorities to Complex Ones

Finally, there is a particularly difficult transition from a system where plans, promotions, and bonuses have been based on the single goal of growth to one where far more complex considerations of debt, environmental impact, and social stress have important roles. It is easy to build a model or motivate an executive or direct a social system toward

---

[15] For a comprehensive review of the outsized role of property in China's economic development, and the risks created by that role, see Meg Rithmire, *Land Bargains and Chinese Capitalism: The Politics of Property Rights under Reform* (New York: Cambridge University Press, 2015).

one particular goal, in this case GDP growth, in the case of most businesses profit. It is orders of magnitude more difficult to create proper incentives for achieving multiple goals (growth, debt reduction, environmental health, expansion of social services . . .), particularly when the officials and executives are operating in a wide variety of different environments. This complex environment can befuddle any economic planner who attempts to do excessively detailed plans, and it can perplex government administrators who try to manage subordinates through an incentive system that is difficult to adjust to varying circumstances.

Financial Squeeze

As noted earlier, if an enterprise is going to evolve from one product line to another, it is crucial to do so at a time of booming prosperity, because then the resources transferred to the new product line won't deplete the resources needed to sustain the old business while waiting for the new one to take over.[16] But the lack of market reform in the Hu–Wen years means that Xi Jinping has to lead the country through its great economic transition at a time of lower growth and a severe financial squeeze.

The financial squeeze has multiple dimensions. Throughout much of the reform era, property, particularly in the big cities, has experienced one of history's great bull markets, but the end of the Hu–Wen administration brought fears of a property market collapse. Those fears were exaggerated in some Western commentary, but the market's great boom, which took another leap upward during Xi Jinping's first term, leaves behind some big problems. The government, knowing that over 10 million people would be moving from the countryside to the city every year, had to get ready for those people. On balance, it did a remarkable job.[17] The other miracle economies were far more chaotic

---

[16] For the broader point about an economy's need for strong aggregate demand in a time of transition, see Rob Johnson, "The China Delusion," *Project Syndicate*, February 16, 2016, www.project-syndicate.org/commentary/china-hybrid-market-delusion-by-rob-johnson-2016-02#eFGZlYDMDZpwY3gu.99, drawing on work by economic historian Michael A. Bernstein.

[17] For an analysis of China's successful urbanization, see Shahid Yusuf and Tony Saich, *China Urbanizes: Consequences, Strategies and Policies* (Washington, DC: World Bank, 2008)

at similar stages of development. For many years Seoul and Pusan in South Korea seemed to be just gigantic slums. Hong Kong people lived in terrible housing, and storms killed many people when tent cities succumbed to "mud slips." While China's big cities have areas near the bus stations where new migrants cluster, they are immaculate by comparison with what happened in the other miracle economies (except Singapore) – not to mention Mumbai or Manila.

To accomplish this, China had to predict where people would move, build extraordinary amounts of housing and other infrastructure, and then attempt to channel people toward the new housing: build and hope they will come – and give some a push. Western doomsayers repeatedly predicted that "see-through buildings" (unoccupied buildings where the lack of interior furnishings meant one could see right through to the other side) portended collapse of Shanghai in the 1990s and collapse of the whole market more recently. The collapses didn't happen, but people often moved to first-tier cities even when the central government prepared nice housing for them in the lower-tier cities. Local officials often overbuilt. As a result there are substantial "ghost areas" where buildings, sometimes many buildings, sit unoccupied. Because the government has been prudent in requiring large downpayments and limiting bank funding of mortgages, Chinese banks aren't exposed to disaster in the way Western banks were before 2008, but they have acquired painful amounts of non-performing loans. The official rate of non-performing loans is 1.6 percent (which is quite manageable), but independent estimates, taking into account unpayable loans that are rolled over automatically, run to at least 6 to 8 percent (a problematic but not disastrous number, far below the problems of the late 1990s). Estimates by some investment banks, such as CLSA, run to twice that level, implying serious financial problems.

The SOEs, with effective government guarantees, borrowed too much and now, as a group, cannot earn back their cost of capital. These are another drag on China's finances, first on the banks and ultimately on the government.

The SOEs and government-related enterprises at all levels had incentives to grow, so they grew without much concern for the size of the market or, in important cases, for competitive efficiency. Many sectors built capacity far in excess of potential demand, even when the economy was growing 10 percent per year. Now that the economy is growing slower, excess capacity has become absurdly excessive. China has more than half of total world steel capacity and proportionate excess in many other sectors. About half of Chinese steel companies are losing money and one CEO estimated that there is a stockpile of five years of supply. Chinese excess steel is spilling out at cheap prices and causing problems for steel companies throughout the entire world. Annual production capacity needs to be cut by as much as 300 million tons. Slimming down so that supply will meet demand is a huge and painful task, punctuated by price wars, layoffs, likely bankruptcies, and, in consequence, slower growth. Official estimates are that reducing steel and coal overcapacity will cost 1.8 million jobs.[18] Some informal estimates suggest that eliminating excess capacity in all industries, from cement to shipbuilding, would cost tens of millions of jobs.

China's corporate debt, around 170 percent of GDP, is extremely high. The government will attempt to control and reduce this number by reducing overcapacity, by merging weak companies into stronger ones, by selling higher proportions of their shares to the market, by moving bad assets into bad banks called asset management companies, and as a last resort through bankruptcies. These processes will be socially painful and the big SOEs and local governments will fight hard against them.

To its credit, the Chinese government accepts a heavy responsibility for workers displaced by reduction of overcapacity (and by globalization). In the previous era of SOE reform under Zhu Rongji most of the 45 million displaced workers found new jobs, mainly in service industries, when growth was 10 percent per year. Current expenditures on retraining and job creation are very large, as are investments in the efforts to create a universal social security system and universal medical care. (This is a sharp contrast with the United States, where Republican budget constraints limit help to displaced workers and Democrats' dependence on industrial unions creates a self-defeating focus on retraining for disappearing industrial jobs rather than service jobs. Unlike Chinese planners, who address the real issues of structural change in the economy, both US parties find it convenient to blame China rather than technological and organizational change. But both would insist that the Chinese government doesn't care about its people whereas the US government does.)

---

[18] For a vivid view of what elimination of steel overcapacity does to a community, see "Death and Despair in China's Rustbelt," *Bloomberg News*, March 1, 2016, www.bloomberg.com/news/features/2016-03-01/death-and-despair-in-china-s-rustbelt.

Analogously to their development of overcapacity, Chinese companies and the government assumed that resources would be expensive, scarce, and in rapidly rising demand for the foreseeable future, so they bought massive inventories of materials at the peak of the market. Then they effectively doubled their bets by buying mines and processing capability all over the world at peak prices and in the riskiest places. Using up the excess inventories and trying to make those expensive mines viable further deplete funds and slow the economy.

The biggest source of financial squeeze is local governments. They too were incentivized to grow as fast as possible, without much regard for cost or other measures of efficiency and sustainability. They borrowed as much as possible from the banks, mostly through Local Government Financing Vehicles, nominally private enterprises that could circumvent constraints on direct local government borrowing. Their direct obligations amounted to US$2.5 trillion in 2015, to which one must add very large informal obligations that are impossible to estimate accurately. Local officials often ask companies to undertake various projects, with oral assurance from local leadership that if they get into difficulty they will be bailed out. Or the companies just assume they have implicit assurances. Thus the official and unofficial debt piled up, sometimes to the point where debt service exceeded total tax revenues. The local governments then acquired land and sold it to service the debt. With land sales coming down, repressed interest rates being freed, and the government signaling that it will require local governments to provide education, medical services, and pensions to rural migrants for the first time, local governments are in a perilous squeeze. The central government is helping them transfer short-term bank debt into bonds with longer maturities, which will help, but difficult decisions about default and central government bailouts lie ahead. The central government restructured about US$48 billion of local government debt in 2015, extending maturities and reducing interest rates at great cost to the banks – but that is just a drop in the bucket.

Because the banks were rigid and tied to the SOEs, a system of shadow banking emerged on a very large scale – equivalent to almost US$5 trillion in 2014, according to an analysis that eliminates the double counting common elsewhere.[19] A later Moodys analysis argued

---

[19] See Andrew Sheng and Ng Chow Soon, *Shadow Banking in China: An Opportunity for Financial Reform* (Hoboken, NY: Wiley, 2016).

that the total shadow banking market in 2015 was US$8.1 trillion.[20] Much of the shadow banking was useful, but there are substantial parts that are Ponzi schemes or bets on uncreditworthy companies. The useful part channeled funds to worthy smaller companies that could not get loans from the official banking system because of complex rules, insistence on land collateral, and the cronyism that predominates in the big banks. But substantial parts of shadow banking are unsavory. The shadow banks serve as intermediaries for "wealth management" products where a company that can't get bank funding issues notes to people who want higher interest rates than they can get at the banks; some of these wealth management products are uncreditworthy.

Much shadow banking is a way to get around the capital adequacy rules. Loans of more than three years require banks to have more capital. So the bank makes a three-year loan to a company with longer-term needs. As the end of the third year approaches, the bank provides funds to an associated shadow bank, which issues a short-term loan to the company at a very high interest rate, then shares the profits with the main bank. The company uses money from the shadow bank to repay the bank loan just before the three-year limit. Days later the bank gives the company a new loan of slightly less than three years. The company gets its money, while both the bank and the shadow bank make an exorbitant profit for a short time. By circumventing the capital adequacy rules, this makes the banking system less sound. Most analysts of the banking system focus exclusively on non-performing loans, but this circumvention of the capital adequacy rules is serious and is more the rule than the exception.

In addition, China's financial burden includes enormous environmental cleanup costs, which are being shouldered for the first time; a rapidly expanding military; enormous startup investments for the health care, pension, and unemployment compensation systems; and, most importantly, a graying population where the ratio of dependent older people to the workforce has begun to rise rapidly (see below).

[20] "PBOC Shines Light on Risks in $8 Trillion Shadow Banking Market," Bloomberg News, www.bloomberg.com/news/articles/2016-05-31/pboc-shines-light-on-new-risks-in-8-trillion-shadow-loan-market. (The Moodys numbers are inconsistent with those in the book by Sheng and Ng, probably reflecting differences about the extent of double counting. The point is the huge scale of the market by either calculation.)

A final aspect of the gradually tightening financial squeeze is the slowing of government revenue growth. For much of the reform period, government revenues have expanded nearly twice as fast as GDP, a consequence of increasing ability to collect taxes and of increasing monetization of the economy. This has had serendipitous results. For instance, China could increase its military budget at double-digit rates while steadily decreasing the military's share of the government budget. To take a hypothetical example, GDP could grow 10 percent, government revenues 18 percent and the military budget 12 percent. Now monetization of the economy is nearing completion, GDP growth is running at 5 to 7 percent, much lower than before, and government revenue growth will eventually have to gradually converge to the same rate as GDP growth. The debt numbers and the declining tax growth will be like a python gradually putting the squeeze on institutions that have not previously had to face the kinds of budget constraints that are elsewhere considered normal.

Ultimately China will need a great tax reform. The last great tax reform, in 1994, saved the central government from penury, but even then China's central government was getting a smaller share of GDP than virtually any other significant country. (See Figure 2.2 comparing central government revenue and expenditure with other countries.)

The 1994 reform channeled the bulk of the country's tax revenues into the central government, which then reallocated funding to the provinces. In this process, the central government retained a

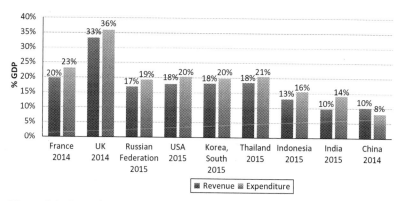

Figure 2.2 Central government revenue and expenditure (data from CEIC Data Company Ltd.).

proportionately large share of the revenues while burdening the localities with disproportionate responsibility (compared with other countries) for most social services and infrastructure spending. This came on top of the earlier decision to force local governments to fund themselves through entrepreneurship.

These multiple financial burdens are cumulatively enormous. The political burden is even more enormous; any one of the many required reforms, such as a fundamental tax reorganization, would be a historic accomplishment for almost any Western government during a four- or five-year term. China has to do them all rather quickly or accept a future of very slow growth.

Having said that, central government debt is low, the country's debt is mostly in its own currency, the savings rate is high, the foreign exchange reserves are large, the economic management institutions are exceptionally competent, and there is tremendous room to reduce the capital requirements of the banks (which are currently more onerous than anywhere else in the world). Above all, the Chinese leadership faces the country's problems. On balance, China is unlikely to have a great financial crisis in the manner of, say, Argentina or even the United States, but deleveraging from these enormous financial burdens means years of slower growth. For our purposes, the most important implication is that this is quite an inauspicious time in China's financial history to have to transfer to a new growth model. As resources are devoted to debt service and poured into new sectors of the economy, the old sectors suffer more and the political costs of change are magnified.

Demography

Demography creates a major challenge and an immediate financial drain, adding to both the difficulties and the urgency of the transition to a new economic structure. China's ratio of working people to total population peaked in 2010–2011 and began to decline as the burden of elderly pensioners began to rise. By 2020 China will already be deep in the problems of a graying society – like Japan, South Korea, and Italy today. Pension and medical systems must be expanded, and their quality improved, at an enormous rate. Dealing with the needs of the elderly population is immensely complex not just because of the scale but because the needs change so fast. Given the years of rapid economic growth, every five years the new cohort of pensioners is living longer, has different medical problems, has substantially more financial resources but also much higher expectations about care, and, because of the one-child policy, has fewer family members supporting it. This is the ultimate economic governance dilemma – requiring big decisions in the face of multiple variables changing quickly.

For a while it was a cliche that the middle of the twenty-first century would be India's period of dominance because it will have a plethora of young workers whereas China will not. Given India's failure so far to build its infrastructure, create manufacturing employment, provide education and health for hundreds of millions of poorer people, and start to address environmental problems seriously, India will be fortunate simply to avoid a nightmare – an era of global competition and environmental distress in which hundreds of millions of malnourished, uneducated people simply cannot function. China has a much more skilled workforce, much better infrastructure, and much better environmental prospects (see the next chapter) for the coming generation and beyond.

China will nonetheless be challenged by becoming gray before it becomes rich. It cannot afford the Japanese scenario of turning inward and stagnating. Stagnation at income of US$40,000+ per capita like Japan can be socially stable, even comfortable, although Japan risks financial catastrophe as its debt metastasizes. Stagnating under US $20,000 in China would be a recipe for social upheaval. Expectations are too high; China's people are determined to live at a standard comparable to that enjoyed by Westerners. One way or another, a limited number of younger people must support the old.

It is not difficult to write scenarios for China to continue growth and prosperity as it ages. The basic formulae have been understood for a long time.[21] Rapid, well-managed urbanization, education, competition, technological upgrading, innovation, and efficiencies from market-oriented reforms could offset, perhaps even fully offset, the effects of a graying labor force. But while it is relatively easy to envisage the mathematical scenario, it is very difficult to implement

---

[21] See for instance Helen Qiao, "Will China Grow Old Before Becoming Rich?" Goldman Sachs Economics Paper number 138, February 14, 2006, and Fang Cai and Yang Lu, "Take-off, Persistence and Sustainability: The Demographic Factor in Chinese Growth," *Asia & the Pacific Policy Studies* 3(2), 2016, pp. 203–225, http://onlinelibrary.wiley.com/doi/10.1002/app5.139/full.

the reforms with sufficient speed and thoroughness. Implementation is everything, and decisive implementation is exceedingly difficult, a theme this book will repeat and refine.

Industrial Structure

Zhu Rongji saved China from a financial crisis by reforming the banks' customers, the SOEs. Under his reforms the number of industrial SOEs fell from 127,600 in 1996 to 34,280 in 2003.[22] In the middle of Hu Jintao's term they were generally competitive and profitable. By the end of the Hu–Wen administration they were once again weighing down the economy. The advantages they had been given, such as cheap land and cheap debt, had led them to excess indebtedness, excess capacity, and excess comfort, not to mention excess corruption.

SOE reform means straightening out the SOEs' finances, making them more efficient, and creating a level playing field between them and the private sector. Freeing interest rates, a task already largely accomplished, will create greater financial discipline and give the private sector fairer access. (When interest rates are held down by the government, it makes no sense for the banks to lend to anyone except very large institutions backed by the state. Low interest rates can't cover the greater risk of lending to smaller or private companies that lack guarantees.)

In 2014–2015, the government tried to create a bull market in equities. Since most big SOEs are listed on the stock market, or have listed arms, rising stock prices would have recapitalized them. But the artificial stock market bubble quickly became a bust in July 2015. Worse, when the government rescued the market, it ended up owning so much of the stock that its exposure to SOE problems increased. Another bust at the beginning of 2016 compounded the problem.

Another theory of financial improvement is to increase the percentage of SOE shares that are listed on the stock markets. The idea is to get more private money invested in the SOEs while maintaining effective government control. More recently the idea of "mixed ownership" has included not just adding private money but also using private shareholders and directors as a check on self-interested managers. But that valid

---

[22] Nicholas Lardy, *Markets over Mao* (Washington, DC: Peterson Institute for International Economics, 2014), p. 125.

concept sits uneasily with the government's emphasis on tightened Party control and predominant state ownership. Xi Jinping has emphasized that Party discipline over the SOEs will be increased. But Party/government control of the SOEs is the most important source of their problems, so strengthening Party authority would seem to be the opposite of reform. Irrespective of whether government ownership is 100 percent, 51 percent, or 25 percent, the Party still will have control. If a Party Secretary in conjunction with the Organization Department still chooses the CEO and reviews major policies, then the source of the problem remains. Selling more shares to the private sector will raise some money, deferring problems but not solving them.

It is possible to have state ownership and efficient, autonomous management. Singapore Airlines is a state enterprise (the Singaporean term is Government Linked Company or GLC), but it is probably the world's best airline. Singaporean GLCs get no special financial privileges from the government.[23] More importantly, they are run by boards that function independently of the government, of the ruling party, and even of the government's GLC holding company, Temasek.

In principle, the Communist Party could strengthen its supervision of an SOE, while allowing the company to have all the benefits of autonomous management, by confining its role to auditing and allocation of additional state capital. But that is precisely what traditional Party leaders do not want. Appointing the CEO and providing general policy direction are the core functions of state ownership and Party supervision. In Beijing today there is quiet but intense political warfare between those who see freeing the SOEs from Party management as the key to China's economic future and those who demand that the Party Committee should retain authority to make or ratify major corporate decisions. This tension between wanting the advantages of market-based decision-making on the one hand, and determination to retain the Party privilege of top appointments and strategic guidance on the other hand, is the core dilemma of the Xi administration's reform program, which has so far strongly reaffirmed that the Party committee in each enterprise must be involved in every major SOE decision.[24]

---

[23] Carlos D. Ramirez and Ling Hui Tan, "Singapore, Inc. Versus the Private Sector: Are Government-Linked Companies Different?", IMF Working Paper WP/03/156, July 2003, www.imf.org/external/pubs/ft/wp/2003/wp03156.pdf.

[24] On continued controls, see Lucy Hornby, "China Rows Back on State-Sector Reforms," *Financial Times*, June 14, 2016, https://next.ft.com/content/

This core dilemma in turn results from the pivot in China's development history, the pivot of fear and courage. Fear gave Deng Xiaoping, Jiang Zemin, and Zhu Rongji the courage, the necessity, and the social support to take risky and socially stressful decisions. At great political risk, they stepped back from control of the farms and took important steps back from direct control of enterprises. By the end of the Jiang Zemin–Zhu Rongji era, the risk of disintegration and chaos was gone. The people were tired of disruptive reform. Complacency and hubris were beginning to replace fear. So Hu Jintao and Wen Jiabao let the country mostly drift through a decade of non-reform.

Now the Xi administration must reform or accept economic stagnation. The country is worried enough that it has geared up economically and politically for a big reform, but the stakes are different now – not war, not chaos, not financial collapse, just slower growth. The key issue in this next phase of reform is whether to take the risk of abandoning the key remaining direct Party controls – over the SOEs, the banks (especially the banks), and the legal system. So far, the leadership's answer is "We will have our cake and eat it too. We, the leadership, will have the advantages of the market in enterprises and banks but we will strengthen Party control. We will have the rule of law but we will strengthen Party control." These are normal politicians behaving in normal times – like US Republicans saying that they will cut taxes, raise military spending, and balance the budget; or Democrats saying that they will maintain all the welfare entitlements without increasing taxes. This Chinese administration says that it will obtain the benefits of the market while maintaining at least 51 percent ownership of the big SOEs and strengthening Party supervision of the SOEs. This shift from the politics of feared social collapse to relatively normal politics is a fundamental transformation of the way Chinese leaders behave.

As it happens, the turn from fear to hubris, from extraordinary politics to normal politics, occurred simultaneously with the GFC.

92e52600-31f7-11e6-ad39-3fee5ffe5b5b?utm_source=The+Sinocism+China +Newsletter&utm_campaign=cbc217ccbe-Sinocism06_14_166_14_2016& utm_medium=email&utm_term=0_171f237867-cbc217ccbe-24564489&mc_ cid=cbc217ccbe&mc_eid=35950f7bcb#axzz4BbEwioXD. On enhanced market discipline, Liu He, who has been Xi Jinping's most influential economic advisor, has strongly advocated greater market discipline through changed shareholdings and greater acceptance of bankruptcies.

That crisis fundamentally reshaped the thinking of Chinese leaders (and many others). No longer is the US market model the ideal toward which all developing economies need to aspire. China's salvation from the GFC came from having control of banks and giant SOEs that could be directed to increase spending and overcome the consequences of the financial tsunami that came from the United States and threatened to engulf China. This has given heart to those in China who resist further surrender of Party control. So the economic plan says that the key to the future is market allocation of resources, but the political goal is strengthened Party control.

Much of the confusion around the discussion of SOE reform derives from failure to observe a classic distinction between ownership and management. Adolf Berle and Gardiner Means[25] taught the West to distinguish ownership of a corporation, which could be dispersed among thousands of shareholders, from management control, which cannot be exercised by thousands of dispersed owners. In a corner bicycle shop, ownership and management control are unified, but in the modern corporation they are quite separate and a share of ownership may convey very little management control. The pre-Berle and Means confusion about corporations has also historically been a confusion in socialist thought.[26] Contrary to much historical socialist thought, government ownership of the economy does not imply government control of the economy or control of the economy by the general populace or management of the economy in the interest of the general populace; it can even give certain interest groups control of the government. Conversely, government may control only 25 percent of the ownership of a company but may have complete management control over that company if the other shareholders are widely dispersed or if there are special control mechanisms inserted into the way the company is managed. Chinese fiddling with the share ownership of SOEs will have little effect on whether those SOEs are likely to achieve the efficiencies of market competition.

South Korea provides an example of the difference between ownership and control. Under Park Chung Hee a dozen big conglomerates (chaebol) were owned privately by families loyal to the President. But

---

[25] Adolf A. Berle and Gardiner C. Means, *The Modern Corporation and Private Property* (New York: MacMillan, 1932).

[26] Ralf Dahrendorf clarified the implications of government ownership of the means of production in *Class and Class Conflict in Industrial Society* (Stanford, CT: Stanford University Press, 1959).

the President's Economic Secretary told them how much to produce and how much to export, and he set the size and interest rates of their loans. Park was a committed socialist who had been talked into allowing private ownership; he conceded socialist ownership but more importantly maintained socialist control. The system worked because the conglomerates were all competing with each other and could go bankrupt if they misbehaved. (The government bailed them out if they got into trouble while honestly and competently seeking to achieve their government-set goals, but let them go bankrupt if the problem was incompetence or dishonesty.)

The same confusion can lead to misunderstanding of the implications of the broader economic balance between SOEs and privately owned companies. Private ownership has spread very quickly in China and is now greater than private ownership in certain European economies that we think of as capitalist. Nicholas Lardy[27] has shown that in China private ownership is more common than state ownership, that Chinese growth comes predominantly from private companies, that job creation comes predominantly from private companies, and that conditions for private companies, including access to credit, have improved enormously. "[B]etween 1978 and 2011 the share of industrial output produced by state firms fell from about three quarters to one quarter," retreating in all product lines. Only 13 percent of urban employees, he shows, work for SOEs. Moreover, he shows that, despite efforts at reform, the SOEs have not performed efficiently. The markets do seem to have defeated Mao, and the statistics seem to refute what Lardy views as the myth that the SOEs became more important during the Hu–Wen administration and especially after the GFC.

And yet there are two anomalies that raise questions about the implications of these figures. When the analysis is presented to Hong Kong tycoons with big operations in China, many adopt a quizzical look and say that such a degree of private sector dominance just doesn't conform to their personal experience of managing in China. Some question the statistics but don't know how they might be wrong.[28]

---

[27] Nicholas Lardy, *Markets over Mao* (Washington, DC: Peterson Institute for International Economics, 2014).

[28] For a different look at state ownership, see Derek Scissors, "China's SOE Sector Is Bigger Than Some Would Have Us Think," *East Asia Forum*, May 17, 2016, www.eastasiaforum.org/2016/05/17/chinas-soe-sector-is-bigger-than-some-would-have-us-think/.

A key anomaly leads me to believe that the role of the SOEs is much more important than the statistics (which I accept) suggest. In the other Asian miracle economies, during the phase of development that corresponds to China's Hu–Wen period (2003–2012), the brightest people tended to lose interest in working for the government and to move into the private sector, because at that level of development the opportunity for bright young people to charge into the government and help save the country has passed. Indeed, in China during the 1990s there was a fad for "jumping into the sea," as moving into the private sector was called. But that reversed in the first decade of the new century. For most of the Hu–Wen period I never met a top student at a leading university who aspired to work for a private or foreign company. The government and the SOEs were the only choice, even more than investment banking and consulting were the top choices for Ivy League American students before the GFC. A Chinese graduate who ended up in the private sector was considered a failure. The government and the SOEs offered easier access to housing, easier access to credit, a more comfortable pace of work, greater ability to get things done, more power, more prestige. And more money. Total compensation at the SOEs – salary, bonus, perks, and bribes – dwarfed what one could obtain in the private sector. My Chinese friends usually didn't go into specifics, but they found it amusing that Americans thought US CEO incomes were so high; taking everything into consideration, top executives at the big SOEs made more.

How could there be such a disjunction between the statistical dynamism of the private sector and the prestige and perks in the state sector? The problem lies in the conclusion Westerners can too easily draw from those statistics.

In China, a major way that the private sector has developed is that the CEO of a state enterprise sees an opportunity, has his SOE borrow from the bank to fund that enterprise, and sets up a private company. If the company does well, the CEO pockets the profits. If it does badly, it's a bad loan for the SOE. Using such socialist means to finance expansion of the private sector has been an extraordinarily effective way to "privatize" the Chinese economy. The phenomenon is omnipresent. But it leaves the private enterprise to some varying extent as an appendage of the SOE.

Another way that private companies get formed is that the mayor of a city has projects to implement but doesn't have the budget, so he supports associates to start private companies, encourages the bank to give loans to the companies, and provides verbal assurance that, if the companies get into a financial squeeze, the problem will go away. This too occurs on a massive scale, encouraging inefficiency and storing up financial trouble. The private companies are doing the bidding of the local government and may be constrained not to deviate too much from their assignments. Thus, while they are privately owned, they function as a hybrid between Western private sector companies and SOEs.

Third, after one sets aside the government and SOE-initiated private companies, there are still a lot of real private companies. But those are subject to the very detailed jurisdiction of the local Party Secretary. There's a regulation for everything, and if there isn't the Party Secretary may invent one. In the World Bank's indicator of ease of starting a company, China comes 151st in the world.[29] That and other obstacles mean that you can't get started and can't survive as a company if you don't have special dispensation from the Party Secretary. Moreover, if the Party Secretary has a pet project that needs a donation – even a very big donation – the private company must instantly provide the donation or it will not be in business for long. What the Party Secretary wants, the Party Secretary gets.

Indeed, there are extraordinarily few privately owned companies in China that can survive without giving shares, jobs, or powerful or well-compensated board seats to government or Party officials. This, plus the exceptional regulatory power of the government, and the ability of the Party to demand that the company support government projects, means that very little of the privately owned sector in China behaves like the private sector in the West. In addition the majority of private companies, including virtually all larger ones, have Party committees inside the company and, while some Party committees are tame adjuncts to management, they are in principle subject to Party discipline and able to influence or control management decisions. Very small companies, and some companies in distinctive locations like Shenzhen, are exceptions, but the rule is substantial government/Party input into management.

---

[29] Professor Chang-Tai Hsieh of the University of Chicago points out that this is the same ranking as the Congo.

In other words, much of the relationship among the big SOEs, the Party, and the private sector is, in aggregate, like a jellyfish called the Portuguese Man of War. There is a big central body (the SOE or the government) with many tentacles hanging down. The tentacles are privately owned companies, but many of them depend very heavily on SOE funding, SOE guidance, Party Secretary facilitation, and local government sponsorship, and they all must move whenever the Party Secretary says to move.

This does not contradict any of Lardy's statistics, nor does it contradict the finding that the private sector is more competitive, that as it expands it makes the overall economy more competitive,[30] and that ultimately the private sector is likely to overshadow a less efficient SOE sector. In Taiwan the Guomindang had 40 big conglomerates (Party-owned, not state-owned) that did a great deal of the kinds of infrastructure building and heavy industry that the SOEs do in China. Gradually the private sector, originally some 200,000 small trading firms, became bigger and more efficient and came to dominate the more modern parts of the economy. In a financial crisis that began in 1990 most of the Guomindang Party conglomerates were consigned to life support. Taiwan's new President, Tsai Ing-wen, has vowed to largely finish the job, albeit for political and social "justice" reasons. Mainland China is indeed going in that direction, but the roles of the Party, the government, and the SOEs so far remain much more powerful and pervasive than the statistics reveal.

The tentacles are much more mobile and, as a group, more resilient than the big blob at the top. As the tentacles multiply and enlarge, the economy becomes more efficient. But the long-run test of reform is not whether legal private ownership expands. It is whether reform modifies the jellyfish structure of the private economy.

The Xi administration is slashing both the salaries and the graft of SOE leaders. This part of reform is very consequential. As I write this, SOE leaders are very unhappy people. Xi wants to retain the kind of power once exercised by the Guomindang's conglomerates but also to gain the efficiency of Taiwan's private sector. The only way to lessen

---

[30] On the way the reform of the state sector and the rise of the private sector have stimulated productivity growth, see Chang-Tai Hsieh and Zheng (Michael) Song, "Grasp the Large, Let Go of the Small: The Transformation of the State Sector in China," Brookings Papers on Economic Activity, Spring 2015, http://faculty.chicagobooth.edu/chang-tai.hsieh/research/CS_large_draft.pdf.

the tension between these goals is to move in the direction of Singapore's more hands-off GLC management. That is not happening, or at least not yet, and to some extent matters are moving in the opposite direction. Roles for Communist Party cells are even being written into the charters of Chinese companies listed in Hong Kong. Moreover, in the Xi era the SOEs are increasingly gobbling up parts of the private sector, using their extraordinary access to capital to buy out successful private sector firms or just overwhelm them. For clarity on future trends, focus on management control, not ownership.

SOE reform is crucial not only to economic efficiency but also to the shape of Chinese society. As we note elsewhere, the sense of universal mobility, the sense that with hard work anyone can move from the bottom of society to the top, evolved during the Hu–Wen era into a sense that a Party–government–SOE elite had sequestered most of the opportunities for itself. The resulting sense of unease is broadly similar to the discontent that motivates youth in the United States to support a Bernie Sanders or a Donald Trump. Alongside great pride in the accomplishments of the Chinese nation, there is a sense of being let down by the establishment. For now, that disquiet is channeled into very strong support for Xi Jinping's anti-corruption campaign. (Ironically the Chinese Communist Party has done a much better job, for the moment, of mobilizing and addressing youthful concerns about the establishment than the US Democrats and Republicans have.) But in the long run the issue is not just anti-corruption or the details of SOE reform. It is whether a pervasive sense of fairness and opportunity will sustain the legitimacy of Communist Party rule. To sustain and restore legitimacy, the anti-corruption campaign and the economic reforms must deliver, and they must deliver in the face of determined opposition from the elites that have in fact sequestered much of the opportunity. There will be more on this in the next chapter. The stakes could not be higher. Youthful support could evaporate quickly.

Entrepreneurship and Innovation

Entrepreneurship

Entrepreneurship has deep roots in Chinese society, thanks to one of Mao Zedong's shortfalls. Like Joseph Stalin, who eliminated Russia's kulaks quite thoroughly, Mao sought to eliminate China's landlords and rich peasants. Although he had perhaps 600,000 of them executed, many remained. Below the radar, village traditions of trading and small business functions proved resilient.

In the reform period Beijing first allowed and then promoted dismantling of the communes, which had provided local officials with resources and power, and brilliantly forced local governments to fund themselves by promoting industrial development.[31] This had two aspects. By giving most of the fruits of the land to the farmers, Beijing deprived the local governments of their principal source of revenues, and at the same time Beijing imposed hard budget constraints on the villages. It also forced the localities to take responsibility for building infrastructure that had previously been funded by the central government. By themselves these measures would have left town and village governments bereft. Simultaneously, however, Beijing empowered local governments with new property rights, namely the right to own and manage local businesses and to retain the revenues from them. Towns and villages were allowed for the first time to retain the taxes from local enterprises. The political result was forcible transformation of local village officials en masse into entrepreneurs. The social consequence was one of the great surges of employment in human history – more than 100 million jobs.

The economic consequences included the rapid emergence of rural industry that actually surpassed agricultural products in value by 1987 and created a huge increase in rural incomes. Although grain production soared to higher and higher records, the biggest success lay with the restructuring of governance and taxes to stimulate rural industrialization. By 2001 rural production by small and medium companies was 140 times the value for 1978.[32]

The strategy of taking away the localities' tax revenue and encouraging entrepreneurship became pervasive. Teachers would give their children fertilized eggs and tell them to come back in six weeks with chicks to sell

---

[31] My understanding of this process is heavily derived from Jean C. Oi, *Rural China Takes Off: Institutional Foundations of Economic Reform* (Berkeley, CA: University of California Press, 1999). The statistics on town and village enterprises, which increased spectacularly and then very gradually faded, are available in the annual national statistics review by the National Bureau of Statistics.

[32] China's Ministry of Agriculture, reported in "China's Market Economy Takes Over the Rural Economy," *People's Daily Online*, October 11, 2002, http://en.people.cn/200210/12/eng20021012_104918.shtml.

to improve the school. The Institute of Marxism-Leninism turned itself into a consulting firm. Wherever one went in China, whether to Beijing or to distant villages, one was offered deals. Everyone had a scheme. (And everyone claimed that the scheme would work in part because he or she was a cousin of China's top leader. Jiang Zemin may never have realized that he had 1.3 billion nieces and nephews. The seemingly universal ability to spin a story was part of the entrepreneurship.)

The center of gravity of this strategy quickly migrated not to the vicinity of Beijing, where the bureaucrats dominated, but rather to Guangdong Province adjacent to Hong Kong. Guangdong got the maximum benefits from early rural reform, the maximum benefits from creation of special market-oriented industrial zones, and, with Hong Kong right next door, maximum benefits from the policy of opening to foreign investment and trade. In addition, Guangdong was blessed by the center with greatly reduced tax rates, while Shanghai in contrast was taxed so heavily that until 1992 it paid one-sixth of the taxes of all of China.

The private and small and medium enterprise (SME) sectors now drive China's growth and jobs, and that is well recognized by senior leaders. Given that recognition, in 2015 a wave of enthusiasm for entrepreneurship swept official circles. At a February 11, 2015 meeting of famous foreign experts organized by the State Administration of Foreign Experts Affairs, Prime Minister Li Keqiang was eloquent about the new emphasis on entrepreneurship, and his annual Work Report for that year emphasized China's benefits from "mass entrepreneurship." The new enthusiasm builds on existing projects designed to promote entrepreneurship, such as the effort in the Zhongguancun area of Beijing that began under Premier Zhu Rongji. There, in an area with over 200 local universities, Chinese returning from foreign study with advanced degrees from reputable Western universities were automatically given grants sufficient to open a business office with a staff of 10. This attracted many participants. As in Silicon Valley, many failed, but according to district leaders almost everyone who failed went to work for someone more successful, with few leaving Zhongguancun.

That initiative shows that China's government has a good idea of what entrepreneurs need, namely a pool of highly educated, highly motivated people with freedom to pursue their own visions. However, implementing that insight in the broader Chinese economy has proved difficult.

The most obvious difficulty is the lack of financing for entrepreneurial ventures. The big banks control most financing in China. They are so committed to traditional customers, namely the big state-owned enterprises, that there is little left over for SMEs and private companies.[33] Even when funds are available, lending to such companies would usually be unwise. As occurs almost universally in emerging markets, smaller Chinese companies invariably produce multiple accounts, one for the tax man, one for potential partners or investors, one for their own management, and sometimes others. Since the figures are unreliable, credit decisions can be made reliably only by someone local with intimate knowledge of the families and their (typically) multiple businesses. But a giant bank headquartered in Beijing or Shanghai will never be able to muster such local knowledge. Thus adequate financing will come only from a (still nascent) proliferation of small local banks or from innovative institutions such as the financing arms of Alibaba or TenCent.

A second difficulty is the overwhelming advantages of the SOEs. Controlled interest rates have meant that banks could never cover the risk of lending to anyone other than SOEs that are large, familiar, and implicitly covered by a government guarantee. The big companies provide higher incomes than the market would support and more relaxed lifestyles than private or foreign companies. They have superior access to government contracts and approvals. They get easier access to land, often at half the price a private company would have to pay. They have superior access to housing for their employees, so young people, daunted by very high housing prices, flock to SOE and government jobs.

A good sign is that, despite the remaining advantages of the SOEs, one is starting to see students from the best universities looking at the private sector again. The anti-corruption campaign is cutting incomes,

---

[33] Lardy's data say that private companies are now paying interest rates similar to those paid by SOEs. It would be valuable to have a detailed investigation of the sources of such funding, which must come heavily from shadow banking. Whether from regular banks or shadow banks, it is totally irrational for private sector interest rates to be similar to the rates for SOEs that have implicit guarantees and usually have more reliable accounting. Hence that finding of Lardy's is a sign of dysfunction rather than a purely positive development. A true market system would free the banks to charge sufficiently high interest rates to cover the risks of lending to various categories of private companies.

Xi Jinping is cutting the salaries of top SOE leaders, and some of the efforts to level the playing field for private companies may be starting to take effect.

The dominant role of the state in relation to business also disadvantages smaller and private companies. During the first decade of the new century, corruption became such a high proportion of officials' income that some started refusing to give permits to small projects. While China's business regulation is not as restrictive or corrupt as India's "License raj," businesses need a permit for nearly everything, and every permit is a source of squeeze. Why give a permit to a project so small that the kickback would be negligible? Moreover, the types of squeeze went far beyond simple kickbacks. In one case where I had personal knowledge, a provincial Party Secretary sent a note to the CEO demanding a large contribution to a favorite new project. The CEO was on holiday, so he didn't see the note for two weeks. Thinking that he was being rebuffed, the Party Secretary used a phony environmental excuse to shut down the biggest operation of the company, which happened to be the country's leading exporter in its sector. The shutdown lasted for months, depriving the country of millions of dollars of exports and costing many workers their jobs.

Underlying that incident, which is typical in relations between local businesses and local governments, is not just corruption but also, and often more importantly, a widespread conception, at least in government and Party circles, of the proper relationship between state and market. Any enterprise, public or private, in this view has priority social responsibilities and those social responsibilities are defined and imposed by the Party Secretary.

When one steps back from outrage over a particular abuse of power, the general problem is one of evolution away from a primitive socialist conception of the relationship between government and business. At the beginning of the reform period, a minister was typically head of a national monopoly, for instance in provision of electric power, serving as both regulator and regulated. This made sense in terms of an ideology that identified the interests of the people with the interests of the Party/state. Then it became permissible to form other power companies, and the minister's family was best positioned to start a new company, so the minister and his family became regulator, regulated, and owner. Modern socialism converged with basic feudalism. Then began a process whereby the central government gradually separated regulator from regulated and began to articulate conflict-of-interest guidelines. Enacting these changes in six levels of government encompassing a sixth of the human race, against the fervent opposition of those with an interest in the old system, takes time.

When academic economists talk about the importance for economic growth of securing property rights, they mean that the Party Secretary shouldn't be able to shut you down for not contributing to his pet project. The difference between China and most Latin American and African countries is the determination to make progress, starting from a low base, and the historically rapid rate of progress. But that is little consolation to an entrepreneur who is being shut down today – or to a Chinese premier faced with rapidly declining growth prospects. Whether China's leadership is able to continue rapid progress will be a primary determinant of future growth rates. It is not at all clear that such progress is consistent with Xi Jinping's effort to increase the power of the Party secretaries inside and outside enterprises.

China's advantage is a highly educated, experienced, and determined leadership. Its disadvantage at the moment is that, in the first decade of the twenty-first century, they fell behind the curve and now they have to try catch up in the face of opposition from central bureaucracies, local governments, banks, state enterprises, and the military that have become enormous and enormously powerful, along with a generation of outspoken youth who inject nationalist and populist fervor into every policy debate.

Meanwhile, the private entrepreneurs and SMEs have developed minds and resources of their own. They know that they account for most jobs and most growth. Small and medium enterprise does not mean tiny and helpless. These companies are typically run by people of exceptional talent, especially organizing skills, who have succeeded on a playing field tilted heavily against them. In the case above, the entrepreneur decided to wait until economic circumstances clearly forced him to lay off most of his workers. He thought that the workers might well demonstrate and that the demonstrations might well catch the attention of Beijing, possibly leading to the Party Secretary's replacement. The emergence of a large class of talented, financially well-endowed people who think such thoughts supplements the challenge of economic transition with a complementary challenge of political transition. More on this can be found in the chapter on politics.

Innovation

China's leaders understand that the era of emulation (copying or importing technology and managerial practices from other countries) is passing and the era of innovation must begin. They have prepared for the era of innovation with typical thoroughness. The Ministry of Science and Technology collected the literature on innovation from all over the world, going back decades, sifting through even obscure journals, translated it, studied it, and circulated the findings in various forms.

A society's ability to innovate depends on many things – education, competition, legal protection, financial support – so it is good to start with the fundamentals. Starting in 1977, China declared that its citizens had a universal right to education. This, along with infrastructure investment, became the foundation of much of China's economic success, including a historic wave of entrepreneurship and local innovation in the towns and villages. Kate Xiao Zhou[34] has best recounted the outpouring of rural entrepreneurship and specifically women's entrepreneurship. Broad basic education was also the foundation for the success of millions of town and village enterprises that were a key part of China's early economic takeoff. As in South Korea, the first commitment was to basic education, and the drive to create great universities came somewhat later. Now Peking University, Tsinghua, Fudan, Shanghai Jiaodong, and many others are universally acknowledged for their quality.

Just as important, and perhaps even more important for innovation, is that China has encouraged the establishment of private schools and private universities. It is far easier to establish an international high school in Shanghai than in Hong Kong – not to mention India. (Having said that, while the initial draft of this book was under review, the government clamped down on the use of foreign subject matter, so some, but not most, of the value of the international schools was curtailed.) The HSBC and Cheung Kong graduate schools of business, to take two outstanding examples, attract top academic, business, and

---

[34] Kate Xiao Zhou, *How the Farmers Changed China: Power of the People* (Boulder, CO: Westview Press, 1996). Professor Zhou attributes all the successes to farmers' and women's initiatives, and thereby neglects the role of government in providing the roads, other infrastructure, education, and rules that enabled the rural outpouring of entrepreneurship, but her description of the outpouring of entrepreneurship is invaluable.

government leaders, and expose students to thinking from all over the world. Leading US and European universities have established campuses and joint venture relationships in China.

China has zones of innovation. Zhongguancun, mentioned above, has companies such as Jingdong (e-commerce), Lenovo (computers), Vimicro (semiconductors for image processing), Xiaomi (mobile phones), and Baidu (search engine). In Shenzhen, north of Hong Kong, which with Deng Xiaoping's support moved from rice paddies in 1980 to one of the world's greatest manufacturing and exporting cities in a mere quarter century, the maker movement pioneers new manufacturing ideas and the biotech industry has thrived. Huawei (electronics), ZTE (electronics), BGI (gene mapping), Tencent (internet), and BYD (batteries and electric cars) are among the globally important companies founded in Shenzhen. While a few of these depend on home market advantages, some (e.g., Lenovo, Huawei, ZTE) are as competitive internationally as any global firm. Tencent has much better social media products than its US counterparts like Twitter and Facebook. Shenzhen and surrounding areas, buttressed by Hong Kong capital and blessed by greater political freedom than other parts of China, are becoming one of the great innovation dynamos of the world.

China also has sectors of innovation. Its finance industry innovates as quickly, and sometimes as destructively, as its Wall Street counterparts. Shadow banking almost overnight became a source of fuel for smaller and private sector companies as well as a collection of Ponzi schemes. Notwithstanding the repression of politically incorrect substance, China's internet sector, with Alibaba and Tencent among others, has created giants in e-commerce, online gaming, and social media. WeChat, Tencent's contribution to social media, has hundreds of millions of subscribers all over the world. China is well ahead of the United States in e-retail and in the technical quality of its social media. (Repression of course subtracts from that quality.)

China has also had innovative successes in electronics, most notably Huawei, which is now a global force. Lenovo, which bought IBM's personal computer business, has been only marginally innovative in physical computers but has succeeded in China and in much of the developing world through innovative distribution.

When the government focuses on a project, it can invent just about whatever it needs in order to achieve its goals. China developed its own space program, which can orbit sophisticated satellites and a nascent space station, impair or kill satellites, and explore the moon. At an international conference in Seoul, in South Korea, I sat between two senior officials of China's Ministry of Science and Technology. They said that, because of US sanctions, China had had to develop its own space technology and had achieved first-class results. They said that, because the United States had not put sanctions on civilian aircraft, China had remained dependent on Boeing and Airbus. So, do you suppose, one of them said, that we could persuade the United States to put sanctions on civilian aircraft too?[35]

While most of China's space program comprises high-tech emulation rather than major technological innovation, it shows how rapidly China can develop its own technology. Space is not the only area of exceptional Chinese accomplishment. It has twice won the competition for building the world's fastest supercomputer, first using arrays of US-manufactured semiconductors, then in 2016 using domestically manufactured ones. Whether the underlying Chinese systems will permit efficient commercial use of these achievements remains to be seen.

Acknowledging these successes, China's progress into the age of innovation still faces high hurdles. Chinese education emphasizes rote drill and discourages critical thinking. This emphasis on rote characterizes virtually all emerging market education, not just China, but in China it is reinforced by the demand for political correctness. When I was managing research teams in Hong Kong, the staff I inherited from China included very talented individuals, but initially most of them lacked the curiosity and skepticism that one expects from researchers in the West. They had been taught to run regressions on the official statistics without digging very much into the reliability or precise basis of those statistics. In one case a couple of them interviewed the local officials about the local education system and were told that an important contributor to the city's success was its great vocational school. They wrote that down as fact. When I asked a knowledgeable senior official about this, he said that Beijing required each of the school's teachers to have a Ph.D., and as a result they knew very little about real business and generally provided very little useful

---

[35] For a more careful exploration of the space/aerospace issues than this casual conversation, see Andrew Erickson, "What Explains China's Comprehensive But Uneven Aerospace Development," www.andrewerickson.com/wp-content/uploads/2014/07/China-Rocket-Satellite-Aircraft-Development_AAS-Vol-40_2013.pdf.

vocational education. The young researchers had never been encouraged to question such things. As soon as the young researchers were put into a different environment, they became as thoughtful and innovative as bright young people anywhere, but in the Chinese context what proportion would be exposed to such a different environment? This is one reason why a very high proportion of Chinese students in the United States remain in the United States rather than returning to China.

Having said that, sometimes when powerful waves hit a shore they create a riptide running in the other direction. The story of rote education, politically constrained information, and hierarchy is true and important, but there is a riptide. Among the Peking University and Tsinghua students who migrated to the United States after what happened in Tiananmen Square in 1989 and who went on to build successful careers in the West, many say that they are surprised when they go back. Their colleagues who stayed behind have seen more change, from more angles, and engaged in more complicated arguments than those who went West and accepted the broad areas of Western consensus. There is so much deadening consensus in the West that the ones who stayed behind seem more interesting, more open to new ideas. And those whose careers did not come to an end in or around Tiananmen Square often made more money in more interesting ways. They are frustrated and worried by political developments in China today, but they are energized by the intellectual and business and human dynamism that coexists. Although I am a writer with strong opinions, I frankly do not know how to weigh this dynamism against the dead hand of censorship and rote. I do know that the political debates in Peking University are much more stimulating, and address more fundamental issues with more sophistication, than those at the US department where I got my doctorate because complacent ideological consensus and methodological faddishness can limit creative thought as thoroughly as an external censor.

In the West, the big high-tech innovations come through a combination of highly trained, inquisitive, often iconoclastic minds; a financial system that searches for big new ideas and continually invests, through many failures, until it finds some big successes; and a legal system that protects innovators' rights in their new products. China does not yet have those.

Silicon Valley in California and Route 128 around Boston developed around great universities, most notably Stanford and MIT, filled with innovative and iconoclastic thinkers. China's efforts to emulate that system go back to 1985, and the government has funded such efforts with increasing abundance.[36] In today's China, the government bestows huge resources on research and development – a goal of 2.5 percent of GDP to be spent on research and development, up from the current 2 percent, which in turn is more than double the proportion spent by other major emerging markets like India. But then much of that is distributed by rank and prestige, not by market judgments as to innovative value, and by administrators who are chosen because they value stability, not disruptive ideas.

In the United States, research grants are distributed to individual scholars who make competitive applications to grant-awarding institutions dominated by scientists. In China, research grants are distributed to universities by ministries. Chinese educational institutions are ultimately run by Party Secretaries whose primary mandate is to safeguard the interests of the Communist Party, not to cultivate iconoclastic thinkers. They typically distribute grants to established scholars with rank and prestige, possibly missing younger, more innovative researchers. After three decades with waves of expanding free expression, only partially reversed by intervals of reactive repression, in the Xi Jinping era university presidents and deans, not to mention the professors, have been severely restricted in what they are allowed to say and do. Everyone is somewhat afraid. That is not conducive to innovative thinking.

While all universities are subject to these constraints, China gains an advantage from encouraging the development of private universities and from its welcome to campuses and joint ventures of great universities from the United States and Europe, as well as from the vast, government-supported exchange of talent between China and advanced countries. Chinese universities are much more welcoming to foreign scholars than those in the other big Asian countries. The Chinese government is also experimenting with more Western-style processes for making research grants.

---

[36] Information derived from a Harvard Kennedy School presentation by Tian Jietang, "Facing Twofold Challenges: The Role of Universities & Colleges in China's Innovation System Today," March 2016.

Successful companies in China must be on good terms with the Party and government. There are layers and layers of licenses and regulations that provide officials with ways to block everything from land acquisition to building permits to staff hiring to funding. While it is fair to point out that the big companies in the United States and EU require major lobbying efforts and large political donations to curry favor,[37] the requirements in China burden companies much more and those burdens fall disproportionately on anyone trying to be innovative. This is particularly true because, as we note elsewhere, a high proportion of private enterprises are actually sponsored and funded by state enterprises or sponsored by local governments; they have special advantages in dealing with the regulatory and political burden and will tend to be the kinds of ventures that state enterprise bureaucrats would think of supporting.

Silicon Valley and Route 128 are supported by a venture capital industry, a private equity industry, a junk bond market, and a banking system that includes many institutions designed to support smaller businesses. China's leaders want to move decisively in that direction, but at best this will take time. The stock market is supposed to move from a system where China Securities Regulatory Commission bureaucrats choose which companies will list, favoring state enterprises, to a system where listing standards will be more objective and transparent. Insiders are suggesting that this listing system transition will take five years, a long delay that means Party power considerations continue to seriously delay more efficient markets.

New kinds of banks, and smaller banks, are being licensed so as to serve a wider range of businesses. The shadow banking market, which provides funding to individuals and enterprises outside the overregulated formal banking system, suddenly became huge. Regulators tolerated it because it was useful, but now are desperate to rein in its excesses. The government plans to develop the corporate bond market, which can become another source of funding for firms that would otherwise have difficulty breaking into the elite circle that the big banks

---

[37] According to a leak by Julian Assange, "Google Is Not What It Seems," https://wikileaks.org/google-is-not-what-it-seems, Google spent US$18.2 million on lobbying in 2012, in addition to donating tens of millions of dollars each to both Republicans and Democrats. There would definitely be value in a systematic comparison of the political rakeoffs involved in major technological and business innovations in the two countries.

serve. Unquestionably China's leaders know where the banking system needs to head, and the financial system is moving in the right direction. But leveling the playing field for banking and capital markets will severely limit the effectiveness of one of the Communist Party's most powerful levers of political control. How they will balance the financial and political imperatives remains to be seen. At the moment they are declaring absolute dedication to both imperatives, but that dodges the core issue of the tradeoffs.

In short, China has created a society with an exceptionally entrepreneurial spirit, and it is devoting exceptional thought and resources to stimulating innovation. It already has a string of major successes, from Alibaba to WeChat to Huawei to space exploration, and it will have many more. A decade ago it was far behind India and now it is far ahead. The entrepreneurial energy in places like Shenzhen is breathtaking. But catching up with the United States or South Korea as economies where innovative entrepreneurship drives economic growth will require fundamental reforms in the way education is provided, the way research funds are distributed, the way scholars are promoted, the way companies are regulated, the ways the law works, and the way funding is provided to entrepreneurs. The indicator to watch is whether the most talented Chinese scholar-entrepreneurs currently based in the United States continue to prefer to remain in the United States or whether they eventually find a more supportive environment back in China.

The risk to China, here as elsewhere, is that it becomes like Japan – less open to foreigners and foreign business, less open to foreign and domestic competition, less interested in sending students and officials abroad, more protective of its national champions as they become uncompetitive, more policies dominated by huge obsolescent interest groups. Some of the trends in Xi Jinping's China, such as the pressure on foreign companies to give up their technology in return for access to the Chinese market, the restrictions that try to drive foreign tech companies out in favor of local companies, and the consolidation of competitors in the effort to create national champions, resemble what happened in Japan when hubris replaced fear after 1975. The alienation of foreign high-tech companies comes at a particularly sensitive moment. Chinese companies trying to upgrade into high tech are often in the position of companies in industries like steel and machine tools back in the early 1980s: they have bought the latest equipment but don't yet know how to manage it. Those skills are typically acquired by working with foreign firms. If the trends toward discrimination against foreign businesses metastasize, China's future prospects become much less optimistic. Here as elsewhere the Xi Jinping administration is taking big risks.

China has a much more open economy than Japan, and a much more open, diverse society than Japan, so a great turning inward seems much less likely. China's exchanges with the rest of the world are so far continuing to expand, not contracting as Japan's did. As I was writing this section, a new Chinese acquaintance told me story after story of Chinese who had received their educations in the United States, gotten into successful US-based careers, then hit seeming dead ends (at Merck and Amgen in particular cases that came up), and found that in China they could earn higher salaries and get more career fulfillment because the government helped them get their new products (in one case a lung cancer drug hastened through disciplined clinical trials) to market more quickly than in the sluggish United States. China welcomes foreign executives, foreign coaches, foreign advice, foreign plumbers, and foreign investment to an extent that is unimaginable in Japan. China's globalization is an enormous asset.

The current repressive state of Chinese politics will not turn China into another Japan, defined by Galapagos sectors and low-productivity protected companies, but making China as innovative as the United States will require not only the success of the current reform program but also a vast improvement of the legal and financial systems and a loosening of Party controls over the allocation of funding for research.

To understand the balance of China's assets and liabilities for innovation, one must go beyond its domestic structures and policies. The overseas Chinese communities, particularly Taiwan and Singapore, but also in the rest of the Asian periphery and around the world, include some of the world's most innovative and entrepreneurial ecosystems. They are constantly inventing new technologies, new products, and new marketing techniques. They have some of the world's most sophisticated legal and financial systems and unlimited access to the world's best education and best information. When they have a new product, they turn to mainland China to get rapid approval and to achieve massive scale. They know how to maneuver around China's intellectual property theft and other problems. One Singaporean told me that his company had struggled for years to achieve commercially viable scale but then had expanded into the Chinese market and achieved valuation of $10 billion within a few years. The combination of basic research in China proper, technological and commercial innovation in overseas Chinese communities, and the scale of the mainland market, added to China's own innovative dynamism, notwithstanding China's domestic weaknesses, assures that China will become a fount of innovation.

Currency

China's currency management has been crucial to its economic stability. Equally it has been a major source of international controversy.[38]

In the early days of reform China's currency was grossly overvalued and the government feared that exposure to international markets would cause it to collapse. Therefore it required foreigners visiting China to use only Foreign Exchange Certificates (FECs), which were purchased at the official exchange rate. Later it started to move toward the market by opening swap centers where businesses could exchange foreign currency for renminbi (RMB) at market rates. Initially the rates at these different centers around China diverged a great deal, but eventually arbitrage caused them to converge. At this point there was a common "swap rate," which reflected the market, and a grossly overvalued official rate that was still maintained in order to subsidize purchases of foreign technology.

China gradually increased the amounts and the range of customers who could use the swap centers, so use of the market rate gradually increased. By 1994, 85 percent of foreign currency trades were at the market rate and 15 percent were at the official rate. At that point, China dropped the official rate and moved the last 15 percent of trades to the market rate. The difference between the official rate and the market rate was 34 percent, so this closure of the official rate amounted to a devaluation of 5 percent (that is, 34 percent of 15 percent). A massive currency adjustment was achieved over a period of many years without destabilizing China's economy or damaging its economic partners. The move to the market was of course exactly what the United States and Europe had advocated.[39] The net effect of

---

[38] For a comprehensive review of China's currency situation and prospects, see William H. Overholt, Guonan Ma, and Cheung-kwok Law, *Renminbi Rising: The Emergence of a New Global Monetary System* (London: John Wiley, 2016).

[39] Protectionist groups like Public Citizen in the United States have created a whole revisionist history of the RMB, which is based on the assertion that China

reducing the overvaluation only very gradually over many years was to inhibit Chinese exports since the currency remained overvalued throughout that process – and until about 2002. This achievement contasts remarkably with the typical pattern, which has occurred often and in many countries, especially Latin America, of propping up an unrealistic exchange rate and then being forced suddenly to conduct a massive, internationally destabilizing devaluation.

For several years prior to 1994 Chinese senior officials had indicated their intent to move toward a freely floating currency. However, in 1997 the Asian Crisis made clear that premature liberalization of the currency could risk a crisis, with huge inflows of money followed by destabilizing outflows. Therefore China fixed the RMB pending domestic financial reform. As it turned out, with that fixing the RMB was severely overvalued from 1994 through 2001. Indeed, it was so overvalued that, when I took my family on visits to Chinese cities such as Guilin, we would be riding bicycles down the street and men on bicycles would converge on us begging to trade our dollars for sub-stantially more RMB than the official exchange rate. American web-sites, such as China Online, published daily black-market rates showing how much the currency was overvalued and foreign busi-nesses made decisions based on those rates.

When China joined the WTO, reforms made Chinese exports far more competitive and China's trade surplus rose. By 2002 this change, and shifts in the real economy of China and its trading partners, were making the RMB undervalued even though the Chinese currency system remained exactly the same. Increasing trade surpluses reached a peak of 10 percent of GDP in 2007. However, from 2006, when the RMB was 8 per US$, it strengthened to just over 6 at the end of 2013 before staging a rebound as the Chinese economy weakened. Because of this strengthening, and because of a rapid rise in manufac-turing wages (roughly doubling in the major export production centers during the five years ending in 2015), China's huge current account

suddenly conducted a massive devaluation of the RMB by 34 percent in 1994 and thereby gained an unfair and destabilizing advantage. Likewise, some nationalistic Japanese analysts traced the currency crisis of 1998 back to this alleged sudden Chinese devaluation (rather than to the real precipitant, which was the Japanese banks' sudden withdrawal of funding from Thailand, Indonesia, and elsewhere). Such revisionist nonsense has been widely accepted in both Washington, DC and Tokyo, to the detriment of sound policy.

surpluses declined by 2010 to below the level (4 percent of GDP) that the IMF uses as an indicator of undervaluation;[40] from 2011–2015 they were at half or less of that level. In 2015 the IMF formally announced that the RMB was no longer undervalued. Indeed, during 2015 China, as always seeking stability, spent around half a trillion dollars propping it up *above* its market levels.

The 1994 system was not designed to create predatory undervaluation, and indeed produced chronic overvaluation for many years. The subsequent undervaluation was caused by efficiency gains stemming substantially from acceptance of reforms imposed by the West as a condition of WTO membership. The US Congressional charges of predatory undervaluation were misguided.

A small devaluation toward the market rate in August 2015 and a change from referencing the RMB against the US$ to measuring it against a basket of currencies in January 2016 did not change these fundamental relationships. China was doing what US and other Western officials said they wanted, namely moving toward a more market-oriented currency while emphasizing stability. Nonetheless, US presidential candidates Bernie Sanders, Marco Rubio, and especially Donald Trump continued to denounce China for undervaluing its currency and thereby stealing US jobs.[41] Democratic members of Congress, led by Senator Charles Schumer of New York, continued to denounce Chinese predatory manipulation in sarcastic, outraged language long after the IMF, market participants, and major publications had widely publicized a new reality that was five or six years old. Protectionist lobbying groups like Public Citizen likewise proved resilient to the new facts.

Of all the major emerging market economies, China handled its currency reform in the most responsible and stabilizing way. But it did have a period of serious undervaluation, including a very short period when this facilitated outsized, 10 percent of GDP, trade surpluses. That could have been handled better; in perspective, it has been

---

[40] This standard was suggested by US Treasury Secretary Timothy Geithner at the G-20 meeting in Seoul in 2010. The United States now uses a standard of 3 percent, which China has remained under since 2011. In 2015 the IMF officially declared that the RMB was no longer undervalued. By 2016 even the US analysts who had earlier made the most extreme estimates of RMB undervaluation were testifying that the currency was no longer undervalued.

[41] See for instance Mark Gimein, "Why the Presidential Candidates Have to Stop Blaming Everything on China," *Money*, December 1, 2015, http://time.com/money/4129837/china-currency-manipulation-imf-yuan/.

handled much better than the persistent trade surpluses of Japan, which, unlike China, managed never to run trade deficits and never to shift toward domestic consumption as the primary driver of growth. Certainly there is nothing in China's development that compares with Japan's massive, roughly 30 percent, devaluation of the yen as part of Abenomics. In Japan's case, the United States decided to accept the fiction that Japan's devaluation was simply a ramification of the use of monetary policy to stimulate growth – a fiction belied by virtually all domestic Japanese commentary. But in the case of China a combination of ignorance and prevarication (paid for by the backers of protectionist lobbies through campaign donations to members of Congress) led to nearly universal public US belief in the fiction of particularly predatory Chinese currency policy.[42] That fiction in turn had an enormous impact on the US presidential primaries, and may have negative consequences for United States–China relations and for the world economy for decades to come.

Stepping back, and looking over the entire reform era, China's currency management has been a force for stability, particularly during the Asian Crisis and the GFC, but also in using incrementalism to avoid the kinds of sudden crises that cause disruption in so many emerging markets from Argentina to Myanmar to Africa. As Western advisors have advocated, its reforms have moved inexorably, albeit with bumps, in the direction of more market-oriented exchange rates. On balance, this has served China and the world well, and is one of the great successes of the reform era.

---

[42] While writing this, I was curious as to why this did not lead to the corrective media and think tank reaction that would typically occur in other cases of gross misrepresentation. If Senator Schumer, for instance, made equally erroneous remarks about German policy, there would be an instant awarding of "Four Pinocchios," the *Washington Post*'s label for extreme dishonesty. Part of the answer, of course, is ingrained hostility toward China, which leads to less careful fact-checking of negative statements about China. But leading think tank experts said the most important factor for them was that Washington think tanks and media are focused on issues that are likely to drive particular pieces of legislation, and the currency issue was not driving legislation. Likewise, a leading international business reporter said that, since there is no longer any serious substantive argument that the Chinese currency is undervalued, the newspapers think it would be a waste of time to correct the views of politicians on the subject. Unfortunately, that has allowed public opinion to be influenced by fictions that could drive not just Sino-American relations but also the whole global trade system in negative directions.

Overview

If China succeeds in its reforms to even a moderate extent, it will become the world's largest economy. It will leapfrog many of the technologies where legacy assets hold the more developed countries back – for instance the shifts to mobile phones, to internet commerce, and to mobile banking. As anyone who uses WeChat knows, it has already leaped ahead in social media, despite government censorship, and has been consistently more versatile than its Western counterparts (Facebook, Twitter, Gmail). It will create scale that overwhelms Western competitors who do not advance into China.

Here's an example of the latter. Around 2008 I was asked to advise the board of a US meat company that was seeking to make a major acquisition in China. I encouraged them to move ahead, because they needed scale to compete in China and they needed global scale to compete in the US market against future Chinese competitors who would inevitably appear. The international leadership of the company was enthusiastic but most of the board members were more comfortable with the US market. The local Chinese Party Secretary in the city of the planned acquisition gave them a hard time, so the US company backed off. A few years later Shuanghui, a Chinese pork company, bought Smithfield Ham for just under US$5 billion, creating a gigantic Chinese-owned competitor right in the meat company's home market. The game is, globalize or be eaten.

Even with only moderate reform success, the center of gravity of the world of fashion, art, and music will shift toward China. Currently the center of gravity of the global market is still the American baby-boomer. In the future it will be millennial Chinese. Already Chinese art has become globally fashionable, commanding extraordinary prices. Western fashions are starting to make use of mandarin collars and many other Chinese touches. A sportswear company that lacks a major share of the Chinese market will be unable to compete with those that do, so Chinese tastes will influence sportswear globally. Hollywood is already tailoring its movies to ensure they attract a Chinese audience. On the West side of Los Angeles, where I used to live, it is difficult to find a fashionable new restaurant whose menu is not strongly influenced by Asian flavors. Some markets may fragment to serve local tastes in different parts of the world, and the extent to which this happens will depend on geopolitical developments, but the big companies will mostly have the Chinese market at the center of their attention. Americans are not ready for this, and indeed most would be shocked to realize the extent to which it is already happening. This will inspire additional protectionist reactions like those of the presidential nomination campaigns of Donald Trump and Bernie Sanders in 2016. Such protectionism, if it happens, will deprive US companies of critical access to the center of gravity of the world market and ensure their relative decline.

To the extent that US politicians stimulate a turn inward against the global market, the United States will lose out to countries that take a longer, more globalized view. France was a great global power, and its language was one of the premier global languages, until protectionism made it just one more medium-size country. Japan is of course the ultimate example of how to lose imminent great power status by retreating from globalization.

In evaluating China's situation, it is well to bear in mind the wave-like process of development and reform. A wave of development builds to a crescendo that creates major problems and then the government seeks to initiate a wave of reform that will solve the problems and take the economy to a yet higher level. By analogy, think of the tech boom in the United States. It gathered force very gradually in the 1980s, built to a crescendo – a massive bubble – in the 1990s, and then crashed, after which users and investors gradually worked out sober ways of using the technology without so much excess. Social movements in the United States are the same – the civil rights movement, the women's rights movement, the gay rights movement. Each of these movements had the same wave-like pattern. If one focuses on the excesses, one misses the developmental progress. The excesses pass, and usually the development remains. This is the story of Chinese infrastructure, the story of Chinese housing, the story of Chinese copying of intellectual property, the story of the Chinese effort to stabilize the currency against the US dollar, the story of Chinese debt. With every wave, the excesses lead some observers to prophesy doom. In China the numbers are so large, the waves so high, that every wave can seem like a devastating tsunami.[43] Usually doom does not happen. But of course the story of financial innovation in the West that led to the GFC

---

[43] Each wave leads to many Western forecasts of disaster. For instance, see the quotations from Patrick Chovanec in Gwynn Guilford, "A Chinese Housing Market Crash Could Be Even More Disastrous Than America's," *Quartz*, March 19, 2014, http://qz.com/189792/a-chinese-housing-market-crash-could-be-even-more-disastrous-than-americas/.

of 2008–2009 shows that real tsunamis can happen; that one could have led to another great depression if slightly mishandled.

China today is experiencing multiple big waves. These can lead to simultaneous waves of reform or they can swamp the ability of the system to cope. The economic plans are the right plans. Implementation in the face of fierce resistance is the issue. Transformation of the growth model of one-sixth of the human race, through a system of six levels of government, is one of the great challenges of human history. The complexity and maneuvering are a more appropriate subject for a great historical novelist than a computational economic model.

If Chinese economic reforms are maximally successful, and if one can assume the United States avoids a leadership disaster, then China will still lag technologically for decades. Although it will be formidable in its immediate neighborhood militarily, it will still lag the United States militarily on a global basis. Its currency will vastly surpass the importance of the yen, the euro, and the pound sterling, but it will not challenge the preeminence of the US dollar without transformative legal reforms. Likewise, without transformative legal reforms, multinational companies will put limits on their China commitments and China's own wealthy citizens will continue to stash nest eggs abroad.

If the backlash against reforms succeeds in stalling or greatly slowing the move to market allocation of resources and to a level playing field, then China's long-term growth will be far less. Some approximation of the Japanese scenario could happen. Japan turned inward after 1975 and, coming off two decades of growth achieved in substantial part through globalization, its politicians spread the belief that the inherent superiority of Japanese culture was responsible for its success. It created protectionist barriers to both foreign and domestic competition and let big traditional interest groups dominate its politics. China would be unlikely to go that far. It is a much more cosmopolitan society than Japan, with a much more open and competitive economy. But a fierce internal struggle could nullify some of these qualities, and there are nativist strands in Chinese politics that could emerge into a stronger role. China cannot afford to stagnate at US$15–20,000 per capita or even fall into an era of extremely low growth at that level.

The struggle over reforms is intense and the outcome uncertain. While I was writing this chapter, one of China's most powerful executives visited my office. He left me with the observation that "The game in Beijing is: you die or I die."

3 | Critical Social Issues of the Transition: Inequality, Corruption, Environment, Globalization

A society of 1.4 billion people undergoing more rapid change than any comparable unit has experienced in world history experiences problems of a scale and complexity that are beyond any human experience and beyond any models or calculations. These gigantic problems interact in ways that are not just complex but often unpredictable. This chapter addresses four of the most important. Is inequality likely to disrupt political stability or economic growth? Will corruption undermine the legitimacy of the regime? Will the anti-corruption campaign reduce that risk? Why does China grow despite the corruption? Is China's political structure and continued growth radically inconsistent with maintaining a livable physical environment? Will globalization sustain economic growth or, as in Japan, will a reaction against globalization undermine growth prospects?

These issues are tectonic plates that lie beneath the economic issues discussed in the last chapter and the political issues addressed in the following chapter. If even one of these major social issues heads toward a disastrous outcome, then economic progress and political stability are threatened. If all of them turn out to be manageable, or are headed in favorable directions, then there is a sound foundation for economic plans and the regime may have considerable resilience in the face of stressful changes.

Inclusiveness and Inequality

Inclusiveness

Two leading economists of our day, Acemoglu and Robinson[1], have compiled historical statistics and a persuasive story arguing that a vital

---

[1] Daron Acemoglu and James A. Robinson, *Why Nations Fail: The Origins of Power, Prosperity, and Poverty* (New York: Random House, 2012).

key to sustained economic growth is an inclusive society. Inclusive societies engage their populations and do not suffer the kinds of instability that disrupt growth in so many societies. But Acemoglu and Robinson conflate socio-economic inclusiveness with Western electoral democracy in ways that lead to fallacies about economies at China's level of development.

Socio-economic inclusiveness properly defined has multiple dimensions: widespread access to jobs, education, and income; avoidance of socially disruptive inequality; including everyone, especially women, in rising incomes; and avoiding economic destruction of important segments of society. The Asian miracle economies, including China, have excelled at inclusionary policies despite politics, in the early phases of development, that Acemoglu and Robinson wrongly disparage as extractive (their term for the opposite of inclusive, namely exploitative systems).

The Asian miracle economies share pieces of a nearly common approach to creating an inclusive society. In Japan, South Korea, Taiwan, and China, the era of rapid growth began with a land reform, followed by the provision of universal education. Those policies, undertaken in every case except Japan by leftist regimes, redistributed society's most important assets so that most of the population acquired a stake in society. Typically they emphasized giving the entire population a solid elementary and some secondary education before focusing on the development of great universities.

In South Korea, General Park Chung Hee was almost Maoist in his fanaticism about equal access to education. Admission to universities was, Confucian-style, by competitive examination, but Park discovered that six elite high schools were providing about half of the entrants to the country's top university, Seoul National University. His reflex was that he wanted to disband those schools in order to give everyone a fair chance. Like Mao's, Park's egalitarianism was extreme, but giving a priority to universal education, fairly distributed, is a hallmark of the Asian miracle economies. Typically, authoritarian China has done an extraordinary job of providing universal education, in sharp contrast for instance with democratic India, although marked inequities persist between rural and urban areas.

The next step is to provide, as much as possible, universal access to home ownership. In Singapore, rental housing was provided to most families at inexpensive rates and then the families were allowed to buy their homes at preferential rates. The housing market was partially shielded from foreigners through measures that made foreigners pay higher, often prohibitive, rates. In China at the dawn of reform, most people were in the rural areas and had, or were given, property rights in their homes. In the city, housing was initially provided by state-owned enterprise (SOE) employers and, primarily in one of Zhu Rongji's great reforms, 1999–2003, was sold to the employees at very low prices. This was one of the great wealth transfers of economic history. Often in China, as vast populations shifted from the country-side to the cities, there was a disjunction between the rural location of the family home and the workplace of the parents, but the system provided most people with a stake in society. Nothing is as important to social stability as the sense of having a stake in society, a foundation of economic security that will not go away.

Since this is a finding crucial to understanding of Chinese society, and largely unfamiliar even to many Western specialists, I provide Table 3.1 with the most important statistical findings.

Thus, by all important studies, homeownership in China is at least 20 percentage points higher than in the United States, where home-ownership was 63.7 percent in the second quarter of 2017 and has varied between about 63 percent and 69 percent in recent history.[2]

Then, in each country, a great asset inflation occurred. Housing prices in particular took off spectacularly in each of these societies. The resultant widely distributed wealth creation has been much more important than the (already proportionately large) savings from wages.

In a study of wealth accumulation in the city of Foshan, north of Hong Kong, Qian Wan, a Ph.D. candidate at Renmin University, compiled official statistics to show how this affected wealth accumu-lation. As shown in Figure 3.1, property wealth quickly outstripped bank deposits (the other principal form of wealth) and became several times per capita GDP. Middle class Americans typically do not have wealth amounting to multiples of per capita GDP. Table 3.2 shows that this pattern occurs in other cities as well. In broad terms the pattern is typical across China and across the Asian miracle econ-omies. This provides families with a very substantial stake in social stability.

---

[2] Federal Reserve Bank of St. Louis Economic Research, "Homeownership Rate for the United States," https://research.stlouisfed.org/fred2/series/RHORUSQ156N.

Table 3.1 *Findings on Chinese homeownership rates*

National Bureau of Statistics of the People's Republic of China
城镇和农村居民收支状况和生活质量的有关报告
Tenure in urban areas (%): owner-occupied units (official numbers):
89.3% (2010); 85.39% (2011); 85.39% (2013)
Chinese Academy of Social Sciences
当代中国调查报告丛书：中国社会和谐稳定跟踪调查研究 **(2013)**
Sample size: 31 provinces, 7,388 residents aged 18–69
Homeownership rate in 2013: 93.5%, 1.9% higher than that in 2011
Urban areas: 89.6%; 1.7% higher than that in 2011
Southwestern University of Finance and Economics and Bank of China
China Household Finance Survey (中国家庭金融调查报告) **(2012)**
Sample size: 25 provinces, 8,438 households
Homeownership rate in 2011: 89.68%; **urban areas: 85.39%**
Centre for Urban Development and Land Policy, Lincoln Institute, Peking
   University
"中国城市化进程中的挑战"研讨会 **(2011)**
Sample size: 500,000 households
Homeownership rate: 84%
Zhejiang University and Tsinghua University
中国居住小康指数 **(2013)**
Sample size: 40 cities; 10,308 effective questionnaires
Ranking of 40 cities in 2012
(1) Changsha 90.1%; (2) Harbin 89.1%; Guiyang 86.0%; ...
(37) Guangzhou 72.8%; (38) Beijing 70.7%; (39) Shenzhen 70.0%; (40)
   Shanghai 67.9%

Of course, asset inflation can exacerbate wealth inequality, but giving the overwhelming majority of citizens a solid stake in society contributes greatly to stability even if the stakes are unequally distributed. People who own a home will be cautious about jeopardizing the system that supported their homeownership.

An ongoing stake in society is also provided by an early economic strategy based on labor-intensive manufacturing, which by definition provides large numbers of jobs in the modern economy and particularly engages huge numbers of women. People feel at home in the modern economy, because they are engaged in it and benefiting from it, rather than experiencing it as a shocking intrusion into a traditional way of life as typically happens, for instance, when a

Table 3.2 *Family assets and income, RMB, various cities*

	Property value per capita		Deposits per capita		GDP per capita	
	2005	2010	2005	2010	2005	2010
Beijing	107,036	379,673	23,453	54,324	45,993	75,943
Shanghai	491,747	491,747	188,361	339,388	49,649	76,074
Guangzhou	95,127	268,784	123,373	226,651	53,809	87,458
Shenzhen	132,929	521,224	Unknown	188,471	60,801	94,296
Foshan	70,796	302,711	67,357	117,547	42,066	80,313

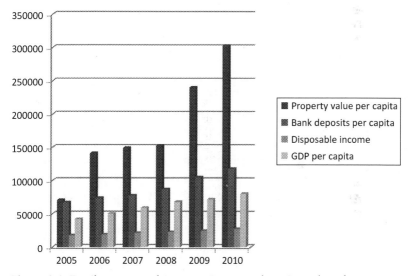

Figure 3.1 Family assets and income, RMB, Foshan City (data from CEIC Data Company Ltd.).

sector of Western-style mining and manufacturing appears in a Middle Eastern country. A country like India is far less inclusive because its inability to provide adequate infrastructure means that the manufacturing sector is small and the widespread modern manufacturing employment typical of the Asian miracle economies cannot emerge.

The Acemoglu and Robinson analysis, although correct in its emphasis on inclusiveness, cannot explain or accommodate the Asian miracle approach to inclusiveness during early stages of development.

Their conflation of democracy and inclusiveness betrays an inability to understand the tradeoffs between inclusiveness and democracy in early stages of development. Democratic elections in societies where there is a powerful elite with money, education, and organizational skills, sitting on top of a vast non-elite almost totally lacking in those resources, empower the elite at the expense of the broader populace. The landlords get organized, win the elections, and rig the system in their favor. Because their social dominance is ensured and legitimized by elections, they are not motivated to invest in the infrastructure necessary to develop a national labor-intensive manufacturing sector.

Democracies cannot accomplish land reforms because the elite is too powerful. (Costa Rica is the sole partial exception.) In India, the Philippines, and Thailand, the power of the elected elite creates a strong bias toward subsidizing world-class universities for the elite rather than elementary education for everyone else. India has some of the world's best hospitals for the elite, but maternal deaths in childbirth, infant deaths, malnutrition, and other social ills are all a substantial multiple of their counterparts in China – and in the other Asian miracle economies in their early developing, non-democratic phases. In poor countries, democratic elections tend to provide legitimacy to socially non-inclusive outcomes. Conversely, the socially inclusive development of the initially authoritarian Asian miracle economies tends to provide a solid foundation for truly inclusive democracy if they make a democratic transition later. *South Korea and Taiwan are the most stable, successful democracies in the emerging world for precisely this reason.*

I elaborate on this theme in the next chapter.

One of the intriguing aspects of the extensive Western literature on sources of stability and instability in China is that the near-universal homeownership is seldom or never mentioned. As an enthusiastic reader of work on Chinese stability/instability, I have never seen an article in the Western literature focusing on it. But it would be hard to find a politician or political analyst who does not understand the importance of homeownership, or lack of it, in Western societies.

In the Asian miracle economies, particularly China, this emphasis on inclusiveness is institutionalized and developed further in two ways. First, the rapid incrementalism and the related one–two system of Chinese development ensure that no major segment of society is left out of the development or suffers huge reverses. Some segments develop much faster than others, with for instance farm incomes taking off first and then urban incomes moving far ahead later, but everyone benefits. Second, the core of development is *labor-intensive* industry – textiles, garments, shoes, radios, televisions, computer assembly, and so forth – that by definition creates vast numbers of basic-level jobs. It accomplishes this by building the infrastructure, providing the needed education, and enabling the competition, so as to make building labor-intensive factories attractive and competitive.

The incrementalism is a sharp contrast with shock therapy in Russia, which reduced GDP by 40 percent and reduced the incomes of many families by far more than that. In many cases, Russians lost their stake in society, namely their homes and pensions. China's focus on developing modern labor-intensive industry is a sharp contrast with India, where the government has so far failed to provide the necessary infrastructure, education, and open, competitive environment. The number of Chinese who own homes is about double the number of Indians who have access to toilets. Inclusiveness in the sense of having assets, jobs, shelter, education, and income is not a problem for China in the way it is for so many poor democracies.

Inequality

Measures of inequality are another way to look at a society's inclusiveness. The Asian miracle economies other than Japan have all been founded on radical left-wing egalitarianism. Japan is only a partial exception, because attitudes and practices in Japan are extremely egalitarian compared with those in the United States and Western Europe. South Korea's Park Chung Hee is often seen in the West as a right-winger, because he came from the military and sided with the United States, but he was a radical socialist by history and inclination. His brother ran a communist front, and Park himself nearly got expelled from the army for his leftist ties. He was persuaded to make the big chaebol (conglomerates) that he sponsored legally private companies, but he charted their paths from the presidential office in socialist detail, with an Economic Secretary setting annual milestones for production, exports, size of loans, and interest rates on those loans. Similarly, in Taiwan Jiang Jingguo, the son of Chiang Kai-shek and the inheritor of his leadership position in Taiwan, was a member of the Soviet Communist Party and, as his father's security chief, a thoroughgoing Leninist. Singapore's People's Action Party was related to the Communist Party in the way that China's Guomindang was related to the Communist Party: a great deal of shared structure and values combined with ferocious competition. But in Singapore no Japanese and Russian intervention tipped the balance toward the Communists and Lee Kwan Yew won decisively. Symbolically, members of his party were required to call each other "Comrade" for years after the victory.

All these economies succeeded by moving gradually from a substantial degree of socialism and Leninism toward acceptance of domestic and global markets, but the image, popular in the West, that they evolved in ways that the Heritage Foundation would approve, toward a laissez-faire, small-government society, is totally false.[3] All have exceptionally detailed regulation, decisive economic planning mechanisms, and strong thrusts toward inclusiveness. Singapore has high levels of government ownership. Even Hong Kong, caricatured in Western thought as the ultimate laissez-faire economy, is dominated by a set of cartels created by government regulations.

Mao Zedong's China fit right into this leftist pattern, but the others integrated their leftist ideology with a solid base of technocratic skill and pragmatic calculation. Mao's China had both, but Mao's agrarian populism rejected the integration. More on this can be found in the next chapter. So Mao did the leftist things, spreading national assets around through land reform, supporting those who had been exploited, and viciously turning inherited advantages into disadvantages by persecuting those from prosperous urban or "rich peasant" families. (Mao's subsequent collectivization of the farms took away the land that had been given to the peasants, but did not undo the egalitarianism. In the

---

[3] Each year the Heritage Foundation awards Singapore and Hong Kong titles as the world's two freest economies. Singapore and particularly Hong Kong fete the Heritage Foundation enthusiastically every year to encourage continued awarding of those titles. In fact, they are two of the most centrally managed and cartelized economies on earth. They do allow free trade and free international investment, but the Singaporean economy is managed as intricately by the government as most economies that would be labeled socialist. The Hong Kong economy is dominated by a system of cartels set up by the British to channel money into British hands – now mostly Hong Kong tycoon hands. On Hong Kong, see William H. Overholt, *Hong Kong: Between Third World and First* (Hong Kong: Nomura, 1999), available in the Hong Kong Publications section of www.theoverholtgroup.com.

reform era, the peasants got their land back, with initial egalitarianism retained.) He went to such extremes that by 1976 the country was ready for a total repudiation of his agrarian populism.

China's repudiation of much of Mao's agrarian populism led it to become in social terms the most right-wing of the principal Asian miracle economies. Japan, Singapore, Taiwan, and South Korea are all more egalitarian than China. Moreover, China's diversity creates additional kinds of inequality.

China's great inequalities include regional, urban–rural, migrant–local, income and wealth, and male–female disparities.

Regional Disparities

China's great geographic diversity makes regional disparities inevitable. For comparison, consider the difference between Manhattan or Silicon Valley and Wyoming or New Mexico. Hence some of these disparities are natural and inevitable. But, beyond the inevitable, they have undergone startling changes over time as China has experienced a pattern of rotating takeoffs. Mao moved China's industry to the deep interior, reflecting security fears that came primarily from the Soviet Union and also from a history of invasion from the sea in the preceding century. With most international trade cut off, this policy made the interior relatively prosperous and left much of the coastal area bereft. Some coastal areas experienced widespread hunger. The co-author of my most recent book, Guonan Ma, faced possible starvation in rural Guangdong during the Cultural Revolution. The industrialized deep interior areas were much better off.

With reform, which germinated at the end of the 1970s and blossomed in the 1980s, trade and manufacturing bloomed all along the coast. Suddenly, the new industries with the good jobs were along the coast, particularly in manufacturing for export. Desperately poor provinces like Guangdong, where many people were on the brink of starvation during the Cultural Revolution (1966–1976), took the lead in economic growth and eventually pulled far ahead of their formerly more prosperous interior counterparts. The big, slow-moving factories of the SOEs in the interior now had to compete and they could not. The lucky ones sold a big share of themselves to foreigners, who would provide technology, international management, and a move to the coast. In the 1980s and 1990s the interior fell far behind the fast-moving economies of Guangdong, Fujian, Zhejiang, and Jiangsu. Xinjiang in the far west, another formerly very poor area, also grew quickly because of its vast mineral resources. (More precisely, half of the province grew quite rapidly, attracting a great inflow into the predominantly Uighur territory of Han Chinese migrants, who captured much of the growth benefit.)[4] This transformation turned many of the formerly poorest provinces into some of the most prosperous. Crucially, it did so not by impoverishing anyone but by lifting the coast's prosperity faster than it lifted that of the also-growing interior.

Meanwhile, development of the national infrastructure of roads, railroads, airlines, and telecommunications was creating the potential to spread the rapid coastal development nationally. In the new century, Hu Jintao's administration made an enormous and successful effort to create development in the interior. The most important places, Sichuan and Chongqing, with huge populations and with positions up the Yangtze River comparable to Chicago's on the Mississippi, got subsidies, regulatory advantages, and proven leaders; they took off with reported growth rates of 15 percent annually, half again faster than the spectacular rates that had marked the coast's rise. This was the great development success of the Hu–Wen era. The area west of Sichuan and Chongqing still has much lower per capita incomes, but only a very small part of China's population lives in that area.

Like the area around Chicago, but on a much greater scale and with much broader reach, the center-west of China, Chongqing and Chengdu, is slated to become the transportation hub of Eurasia, with roads and railroads stretching southward into Southeast Asia and northward across central Asia to Europe. The "One Belt" part of China's grand One Belt One Road development plan (now called the Belt and Road Initiative or BRI) envisions this core of China, which was once isolated from the rest of China by mountain ranges, becoming the center of gravity of Chinese development and of Eurasian commerce. Figure 3.2, showing the size of the economies of different

---

[4] In the prosperous half of Xinjiang the economic benefits of the Uighurs have been sufficient that, despite independence sentiments, Han Chinese and Uighurs work together smoothly and there is minimal terrorism. Uighur women hold influential positions in Hong Kong-owned factories and invite their Hong Kong counterparts to parties and dances at their homes. (I learned a couple of Uighur dances, very awkwardly, at one of those occasions.) There is little such camaraderie in Tibet.

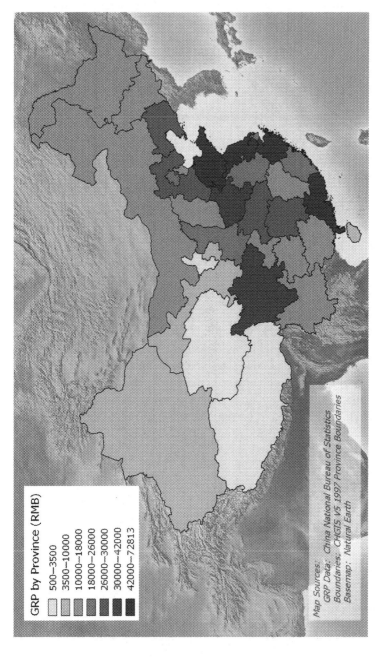

Figure 3.2 Gross regional product (GRP) by province, 2015, 100 million yuan (map by Lex Berman, Harvard Center for Geographic Analysis).

GRP by Province (RMB)

500—3500
3500—10000
10000—18000
18000—26000
26000—30000
30000—42000
42000—72813

Map Sources:
GRP Data: China National Bureau of Statistics
Boundaries: CHGIS V5 1997 Province Boundaries
Basemap: Natural Earth

parts of China (gross regional product, GRP, not per capita income), shows how the heavily populated center of China has become economically important. (The light-shaded areas of the far west contain very few people.) Meanwhile, "One Road," the maritime part, is intended to continue the coastal takeoff of earlier years.

Next due for revitalization is the industrial northeast, the heavy industry center of gravity of China. For most of the twentieth century, this was the highly developed region, with the heavy industry that much of the rest of the country lacked. But now the steel mills, coal power stations, aluminum smelters, and cement factories are the old China. They are predominantly SOEs, inefficient, environmentally destructive, heavy with overcapacity, the core of China of the previous century.

Regional disparities will always be present in China, but all regions have developed, and the proven ability of the government to pivot its talent and resources into areas that need development creates successive waves of regionally equalizing development in each area. Importantly also, Chinese are highly mobile, in contrast for instance with Indians, who are often limited in mobility by language and caste considerations, constantly moving to where the opportunities are. So long as this pattern continues, the regional disparities will not be destabilizing. Risks would arise from stagnation such as has happened in Brazil, but for now China's prospects seem to be for an extended period of slower but not slow growth rather than stagnation. Among large countries, China's success at pivoting development to previously impoverished areas is unique. Brazil's similar efforts to develop its vast impoverished north and interior rapidly led to national financial collapse without achieving the desired development.

Rural–Urban and Resident–Migrant Disparities

Rural incomes are about one-third of urban incomes, a ratio that sounds large but is not disconcertingly high at this stage of development. In egalitarian Taiwan and South Korea, rural incomes were sometimes just a little better, about 40 percent of urban incomes.

The farmers were the first big beneficiaries of reform. When the communes were dismantled in the first few years of reform, farm families began to receive the full benefits of their labor, along with (for some) most of the costs of being lazy, and incomes skyrocketed. Then Deng Xiaoping's budget reforms created an explosion of town and village enterprises, creating more than 100 million jobs. The jobs were important because, as in the cities, everyone had been officially employed in the commune or factory, but Mao's feudal residence and job system locked large numbers of people into roles that no longer had value; on the books they had jobs but in the United States they would have been considered unemployed and on welfare. Meanwhile the creation of a national network of roads, railroads, and communications, along with the gradual move to market pricing and markets rather than rations, created a national market and improved rural welfare.

Subsequently the government's emphasis has been on creating modern cities, to some extent at the expense of the countryside (which continued to grow but much more slowly than the cities). The contrast between the shimmering skyscrapers of Shanghai's Pudong and the underdeveloped countryside of much of the country is striking, although nothing like as stark as the contrasts between wealth and subsistence poverty in India. The continued existence of Mao's feudal hukou system, which ties a family's ability to get social services to a local residence permit, has created a deep division between those with a residence permit for the city and those tied to the countryside. People move to the cities by the hundreds of millions, but they continue for long periods to lack equal access to education, medical care, and pensions.

Throughout the country families have been moved off their land by takings (government acquisitions, usually legal, sometimes illegal, frequently abusive) for industrial and property development, often with limited compensation, and rural people have been much more vulnerable to such takings than urban people (who since the later 1990s have increasingly organized to resist unfair takings). Unfair takings have understandably been the largest source of social unrest in China; ruthless local officials in collaboration with ruthless developers have given local government a bad name throughout the country, as has been made clear by periodic outbursts of rioting and documented by every significant opinion survey.

In the first decade of the new century, Beijing began to address these disparities, primarily by lifting a variety of fees and extortions that local governments, desperate for revenue, had imposed on rural people. Hu and Wen abolished China's ancient agricultural tax and provided large subsidies for primary education. Now there is an emerging effort to make it easier to get an urban residence permit, to provide increasing social services to rural migrants who lack such

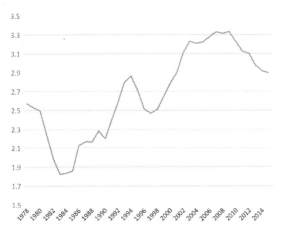

Figure 3.3 Urban to rural income ratio (data from National Statistics Bureau).

permits, to reduce unfair takings, and to enhance the property rights of rural people so that they will be able to borrow against their land, lease their land, and consolidate their holdings with others to enable larger scale, more efficient production. As with other reforms, these move forward at an excruciatingly slow pace for those who watch from day to day but at a very rapid rate in historical terms. Reforms under Hu Jintao had a substantial impact, as shown by Figure 3.3.[5]

In short, rural–urban disparities are substantial and compel policy attention, but it is always important to remember that rural people were the first beneficiaries of reform and have continued to be substantial beneficiaries despite falling behind their urban counterparts. A flow of over 10 million people per year to the cities relieves pressure on the rural areas. The residual Maoist restrictions on sale of rights in rural family plots (technically the government still owns all the land) have constrained agricultural modernization, but more importantly they have also prevented predatory developers from grabbing everything and leaving a bereft peasantry. The fact that each peasant family, and ex-peasant family, has a place to call home has been fundamental to social stability.

Despite serious inequalities, the authorities' successful implementation of successive waves of strategies that ameliorate regional and urban–rural disparities, coupled with incrementalism which ensures

[5] I am indebted to a presentation by Chen Zhao for calling my attention to this improvement and providing the data.

that every major group experiences improved standards of living, has thus far been a source of strength and stability for Chinese society.

The Role of Women

One of the great triumphs of contemporary China is a drastic, although blemished, improvement in the status of women. Mao proclaimed formal equality for women soon after the Communist victory in 1949. The foundation of actual improvement is that China has educated men and women universally and roughly equally. Indeed, the average Chinese woman gets 13.2 years of education while the average man gets 12.9. In higher education, women consistently outnumber men, even though there are more men in the general population. On the UN Human Development Index, Chinese women's score (0.705) is comparable to that of men (0.747).

This is a sharp contrast with India, where women get, on average, half the schooling of men (3.6 years versus 7.2), and 27 percent of Indian women get some secondary education as compared with 57 percent of men. On average Indian women make less than one-quarter of what men make. Twenty-seven percent of Indian women are in the labor force, as compared with 80 percent of men.[6] India's gender inequality index is a high 0.563, whereas China's is a low 0.191. (Smaller numbers indicate less inequality.) China's Gender Development Index is a high 0.943, whereas India's is a lower 0.795. The situation of Chinese women also contrasts favorably with that of women in Japan, a far more developed country, who find it much harder to combine child-rearing and work.

As one travels throughout China, one constantly meets powerful women mayors and women Party Secretaries. As elsewhere, women are underrepresented, particularly at higher levels, in comparison with their proportion of the population,[7] but their pervasive importance is a

[6] *United Nations Human Development Report 2015*, http://hdr.undp.org/en/countries/profiles/IND.
[7] On the dearth of women on the Central Committee and above, see Cheng Li, "The Dire State of Female Representation in the Chinese Government," http://supchina.com/2017/04/10/dire-state-female-representation-chinese-government/?utm_source=SupChina&utm_campaign=36a908d39c-20170425-278newsletterRobotChineseJournalists&utm_medium=email&utm_term=0_caef3ab334-36a908d39c-164721977.

sharp contrast both with China's past and with many other emerging economies. In the National People's Congress, 23.4 percent of the delegates were women in 2015. Internationally, China is ranked number 61 globally in the political role of women, whereas South Korea is 91, India 111, and Japan 127.[8] In business life, although top male executives are much more numerous, one constantly meets wealthy, powerful women and the role of women is much more prominent than in politics. China has more self-made female billionaires than any other country.

The combination of universal education, the reversion to family farms, and the flowering of the town and village enterprises created a wave of rural entrepreneurship in which women played a crucial role.[9]

Above all, what has transformed Chinese society is the role of the manufacturing industry. In agriculture, which until a generation ago employed most of the labor force, the decisive, sometimes life or death, advantage went to the family that could deploy more muscle power. Men are bigger, so in most pre-industrial societies there is a strong preference for male children.[10] In China the one-child policy combined with the traditional preference for males to create a tendency to abort female children. (Having said that, the gender imbalance in India is roughly comparable.)

When China became the world's center of labor-intensive manufacturing, the incentive system changed decisively. In the textile factories employers want women. In the computer assembly factories they want women. In most but not all manufacturing, attention span and fine motor control are prized while muscle power is increasingly irrelevant. (Traditional steel mills, car assembly plants, and the like are exceptions to this rule, but even there automation increasingly substitutes for muscle power.) These jobs offer far better income and living conditions than the villages, so it is not unusual for young women to journey to a

---

[8] See http://gb.cri.cn/42071/2014/03/05/6071s4449057.htm.

[9] The role of rural entrepreneurship and particularly the role of women is documented in Kate Xiao Zhou, *How the Farmers Changed China: Power of the People* (Boulder, CO: Westview Press, 1996).

[10] One frequently hears even scholars ascribe the preference for boys to culture. There are of course real cultural differences, but the concept of "culture" too often becomes an intellectual dumping ground to explain behavior that has roots in the economy or the broader social context. Most (not all) traditional societies prefer boys because their livelihoods, even their survival, require muscle power; culture shapes itself around that imperative.

different province, where the dialect is different, often traveling 500 or even 1,000 miles to get these jobs. The consequences are socially transformative.

In the village, and in the traditional family, these women are totally subordinated to men. The men are the ones who experience the working world and learn to make decisions and exercise authority. The men control all the assets. The manufacturing world turns this on its head. A shy, frightened girl leaves the village for the opportunities of the big city and gets bumped around. Her early days are hard. But she quickly learns to cope with a difficult, competitive situation and to take care of herself in an environment of sharp elbows. She develops an independent mentality of "There's only one person who can help me and that's myself." After a few years, she, not the village boys, is the one who knows how to function in the formerly strange world of modern enterprises and urban culture.[11] She is the one with the financial assets to buy a home. In this situation, while the bosses of the big companies are still men, and while many women settle into what is outwardly a traditional Confucian marital relationship, the balance of opportunities, the balance of skills, and the balance of confidence in Chinese society have been transformed. This deep transformation underlies the explosion of female entrepreneurship, the increasing prevalence of female executives, and the fact that large numbers of women have become extremely wealthy.

Having come a long way, and being far better off in gender fairness than Indian or Japanese women, does not of course mean that life is fair for Chinese women. A preponderance of families still emphasize having a male heir to carry on the family name. Leta Hong Fincher[12] reminds us that the centuries-long tradition that the family home should be held in the husband's name disadvantages women,

---

[11] This is the core message of Leslie Chang, *Factory Girls: Voices from the Heart of Modern China* (New York: Picador, 2008). She emphasizes that the women migrants of this generation "are driven out [of the village] less by the poverty of the countryside than the opportunities of the city." (p. 105). The same phenomenon occurs in India, as shown in, for instance, Ellen Barry, "Young Rural Women in India Chase Big-City Dreams," *New York Times*, September 24, 2016, www.nytimes.com/2016/09/25/world/asia/bangalore-india-women-factories.html. The difference is that in China the opportunities are orders of magnitude more numerous and the urban conditions far better.

[12] Leta Hong Fincher, *"Leftover" Women: The Resurgence of Gender Inequality in China* (London: Zed Books, 2014).

particularly in an era of extraordinary housing price inflation. Aside from the straightforward inequality of assets, this particularly disadvantages women who get divorced at a time when divorce rates are rising. But this cannot be generalized, as Fincher does, to an argument that women are generally becoming worse off relative to men. Indeed, the focus on "leftover" women in Fincher's title shows the opposite. There are 33 million more men in China than women, because of the lingering effects of the demand for muscles in a formerly agricultural economy, but China has a substantial number of women who cannot find suitable husbands. Everywhere one meets educated, successful, attractive women who hold their heads up with well-earned pride but in private moments express the wish that they could also fulfill the other side of their lives. Women who have achieved what Chinese call "the three highs" (high education, high professional status, and high income) often cannot find what they view as a suitable partner unless they marry a substantially older man. Government efforts to help them are not a form of repression, but rather efforts, sometimes clumsy, to address a legitimate problem that is increasingly pervasive throughout the region and the world.

Japan and Singapore also worry about fertility and try to encourage women to marry earlier and have more children. When I lived in Singapore, the government was providing free cruises to college-educated singles. One (female) Singaporean scholar recently recommended that Singaporean businesses should turn off the air conditioning at 7:00pm to pressure young people to leave the office and have some fun together.[13] For years the Japanese government has been trying to persuade women to have more children as well as to join the work force in higher numbers; compared with Chinese women, Japanese women are more frustrated in both aspects of their lives.

The rising incidence of divorce is also, ironically, an indicator of rising women's self-confidence. In the old days, male control of the family assets created an inescapable cage for unhappy women. The problem remains, but more and more women have the confidence and resources to break out of the cage.

---

[13] See for instance Charissa Yong, "More Young People in Singapore Staying Single," *The Straits Times*, March 11, 2016, www.straitstimes.com/singapore/more-young-people-in-singapore-staying-single.

The one-child policy, which has recently been abandoned, cut two ways in reformist China. Most importantly, it led to frequently abusive treatment of women and added to the incentive to abort female children in order to ensure a male heir. (Female abortions are also common in India, where there is no one-child policy.) Importantly, the positive side of this bad coin was that families whose only child was a girl had a strong incentive to encourage her success in education and work in order to have someone to support them in old age.

A pervasive problem for Chinese women (and women in most developing societies) is the universal effort by men to trade business favors for sexual favors. It has taken a long time to get this problem mostly under control in Western societies, and in China it has barely begun. In the textile and electronics factories, male executives sometimes refer to the factory floors of women as "peach orchards." But it is not just on the factory floor that such attitudes are found. In the investment bank where I worked the longest, women wanted the powerful, highly paid marketing jobs but dreaded being assigned to market in China. They would come to me and say, "My customer is offering me a million-dollar trade but only if I sleep with him." We would call up the customer and inform him that the woman had been promoted to a new job and his new marketing exec was a man. Unfortunately, at many companies the women are afraid to speak up and the corporate attitude is less supportive.

More subtly, women complain that they are expected to be beautiful, not just smart, whereas no such standard applies to men. Some women glory in this, but many find it unfair and burdensome.

Having said that, the ultimate sign that the situation of women is improving is that, when one asks sophisticated urban women whether they would prefer to have a boy or a girl, the answer is as likely to be a girl as a boy. That is a huge change from previous generations.[14] Chinese women are far better off than in recent centuries, are far better off than their counterparts in India, and have been delivered from the degree of bondage to husbands and family that led to high suicide rates for women in traditional families. Universal education and the manufacturing economy have changed the balance of a society away from the oppressive patriarchy of the past. The path to elimination of all

---

[14] This assertion is based on my personal experience, obviously a very limited sample of very successful women.

unfairness remains long, but in a developing society perfection is never the right standard. After acknowledging residual source of unfairness, Leslie Chang, in a summary of her numerous, lengthy interviews with "factory girls" who had escaped the villages, says,

> The migrant women I knew never complained about the unfairness of being a woman ... The divide between countryside and city was the only one that mattered. Once you crossed that line, you could change your fate.[15]

Notwithstanding the problems, they feel in control. Many feel exhilarated about their newfound liberation. It is fair for feminists to gear up for the next battle. To understand today's Chinese society, it is important to know how empowered Chinese women are compared with their predecessors and most of their counterparts in neighboring countries. They are acquiring the wherewithal to win their future battles.

The speed of change is breathtaking. When I was running research teams for Bankers Trust in Hong Kong, I always had a smaller team than my competitors at other banks. One strategy that worked for me was to seek unrecognized female talent. I hired the first stock analyst from the mainland ever hired by a Hong Kong bank, a woman who went on to spectacular success. At one point we calculated that every 18 minutes she earned as much as her brother back in China earned in a month, and that was at the beginning of what became her spectacular career. A couple of the women to whom I gave a boost, and who gave my teams a disproportionately large boost, earned wealth that dwarfs anything I ever imagined achieving. Today such a strategy would have limited value; the companies and banks are full of powerful Chinese women and competition for them is intense.

China's superior movement toward improved gender equality is a major social strength.

General Income and Wealth Inequality

China is a very unequal society, more in line with the right-wing systems of Latin America, the United States, and Hong Kong than with the relatively egalitarian systems of the other major Asian miracle economies (Japan, South Korea, Taiwan, Singapore). On the

---

[15] Leslie Chang, *Factory Girls: Voices from the Heart of Modern China* (New York: Picador, 2008), pp. 57–58.

Gini Index scale of income inequality, where 0 is perfect equality and 1 is perfect inequality, China's official statistics lead to numbers like 0.47[16] (depending on which year), and one university survey came up with an extreme 0.61.[17] The World Bank's Gini Index compilation,[18] which omits a Gini index for China, presumably because the statistics are just too uncertain, shows extremely unequal Brazil as 0.529, relatively egalitarian Switzerland as 0.316, extremely egalitarian Sweden as 0.273, and the relatively unequal United States as 0.411. In income, China is definitely one of the world's more unequal societies.

The first point is that all the Chinese estimates show very high income inequality, and wealth inequality is much worse because those who had substantial assets experienced extraordinary gains through a generation of asset inflation. The second point is that the inequality derives from some of the prosperous becoming spectacularly wealthy, not from any significant group being absent from reform's benefits or experiencing income declines. All major groups in China have been gaining. All social groups can look at their parents and grandparents and see that the current generation has been elevated to a standard of living their predecessors could hardly have imagined. Almost everyone who wants a job has one, and even the great layoffs of the SOE reforms under Zhu Rongji were compensated for by opportunities elsewhere, mainly in services and to some extent in the private sector. So far, China has done a superb job of retraining and relocating workers, in sharp contrast with the United States. Wages of coastal manufacturing workers have risen spectacularly, almost doubling in the five years from 2011 onward. The government puts a floor, a low one but one that would transform Indian society, under everyone, and under the five-year plan

---

[16] See for instance Ryan Rutkowski, "China Chart of the Week: Inequality Continues a Steady Decline," Peterson Institute, January 30, 2015, http://blogs.piie.com/china/?p=4257, showing a decline from 0.49 to 0.47. See also Terry Sicular, "The Challenge of High Inequality in China," *Inequality in Focus* 2(2), 2013, pp. 1–5, http://documents.worldbank.org/curated/en/254081468218393028/pdf/825220BRI0Ineq00Box379865B00PUBLIC0.pdf.

[17] Shen Hu, "China's Gini Index at 0.61, University Report Says," *Caixin Online*, http://english.caixin.com/2012-12-10/100470648.html.

[18] World Bank, "Gini Index (World Bank Estimate)," http://data.worldbank.org/indicator/SI.POV.GINI. The World Bank report multiplies all the indices by 100 to come up with a whole number, but I have followed the more usual scholarly convention.

just completed told local governments that they should raise the minimum wage at least 13.1 percent per year. Most families have significant assets, including a home. Most are literate and have basic appliances – the accoutrements of modernity. This is one of the great achievements of human history, and Chinese families are intensely aware of that and appreciative.

Recently a prominent scholar has claimed that the Chinese government is highly extractive and just gives its people the minimum required to maintain stability, in contrast to democratic governments that give priority to taking care of their people.[19] He arrives at this result by lowballing Chinese economic growth; by comparing China with Britain and modern democratic South Korea while eschewing comparisons with India, South Korea when it was at China's stage of development, and other peer comparisons; and by systematically ignoring all evidence, such as housing, longevity, malnutrition rates, infant death rates, maternal death rates, and disease rates, that shows China providing superior support for its citizens than its peers like India.

The most appropriate comparison with China is India, which a few decades ago had per capita incomes similar to China's. Now the UN categorizes China as having High Human Development and India as having Medium Human Development. In India, a third of the population is illiterate (and much more if properly measured), half do not have toilets, women are widely treated as chattels and playthings, infant and maternal deaths are a multiple of China's, and malnutrition and disease are omnipresent.[20] Table 3.3 provides representative comparisons; all other human development comparisons point in the same direction.

At a conference in Mumbai's Grand Hyatt Hotel in 2005, CEOs from India, China, and the United States came together for several days of exchange. Some of the sessions were held across town in a Taj hotel. One day the normal bus route was blocked by a political demonstration, so we were re-routed through a slum area. The Chinese delegates, amazed at what they saw outside the bus, took some time to learn

---

[19] Stein Ringen, *The Perfect Dictatorship: China in the 21st Century* (Hong Kong: Hong Kong University Press, 2016). My review of this book is "Cartoonish Sketches of China As a Villain," *GlobalAsia* 12(1), 2017, www.globalasia.org/bbs/board.php?bo_table=articles&wr_id=9188.

[20] A very convenient source of comparative statistics is "World Bank Open Data," http://beta.data.worldbank.org/. The specific data I cite are from United Nations, *Human Development Report 2015*, http://hdr.undp.org/sites/default/files/2015_human_development_report.pdf.

Table 3.3 *Human development indicators, China and India*

	Infant mortality	Child mortality	Child malnutrition	Public health expenditure	Deaths from tuberculosis
	(per 1,000 live births)	(per 1,000)	(%)	(% of GDP)	(per 100,000)
China	10.9	12.7	9.40	5.60	3.2
India	41.4	52.7	22.70	4.00	22

Source: United Nations, *Human Development Report 2015.*

about the slums. At the closing session, a leader of the Chinese delegation led off with a comment to his Indian counterparts: "If we treated our people the way you treat your people, we would have a revolution overnight." That was the only time I have ever seen top Indian executives, who are not shy, without a retort. It was just true. China has very big problems of fairness, but its citizens are taller, healthier, better housed, better educated, more modern, and longer-lived than their Chinese counterparts of a generation ago and their Asian counterparts except for the earlier Asian miracles. Importantly, they are sufficiently well informed to know that.

The vulnerability created by Chinese inequalities does not lie in the numbers per se. It lies in whether the economy continues to make gains, whether policy continues to address the (very substantial) problems effectively, and whether the leadership is perceived as conducting itself properly, in service to the larger society. Like Americans, the Chinese will tolerate some people becoming extraordinarily wealthy if the foundations of that wealth are believed to be legitimate. Like Americans of earlier generations, they are inspired by a sense of upward mobility and universal opportunity, the sense that hard work can carry anyone from the bottom to the top. All those things were universal perceptions throughout China during the last two decades of the twentieth century, but have come increasingly into doubt in the early twenty-first century. By the second term of Hu Jintao, 2008–2013, there was a strong sense that a Party–government–SOE elite was sequestering the opportunities. Home costs in the Tier 1 cities rose spectacularly high, and earnings for college graduates – unlike those of manual workers – went into sharp decline. Resentment spread that a lot of the elite gains came not from hard work and brilliance but from corruption. This puts the legitimacy of the system at risk. That risk is greatly magnified by corruption.

Corruption and the Anti-Corruption Campaign

Chinese President Xi Jinping's anti-corruption campaign has highlighted the seriousness of China's official malfeasance. The outcome of Xi's campaign will shape a new era of China's politics, economy, and foreign policy.

"Corruption" covers quite disparate phenomena with different consequences. It may mean graft, which is taking a bribe (tantamount in this case to a tip – even a multi-million-dollar tip) for doing your job, or it may mean corruption in the stricter sense, taking money in return for undermining national policy or the national interest. When a Chinese official accepts an illegal kickback for building a good road, that is graft.

Chinese "corruption" is overwhelmingly graft, whereas, for instance, in the Philippines under former president Ferdinand Marcos and in India, corruption in the narrow sense, corruption that defeats national goals, has predominated. How can we tell? We can do case studies. In the Philippines, for instance, many important projects were designed to fail. A hotelier would borrow US$100 million with a government guarantee, then steal US$40 million for personal use and let the hotel go bankrupt during an economic downturn, leaving the government with the debt. That is corruption.

Beyond case studies is the Biblical saying "By their fruits ye shall know them." A modern-day equivalent is "The proof of the pudding is in the eating." In China, good roads, good railroads, good airports, and good ports get built, consistently. In India they don't. In China, when the government announces a major project, it almost always gets done and done well. In India, the government will announce a cleanup of the Ganges River and nothing will happen. This simple fact is beyond dispute. Likewise with primary education, and with events like the Olympics and the Asian Games; China's hosting of the Olympics in 2008 and Shanghai Expo in 2010 set the all-time standard, while India's hosting of the Asian Games was markedly shoddy. In China graft predominates while in India corruption predominates.

An Indian insider gave me a representative example. India was severely short of electric power, and that was seriously harming the economy. Solving the electric power problem became one of the highest priorities for the government, which signed a landmark contract with Enron (a company with its own fatal corruption problems). To move forward, Enron had to pay off a legion of regulators and legislators, paid for out of its "education budget." According to the Indian executive, after everyone had been paid off officials decided there was no more milk in the cow and just let the project die. That defeats urgent national policy.

Even worse is what the Japanese term "structural corruption." In Japan virtually all government officials and senior executives are personally honest: no bribes, much hard work. But five major interest groups – agriculture, retail, construction, property, and banking – dominate the legislature to the extent that they can, to an extraordinary degree, pervert national policy to their benefit. The construction lobby, itself connected to organized crime as occurs in many countries, provides the template. For a long period, Japanese infrastructure spending (for a country the size of California) exceeded US infrastructure spending. There are world-class "bridges to nowhere" used largely by deer and rabbits, and bullet trains to small towns. Almost every river and stream is gratuitously lined with concrete. The waste of national resources was spectacular.

Moreover, so powerful was the grip of the construction lobby on the nuclear regulators that the operators of the Fukushima nuclear plant were allowed to build in an inappropriate location, to inappropriate standards, ignoring even crucial explicit safety rules like the one requiring a fire station inside the plant. And all the while public discussion was smothered by government propaganda about safety. The Fukushima nuclear disaster was only the most dramatic of the costs of Japanese structural corruption; alone it is more costly than the corruption in China.

The economic costs of Indian corruption are far greater than China's graft, severely limiting social progress. The economic costs of Japan's structural corruption dwarf both. Notwithstanding the relatively favourable comparisons of economic costs, the scale of graft in China has become a potentially fatal *political* problem for the Chinese regime. The Chinese regime is particularly dependent on its reputation for economic efficiency and meritocracy. It does not have the procedural legitimacy of elections and as a corollary it lacks the periodic venting of popular frustration that comes from holding elections and changing officials.

The varieties of corruption obviously overlap, and Chinese graft was gradually tilting into more corruption in the narrower sense. But the overall patterns are quite distinctive and predictive.

Probably the single greatest consensus in the Western political science literature about corruption in China is that the authoritarian system inevitably causes corruption and that China would be much cleaner if it became more democratic. As the examples of the Philippines, Thailand, and India show, this is an ideological conceit that ignores problems widespread in the democratic developing world. Democracies in poor countries typically have much more crippling corruption than China, and it is rooted in the process of democracy. In very poor countries, peasants and subsistence workers can't donate to political candidates. Two kinds of funding predominate. Overwhelmingly the most important is bribes. Second, wealthy candidates fund themselves in the expectation that their "investment" will yield a high return. In very poor democracies, the complexity of democratic judicial systems makes it very difficult to convict criminals and therefore empowers wealthy criminality. The Indian legislatures are full of felons. In Taiwan, a reforming Leninist[21] government under Jiang Jingguo cleaned up world-beating corruption, but the advent of democracy under Lee Deng-hui and Chen Shui-bian partially revived it; President Lee Deng-hui quickly fired a crusading prosecutor who tried to push back the rising tide of corruption, members of local mafias became common in the legislature, and his successor Chen Shui-bian went to jail for corruption.

Japanese corruption provides a crucial template for comparison with China. The governing Liberal Democratic Party (LDP) was constituted through corruption. After being defeated in World War II, the conservative nationalist elite sold off military supplies illegally to fund a conservative political force. Its funding gave it a decisive advantage. After 1955, when a broader conservative party was formed through the

---

[21] A Leninist government is an authoritarian, hierarchical polity structured around powerful top leaders, a Politburo, a Central Committee, a party with a wide-ranging cell structure, and some degree of commitment to Marxist ideology, along with a doctrine that the party is a vanguard that must lead the people. As noted earlier, Jiang Jingguo, the son of Chiang Kai-shek, began his political life as a member of the Soviet Communist Party.

merger of the Liberal and Democratic parties, conservative groups colluded to siphon off vast funds from many sectors of the economy. For instance, when the United States forced Japan to open up to imports of US beef, the LDP gave an American the right to organize such imports. He was required to funnel the imports through a Korean-Japanese. (They typically chose either Korean-Japanese or burakumin for such roles because their low status made them easy to control.) The American had to turn over a high proportion of his profits to the Korean-Japanese, and the Korean-Japanese was required to turn over most of his profits to the LDP. Multiply such arrangements across many sectors and one has funding for an insuperable political force. Control over these flows of funds was the Japanese LDP counterpart of the Chinese Communist Party's control over funds from SOEs. In the face of these arrangements the United States kept its eyes firmly closed; the possibility of the LDP losing its sources of political dominance was unthinkable to Cold War Washington. Contrast this with the current (2017) US investigations of possible high-level corruption in the 1MDB scandal in Malaysia, whose system is similar to Japan's.

The combination of elections, a partially Western-style legal system, and a certain acceptance of international standards made it possible to clean up, gradually, over decades, the personal corruption and many illegal fund flows, while leaving LDP dominance of the political system intact. The legacy of the system, however, was control of the LDP by the five major interest groups and acceptance of systematic protection from foreign and domestic competition to a degree that has crippled Japan's development and allowed very serious abuses by key groups – most notably the misbehavior that led to the Fukushima nuclear crisis because the power of the construction lobby overwhelmed any possibility of effective regulation.

The Japanese template reveals two challenges for China. One is that cleaning up graft and simple corruption in Japan was possible because of the framework of the legal, media, and political system, a framework that is lacking in China. Similarly, in Hong Kong the Independent Commission Against Corruption was able to be effective because it operated within a legal, political, social (outspoken individuals), and media framework that supported it, institutionalized it, and oversaw it. It is not clear, or at least not yet, how China will institutionalize its gains in the battle against corruption. Xi Jinping's administration has announced an intention to create a permanent network of local corruption-fighting institutions. While the objective is admirable, it remains to be seen how effective such institutions can be unless the public and media are allowed to speak freely and unless a depoliticized legal system is created. A principal risk is that such institutions could degenerate into instruments of local power struggles or even instruments of corruption themselves.

The second and more important lesson from Japan is that the power of the major interest groups over the polity became institutionalized, in the system called structural corruption, holding the Japanese economy back ever since. That could happen in China. As early as 2005, influential Chinese scholars started privately expressing worries that the interest groups and rising provincial influence would take China back to the bad old days when the center could not implement policy effectively. Fear of such centrifugal forces was the most important reason why Party leaders agreed to centralize so much power in Xi Jinping's hands.

In China, as in virtually all emerging economies, most officials supplement their salaries with irregular income. But the forms and intensity vary. One characteristic of the Asian miracle economies is that the values of the top leaders have generally given priority to national service; they focus on how they will be seen by future historians. In the Marcos Philippines and in numerous Latin American and African countries, the motivation to become president is that the president can become richer quicker. While some of their family members did well, nobody has accused Park Chung Hee, Jiang Jingguo, Lee Kwan Yew, Deng Xiaoping, or Zhu Rongji of being in it for the money. They were obsessed with saving their countries through economic growth.

The core reason why graft rather than policy-defeating corruption prevails in China is that the growth-focused system demands performance at all levels. China is run like a business. Every village head, city mayor, provincial governor, and party secretary has performance requirements – economic growth, domestic and foreign investment, building key roads and bridges, and improvements in children's education – that must be met to gain promotion and avoid punishment.

And Chinese officials are held to high standards. Even in poor provinces like Anhui (where I have driven for many hours), the main Chinese roads appear better than their US counterparts. In the Hu–Wen administration China's railroad minister became obscenely rich but built extraordinary railroads. To get a promotion a mayor or other official must not just fulfill his targets but also outperform ambitious colleagues. Although politicians everywhere orate about fostering growth, most countries do not hold political leaders at any level to performance standards. Much more on this, and on controversies about it, can be found in the next chapter.

Jiang Zemin and Zhu Rongji oversaw an economy characterized by pervasive graft, but they knew how to keep it under control by using structural reforms. They sought to cut the top levels of government in half, while quadrupling salaries, to ensure that officials could live on their incomes. They gave every government and party bureau a quota of regulations to cut, to reduce the number of opportunities for squeeze. They drastically reduced the number of SOEs and put the remaining ones on more of a market basis. They forced the military to give up over two-thirds of its non-military businesses. And they promoted competition and demanded increased transparency of various kinds. So graft, while still pervasive, remained within limits and was not allowed to evolve into performance-destructive corruption.

Their successors, Hu Jintao and Wen Jiabao, reversed many of the reforms, expanding the bureaucracy, ceding central power to the localities and interest groups, and allowing the military back into business. In coping with the Global Financial Crisis that began in 2008, like leaders everywhere they poured money into the only institutions that could create rapid increases of production: the big companies. The government and party bureaucracies nearly doubled, from 40 million officials to 70 million, reversing Zhu Rongji's reform. The SOEs revived their preeminence (notwithstanding the caveats in the economics chapter) and the 1990s campaign to increase competition dissipated. Senior military officers reverted to managing numerous and often huge side businesses and driving Mercedes 500s. Some top leaders and their families began making the equivalents of hundreds of millions of dollars or even, as in the case of Prime Minister Wen's family, billions of dollars. The combined wealth of members of China's legislature came to exceed half a trillion dollars.

Graft opportunities rose much faster than economic growth. As property development reached a huge scale, and as asset inflation magnified the fortunes available from property, official control over property allocations became the basis for great fortunes. Private equity Chinese-style became a particular specialty of many princelings. In the

West, private equity means buying a company, reorganizing it, and selling it profitably on the basis of its arguably improved value. In China, it often (perhaps usually) meant persuading the local Party Secretary to allow you to buy into a good SOE just before stock market listing – with stock market prices at three times the level of Western market prices for much of the Hu–Wen era. The scale of graft became astronomic.

Graft became such a high proportion of local officials' income that some of their behavior began to shift in the direction of the Philippines' Marcos-era officials. Many became reluctant to approve smaller projects because small projects provided so little squeeze. This was corrupt in the narrow, more deleterious sense.

That observation leads to the broader point that, although the different types of corruption described above are the central tendencies for the respective countries, there are aspects of all three kinds of corruption in every country. As China developed in the new century, it became clear that deleterious corruption was affecting many aspects of society, including even universities.

Chinese universities follow the pattern of efforts to govern by objective standards. Students are admitted on the basis of a rigorous exam. Professors are promoted in substantial part on the basis of objective standards, notably publications in respected journals. As with infrastructure, one can see everywhere that the effort to uphold objective standards leads to positive results. Chinese roads are better than Indian roads, and Chinese universities are generally better than Indian universities. But deviation from the rules and gaming of the standards is also severe. In China, plagiarism and faking are pervasive. Groups of professors review each other's papers for publication and then cite each other's publications frequently in order to ensure that group members perform well on measures of publications and citations. As the economy develops, this becomes increasingly consequential because the economy becomes more dependent on genuine findings and genuine innovation.

Moreover, the corruption spreads beyond mainland China and creates scandals. Hong Kong universities, which have hired many mainland scholars, now have the same kinds of groups gaming the system (and scratching each other's backs in even more unethical ways) as the mainland does. The consequences have even spread to the United States. Chinese applicants to leading US high schools and

Box 3.1 Japanese and Chinese Anti-corruption Tactics

Some of the tactics of China's anti-corruption reform are similar to those used in Japan. Both societies have had extreme abuses of entertainment. In Japan, getting the financial and economic ministries to approve deals required exotic entertainment. In China, the entertainment budgets became so enormous in the Hu Jintao era that Beijing's restaurant scene became startlingly luxurious. For example, a former colleague from a financial project took charge of a moderate-sized government unit. Every meal for a week he took me to a fabulous restaurant. Familiar with straitened US government entertainment allowances, I asked how a civil servant could afford this; he said, oh, his unit's entertainment budget was US$34 million.

In Japan, financial approvals often required taking government officials to no-pan shabu shabu. Eating shabu shabu, you cook meat and vegetables in a pot of boiling broth centered in the table. In no-pan shabu shabu, short for no-panties shabu shabu, the bottles for drinks are on a shelf high above the table. When a customer wants a drink, the waitress, wearing a mini-skirt and no panties, steps onto the table and reaches up high to get the bottles. In 1998 the media chose to scandalize this and suddenly severe rules were imposed on all entertainment of government officials. When I was chief Asia strategist of Nomura, Japan's largest investment bank, in the year 2000 I was asked to set up a lunch with two top regulators from Hong Kong's Securities and Futures Commission. As we were driving toward Hong Kong from Shenzhen, my boss asked me where lunch was. I told him I had reserved a table in a Mandarin Hotel restaurant – the kind of venue that a Western investment banker would choose. He said, "Oh no, I could go to jail." I had to make an extremely embarrassing phone call to the regulators to tell them we would have simple sandwiches in the bank conference room instead. Only two years after the new rules began, they were extremely effective.

Chinese business entertainment tends toward lavish food and drink, often with karaoke in the evenings. Waitresses keep their panties on at dinner, but on important occasions may be serving dishes made from endangered species. In the past, when a foreign scholar visited a university, they would take him out to a lavish dinner with local scholars. Now the standard is a simple dinner one on one. If the professor hosts a more expansive dinner with his own money, the government investigates his ability to pay for such entertainment.

Box 3.1 *(cont.)*

To enforce their rules, the Japanese have a highly effective administrative system and a vigilant public (media and angry wives). The rules affect only meetings with government officials, not private parties. (When I worked for Nomura, based in Hong Kong, I had to go to karaoke every night that I was in Tokyo; enforcing austerity on private business in Japan would be enormously beneficial to family life but business relationships would be severely disrupted.) The Chinese entertainment crackdown extends to family celebrations of Chinese New Year, causing resentment. It remains unclear how much of the Chinese crackdown can be institutionalized. In China, the administrative system can enforce these rules as long as it focuses on the issue, but may eventually have to shift its attention. The government fears too much citizen whistle-blowing and, while welcoming some reports, punishes people severely for excessive zeal reporting corruption. China's anti-corruption campaign risks ranging too far into private life and being inadequately institutionalized.

universities frequently hire professors to write or vet their applications, including their personal essays, for them. Some American scholars become wealthy doing this. Gradually, everyone is affected by the need to compete with applications written by senior professionals. When I was an applicant to Harvard, it would never have occurred to me to ask someone to vet my application and rework my essays; now such vetting is commonplace.

Prospects

The history of anti-corruption campaigns (see Box 3.1) suggests that structural reforms are crucial and sending in the cops is necessary but insufficient.[22] Under Xi there are glimmerings of structural reform, particularly in the judicial system. Centralization of judicial appointments, for instance, could radically reduce conflicts of interest in the courts compared with the current system where the local mayor

---

[22] For a nuanced description of China's anti-corruption process, see Hualing Fu, "China's Striking Anticorruption Adventure: A Political Journey Toward the Rule of Law?," in Weitseng Chen, ed., *The Beijing Consensus? How China Has Changed the Western Ideas of Law and Economic Development* (Cambridge: Cambridge University Press, 2017), pp. 249–274.

appoints the local judge. Marketization and competition, somewhat compromised by efforts to consolidate national champions, would, if successfully implemented, reduce the margins available for corruption. Successful implementation remains an "if."

Starting with the fourth plenum, the leadership has expressed determination to reduce the costs of opaque, unpredictable, politicized governance. The most promising strategy is a determination to delineate property rights clearly, in both agriculture and industry, which should reduce theft of state assets and sequestration of private assets.[23] But these are initial plans that have not yet been implemented.

Implementing economic reform has a paradoxical relationship to the anti-corruption campaign. The campaign is vital to nullify interest group opposition, but it also frightens and immobilizes the officials who should implement reforms. Any reform hurts someone, and the offended person may respond with an accusation of corruption – which is very frightening because the majority of officials in China are to some degree vulnerable to such accusations. So, until the

---

[23] Ambiguous property rights are the center of gravity of Chinese corruption. Long after this analysis was published as an article, and months after this book was submitted for publication, Minxin Pei's analysis of Chinese corruption became available: *China's Crony Capitalism: The Dynamics of Regime Decay* (Cambridge, MA: Harvard University Press, 2016). Pei's impressive study illustrates both the great strengths and the weaknesses of Western political science. He provides an extraordinary compilation of data and case studies about Chinese corruption, along with an elegant theoretical discussion showing how Chinese corruption is rooted in a structure that gives decentralized authority to officials over property in a context of ambiguous property rights. Anyone who wants to understand the mechanisms peculiar to Chinese corruption must read Pei's book. But then he jumps to a generalization that democracies would not generally suffer from such problems – on the basis of no evidence other than a wave to several East European regimes whose levels of economic and institutional development were far higher. This assertion ignores all the readily available evidence from India, the Philippines, Thailand, and many other countries; in this, Pei mirrors the US discipline of political science, which too often substitutes an ideological conceit for evidence. For a comparison with India, where the corrupt system is much more violent, and where over one-third of legislators are typically felons, see Milan Vaishnav, *When Crime Pays: Money and Violence in Indian Politics* (New Haven, CT: Yale University Press, 2017). Second, Pei treats the scale of corruption as inevitable, in China and in other authoritarian countries. It is not, as one can easily see by contrasting the Zhu Rongji era with the Wen Jiabao era or, to take a Taiwan example, seeing the extraordinary job that the authoritarian Jiang Jingguo did in cleaning up corruption while his democratic successors enabled a relapse.

intensity of the anti-corruption campaign diminishes, economic reform will be limited. And that could take a while.

Fortunately, financial reform is politically easier than judicial, regulatory, or SOE reform. Liberalization of interest rates, stock market listings, and the currency, and opening of stock markets, are accelerating and will be transformative. A campaign to internationalize the currency was initially being used the way Zhu Rongji used the WTO: to force the pace of domestic reform.

Premier Li Keqiang has spoken of the need for small government, seemingly an echo of Zhu Rongji's efforts to slash the bureaucracy. But the current efforts seem weak and frequently nullified. An example of what happens is as follows. The premier's office instructs the Education Ministry to reduce controls. It eliminates the requirement that universities get Ministry permission before inviting foreign professors or students. But it forbids them from raising any money for those purposes without permission. That way, it can report to the premier that it has eliminated a requirement, but it keeps near-complete control. Bureaucrats everywhere are very good at this. In Zhu Rongji's years, the required staff reductions were cushioned by keeping on many of the former employees in consulting and contracting relationships. But Zhu's efforts had major consequences; at the time, I visited office after office where officials were sincerely working to reduce the number of regulations in order to meet Zhu's quota. As I write this, the stories are mostly about successful deflection of the new rules.

The outcome is uncertain. Xi's experienced, able leadership team has the initiative. They have a brilliant economic strategy. And, for now, overwhelming public support buoys the anti-corruption campaign and the idea of market-oriented reform. But bureaucratic resistance is coalescing and even becoming open. Continued popular support depends on delivering economic reforms and limiting an economic downturn, while coping with a financial squeeze. To do this President Xi must resolve the paradox that the anti-corruption campaign is a prerequisite to economic reform, but at the same time inhibits immediate reform. Does he curtail the anti-corruption campaign in the interest of bureaucratic decisiveness? He has promised not to. Does he fire whole layers of officials in order to get rid of the ones who are not moving? With such broad resistance, does he know whom he can rely on?

Environment

China's physical environment today is as horrible as news articles suggest. The air in major cities is filthy and hazardous to health. Fossil fuel use, which has now surpassed the United States, worsens global warming, of which China will be one of the most seriously affected victims. (Northern China is arid and dependent on runoff from Himalayan snows; if warming curtails the snowfall, habitation in much of the north could be limited.) The soil is polluted with dangerous metals. Water, particularly clean water, is scarce in vast areas, ground-water tables are declining, and the majority of the country's rivers and lakes are unfit for drinking, cooking, and even swimming. Surveys in early 2016 found that the water in 80 percent of tested wells was unfit to drink. The air in Beijing is typically a yellowish haze, sometimes so thick that buildings on the other side of wide avenues look fuzzy. On most days the concentration of PM 2.5 particles, which are so small that they penetrate deep into the lungs and build up, endangering health, is far above safe levels. Food is often unsafe. Perhaps because of the water and food contamination, more than 80 percent of young Chinese men in Hunan applying to be sperm donors had insufficiently healthy sperm to qualify.[24]

These environmental problems (possibly excluding the "sperm crisis") are typical of countries undergoing early industrialization, exacerbated in China's case by the country's large scale, enormous population, concentration of people in huge cities, and speed of development. Notwithstanding China's scale problems, understanding the Chinese environmental dilemma requires the perspective of what has happened in other countries. Even with major regional variations, if the process of environmental reform gets under way, different regions can in principle be reformed sequentially. Western political scientists have argued that, as with corruption, the severity of China's environmental pollution results from its communist political system; as with corruption, even a cursory glance at other countries at similar levels of economic development with different political systems shows this conclusion to be false.

---

[24] Yuan Yang and Hudson Lockett, "Sperm Crisis As Fertility Slides," *Financial Times*, November 28, 2016, www.ft.com/content/d4b5325c-abad-11e6-ba7d-76378e4fef24.

The first great industrialization concentrated in Britain, and every description of the London fog, caused, as in China's case, by coal dust and exacerbated by other pollutants, makes the problems of Beijing and Shanghai seem highly diluted by comparison[25]:

The fog was so thick that the shops in Bond Street had lights at noon. I could not see people in the street from my windows. I am tempted to ask, how the English became great with so little day-light? It seems not to come fully out until nine in the morning, and immediately after four it is gone.

...

On the 22nd of the month, accidents occurred all over London, from a remarkable fog. Carriages ran against each other, and persons were knocked down by them at the crossings. The whole gang of thieves seemed to be let loose. After perpetrating their deeds, they eluded detection by darting into the fog. It was of an opake, dingy yellow. Torches were used as guides to carriages at mid-day, but gave scarcely any light through the fog. (Richard Rush, *A Residence at the Court of London*, 1833)

SUCH of our readers as have never been in London in November can scarcely imagine what it is to grope their way through a downright thorough London fog. It is something like being imbedded in a dilution of yellow peas-pudding, just thick enough to get through it without being wholly choked or completely suffocated. You can see through the yard of it which, at the next stride, you are doomed to swallow, and that is all. It is a kind of meat and drink, and very sorry sustenance for those who are asthmatical, as you may tell by hearing one old cough answering to another from opposite sides of the street, ... (Thomas Miller, *Picturesque Sketches of London Past and Present*, 1852)

Britain began to take action to clean up the environment only after a December 1952 smog killed 12,000 people. Nothing comparable has occurred in China. One of the lessons of history is that decisive change requires a shock.

Because of its broad expanses of land, the United States fared better, but it took a social movement triggered by Rachel Carson's book *Silent Spring*, published in 1962, to roll back the poisoning of the land by pesticides. For a century from 1869 to 1969 the Cuyahoga River in Ohio periodically caught fire. A 1968 description of the river sounds like a contemporary article about a Chinese river:

---

[25] These two selections are from a collection on the internet website www.victorianlondon.org/weather/fog.htm. For a modern account of those times, see Lee Jackson, *Dirty Old London: The Victorian Fight Against Filth* (London: Yale University Press, 2014).

The surface is covered with the brown oily film observed upstream as far as the Southerly Plant effluent. In addition, large quantities of black heavy oil floating in slicks, sometimes several inches thick, are observed frequently. Debris and trash are commonly caught up in these slicks forming an unsightly floating mess. Anaerobic action is common as the dissolved oxygen is seldom above a fraction of a part per million. The discharge of cooling water increases the temperature by 10 °F (5.6 °C) to 15 °F (8.3 °C). The velocity is negligible, and sludge accumulates on the bottom. Animal life does not exist. Only the algae *Oscillatoria* grows along the piers above the water line. The color changes from gray-brown to rusty brown as the river proceeds downstream. Transparency is less than 0.5 feet in this reach.[26]

The US Environmental Protection Agency was established after the Erie River caught fire in 1969.[27]

More directly relevant for China were the experiences of the other Asian miracle economies. When I first visited Japan in the early 1960s, Tokyo's air was like Beijing's today. Leading US magazines created the image of Japanese industrialization by publishing vivid pictures of stunted, twisted children suffering from what was called Minamata disease, caused by extensive mercury pollution in Japanese soil and the sea, particularly poisoning shellfish in the seas off the cities of Minamata and Niigata. There were scandals around the methylmercury poisonings in Minamata and Niigata, horrible air pollution from sulfur dioxide that was associated with asthma in Yokkaichi, and cadmium poisoning that led to skeletal deformities and kidney disorders in Toyama, which became known as the Four Big Pollution Diseases. In Yokkaichi prefecture, 5 to 10 percent of all inhabitants suffered from chronic bronchitis due to the failure to scrub sulfur dioxide from emissions. These scandals led to the creation of Japan's first Environmental Agency in 1971 and subsequently a vast effort at environmental cleanup.

Although legal proceedings about Minamata disease continued until 2010, today Tokyo is noteworthy for its blue skies and clean air (a great source of relief for those of us who fly there from polluted Hong Kong).

---

[26] From *The Cuyahoga River Watershed: Proceedings of a Symposium Commemorating the Dedication of Cunningham Hall, Kent State University*, November 1, 1968. Quoted in Wikipedia, https://en.wikipedia.org/wiki/Cuyahoga_River.
[27] See Hugh McDiarmid, Jr., "When Our Rivers Caught Fire," July 2011, www.environmentalcouncil.org/priorities/article.php?x=264.

With an important caveat for the aftermath of the Fukushima nuclear disaster, Japan today has clean water, clean air, and clean soil. South Korea and Taiwan have followed a similar path, with a lag of more than a decade. South Korea's pollution was particularly severe, but environmental movements in both places, new laws, and increasingly effective enforcement have steadily improved environmental conditions.

In this area as in others China is just following the path of its predecessors. Contrary to the writings of many Western political scientists,[28] China's environmental degradation is a typical phenomenon at this stage of development. India's pollution is much worse. The average concentration of PM2.5 particles in Delhi in 2015 was about twice the level in Beijing and, as noted elsewhere, the overall damage caused to human health by air pollution is many times greater in India than in China. The question about China's future is whether the extraordinary scale of the problem, created by China's large size and densely populated coastal and central areas, can be matched by the combination of political will and China's extraordinary resources to address problems.

The scale of the problems is daunting.

Of the 13 major lakes, only 2 are safe sources of drinking water, and 5 are unsafe for any use. Of seven major rivers, three have a substantial proportion of segments where the water is unsafe for any use. Moreover, the water quality in densely populated areas is in general very poor.[29] North China's water, as noted above, comes heavily from Himalayan snow melt, whose vulnerability to global warming puts China at severe risk. Fifteen of China's major lakes are suffering some degree of eutrophication. Water tables in key areas, most notably Beijing, are declining to a shocking degree. In 2014 official statistics indicated that 81 percent of aquifers were of either poor or very poor quality.[30]

---

[28] In sections such as the ones on corruption and environment, I have for the most part chosen not to cite, or pick on, particular political scientists who advocate the view that China's corruption and environment problems are unique to its communist/authoritarian political system. A proper list would take pages; every specialist knows the major works.

[29] See the figure in J. Zhang, D. L. Mauzerall, T. Zhu, S. Liang, M. Ezzati, and J. V. Remais, "Environmental Health in China: Progress towards Clean Air and Safe Water," *Lancet* 375(9720), 2010, pp. 1110–1119.

[30] Peter Cai, "A Patch of Blue Sky for China from Under the Dome," *East Asia Forum*, March 11, 2015, www.eastasiaforum.org/2015/03/11/a-patch-of-blue-sky-for-china-from-under-the-dome/. In addition to the connivance of officials in

Average levels of air pollution from the most dangerous particulates, the tiny PM2.5 particles that can lodge deep in the lungs, are more than five times higher (62) in China than in the United States (12). In China the acceptable daily limit is set as 35, higher than in most other countries, but in major cities it often runs to a multiple of that level and sometimes very dangerously higher: Beijing measured 568 on January 15, 2015, and 700 on January 13, 2013.[31] China offers free home heating to everyone north of the Huai River, and that heating causes so much air pollution that the average life expectancy of the recipients is reduced by 5.5 years compared with those south of the river.[32] Awareness of the dangerous degree of the PM2.5 pollution became general shortly before the 2008 Olympics when the US Embassy began tweeting the levels. People began wearing gas masks. Wealthy private schools installed expensive filtration systems. An air pollution documentary, *Under the Dome*, directed by Chai Jing, demonstrated not just the seriousness of the problem but also the conniving of officials to evade the rules; it attracted over 200 million viewers and 280 million social media posts before being taken down by the government.

Soil pollution is also pervasive. According to China's Ministry of Environmental Protection, in 2014 the percentage of samples found to be polluted was 36.3 percent for areas surrounding heavily polluting plants, 34.9 percent for abandoned industrial land, 29.4 percent for industrial parks, 21.3 percent for solid-waste treatment sites, 23.6 percent for oil-producing sites, 33.4 percent for mining areas, 26.4 percent for irrigation sites using waste water, and 20.3 percent

---

evading environmental rules, there are serious abuses of environmental policy such as the use of anti-desertification policies to bring nomadic herders under control. See for instance Edward Wong's interview with Troy Sternberg in "How China's Politics of Control Shape the Debate on Deserts," *New York Times*, October 27, 2016, www.nytimes.com/2016/10/28/world/asia/china-desertification-troy-sternberg.html.

[31] BBC, "China Pollution: Beijing Smog Hits Hazardous Levels," January 15, 2015, www.bbc.com/news/world-asia-china-30826128; and AP, "Beijing Air Pollution off the Charts," January 13, 2013, www.cbsnews.com/news/beijing-air-pollution-off-the-charts/.

[32] Yuyu Chen, Avraham Ebenstein, Michael Greenstone, and Hongbin Li, "Evidence on the Impact of Sustained Exposure to Air Pollution on Life Expectancy from China's Huai River Policy", *Proceedings of the National Academy of Sciences* 110(32), 2013, pp. 12,936–12,941, www.pnas.org/cgi/doi/10.1073/pnas.1300018110.

for the sides of highways.[33] Acid rain affects about 30 percent of China's land.[34] Deforestation and desertification are rampant in northern China despite vast tree-planting campaigns. In 2002 the Ministry of Agriculture found that 10 percent of rice samples nationally contained excessive cadmium, and in 2013 Guangdong's provincial government found that 44 percent of rice samples contained excessive cadmium.[35] (Cadmium can damage the lungs, nasal passages, kidneys, and stomach, and can cause cancer.) These scandals, together with widespread instances of deliberate adulteration of food, such as the addition of melamine to milk, have created near-universal concern about the quality of food.

Just as the United States was awakened by *Silent Spring* and rivers catching fire, and more pertinently just as Japan was awakened by the four scandals of 1970, China has been awakened by air pollution and food safety problems. Hong Kong had to put limits on how much powdered milk visiting Chinese could buy for their babies, since stocks were being depleted. The run on milk powder by Chinese tourists spread as far as Germany.

Large numbers of people wear masks, and masks have become for many people fashion items, with interesting designs and increasingly high technology. When my assistant was headed to Beijing and Shanghai from Cambridge, her Chinese friends gave her a gift of two respirators to use when outside. The smog has become a rich source of humor:

A coworker's mother asked her son to go find a girlfriend, to no avail. He asked his mother, "Why now? With the smog so bad, I can't even make out the girls' faces." "That's exactly the point," his mother replied. "With looks like yours, you'd better go grab one while the smog lasts."

A reporter is working the streets. He asks a senior citizen, "Grandma, has the smog brought any inconvenience to your life?" Granny replies, "Too much inconvenience. If you could see, you'd know I'm a Grandpa."[36]

---

[33] Ministry of Environmental Protection, www.mep.gov.cn/gkml/hbb/qt/201404/W020140417558995804588.pdf.

[34] Gregory C. Chow, Princeton University, "China's Energy and Environmental Problems and Policies," undated mimeo, p. 3, gchow@princeton.edu.

[35] See Kevin Brigden, Samantha Hetherington, Mengjiao Wang, and David Santillo, "Distribution of Metals in Soils from Uncultivated Land, Soils from Rice Fields and in Rice Grown in the Area of an Industrial Complex with Metal Smelting and Processing Facilities in Hunan Province, China," April 2014, www.greenpeace.org/eastasia/Global/eastasia/publications/reports/toxics/2014/Heavy%20metal%20pollution%20of%20China's%20rice%20crops.pdf.

[36] These two jokes are from ChinaFile, www.chinafile.com/reporting-opinion/green-room/china-joking-smog.

Finally, China is now the world's largest emitter of climate-warming carbon dioxide, although per person it emits only about a third of the US amount, according to World Bank figures for 2010. Carbon dioxide emissions are particularly high because China's use of energy has been exceptionally inefficient – 36,000 BTUs per dollar of economic output in 2001 compared with 4,000 in Japan and 11,000 in the United States.[37]

By the end of the first decade of the twenty-first century, public opinion in China had become quite mobilized, like the Japanese after the Four Big Pollution Diseases and Americans after *Silent Spring*. Moreover, China's leaders in Beijing could not isolate themselves from the air pollution; notwithstanding indoor filtration systems, they know it is shortening their lives. The intensity of feeling showed itself, for instance, in demonstrations against plans intended to manufacture paraxylene (PX), a chemical essential to making plastic bottles and polyester. If inhaled or absorbed through the skin, PX can damage the nervous system and abdominal organs. China is the largest producer and consumer of PX. Awareness of this, spread through social media, led to an impressive series of demonstrations.

- 2007: Xiamen, thousands of people protested in June about a PX project that had been under construction since 2006. The provincial government decided in December to relocate it to another site in the same province. The relocated plant has had several explosions since then.
- 2008: Chengdu, protest.
- 2010: Dalian, explosions of an oil tank affected a nearby PX plant leading to PX leakage. The municipal government decided after one year to relocate the PX plant.
- 2012: Ningbo, hundreds of villagers protested and petitioned the local government against a PX project that had been approved. Within a week, the municipal government decided not to take on PX projects again.
- 2013: Kunming, thousands protested several times in front of the provincial government after China National Petroleum Corporation announced plans to build a PX plant 17 miles from the city center. Protesters talked with the mayor in a confrontational setting.
- 2013: Jiujiang, protest (soon banned).

[37] Gregory C. Chow, Princeton University, "China's Energy and Environmental Problems and Policies," undated mimeo, gchow@princeton.edu.

- 2013: Chengdu, protest (soon banned).
- 2014: Maoming, protest, turned into violence late at night.
- 2015: Shanghai, thousands protested.

In at least three of these cases, Xiamen, Dalian, and Ningbo, the local government was forced to cancel or relocate the plant. The examples of reactions to PX factories show how heightened consciousness and popular determination to act are changing the political–industrial game in China. Similar protests have recently forced the government to abandon other chemical plants and nuclear-waste disposal plans.

As in Japan, heightened awareness led to rapid changes in regulation. China has always had laws designed to protect the environment, dating back to a 1979 environmental protection law and articles in the 1982 constitution,[38] but the laws and institutional enforcement structure have been ineffectual – as is virtually universal in developing countries. In many cases, coal-fired power plants were required to purchase scrubbers to remove pollutants from their exhaust, but the plant managers did not turn them on because that costs money and the government wasn't able to monitor them.

Recent years have seen a tremendous effort to improve the laws, the norms, and the enforcement. Perhaps most important is that local officials are now being judged not just on whether they increased the size of their local economy but also on environmental performance. Implementation of the new standards takes time in a place as large as China, but it is beginning to bite. I approached the government of Foshan, a successful manufacturing city north of Hong Kong and asked officials whether they would be willing to work with a German company on a pilot project to clean up the water supply. They said yes. As it happens, the Foshan area includes a major luxury garment firm, Esquel, which produces one out of seven high-quality shirts sold in the United States. Esquel needs very clean water to produce bright-colored shirts, so it cleans the water before using it, and the socially conscious CEO, Margie Yang, insists on cleaning the (very polluted) water to drinkable standard before it leaves the plant. I asked one of her engineers whether she thought the mayor was sincere in wanting to clean up the city's water supply. She said, "Oh yes. These days he'll get

---

[38] A good concise summary of the legal background and environmental issues can be found in Gregory C. Chow, Princeton University, "China's Energy and Environmental Problems and Policies," undated mimeo, gchow@princeton.edu.

promoted faster for cleaning up the water than for improving the economy." That response is not necessarily representative of the situation throughout China, most of which is far less progressive than Foshan, but it is a significant bellwether. Chinese officials respond to the incentives for promotion and bonuses.

The leadership has steadily upgraded the institutional structure of environmental protection. This actually started in 1972, when a massive fish kill in the Guanting Reservoir near Beijing led them to establish the Guanting Water Protection Leadership Group, reporting to China's cabinet, the State Council. The following year they established the first national environmental bureau, the Office of Environmental Protection Leadership Group. During 1982–1988, however, the environmental protection bureau was subordinated to the Ministry of Housing and Urban–Rural Development, or Ministry of Construction, which was not a propitious platform since it created a direct conflict of interest. In 1988 it was renamed the State Environmental Protection Administration and upgraded to vice-ministerial level, directly under the State Council. In 2008 it became a full ministry, the Ministry of Environmental Protection (MEP), hence a full member of the State Council. It has a vast mandate: draft laws and regulations, and formulate administrative rules and regulations for environmental protection; implement overall coordination, supervision, and management of key environmental issues; enforce emissions control; channel environmental investment; monitor pollution; and disseminate environmental information.

In November 2012, at the 18th Communist Party Congress, leaders articulated the concept of "Building a Beautiful China." In characteristic Chinese fashion, they emphasized the need for six steps: articulating an overall strategy for an "ecological civilization"; establishing an efficient pollution control system; devising an environmental evaluation system; improving environmental regulations and policies; enacting environmental protection laws; and engaging the whole population in environmental action.[39] This sounds very abstract, and it is, but articulating a broad strategy and then gradually filling in a consistent framework is one of the reasons why China's economic policies have so often succeeded. In 2013, Beijing changed the promotion

---

[39] I am indebted to a presentation and notes by Professor Zhu Yan regarding "Building a Beautiful China."

criteria for Chinese officials to incorporate proper care of the environment, and that same year it amended China's Constitution to specify one of the country's core purposes as "building an ecological civilization." And the government started putting its money behind the rhetoric; a Harvard colleague who had studied Chinese air pollution for two decades estimated at a seminar that, in the decade to 2016, resources available to study air pollution and remedies had risen by two orders of magnitude (i.e., 100 times).

This steady upgrading of the stature of the environmental protection bureaucracy mirrors the rising level of social and leadership concern. But of course, as in the United States, the ministry has to build a national infrastructure and fight entrenched interests. The other ministries want to build power plants to fuel growth and, as in the United States, they are frustrated that environmental rules slow them down or raise their costs. Local governments are often determined to charge ahead despite the environmental rules. Millions of small, polluting factories and hundreds of millions of farmers strongly resist anything that will raise their costs. As in the United States, the companies that own the distribution grid drag their feet when it comes to allowing renewable energy producers to feed into their grid.[40]

In April 2016, China's cabinet, the State Council, issued its "Water Pollution Prevention and Control Action Plan," its water cleanup plan from 2016 to 2050.[41] The plan mandates closure in 2016 of small factories in 10 industries such as textile dyeing, leather, paper, and oil refining that cannot meet environmental standards, and it plans upgrades in an overlapping group of 10 industries to achieve clean production. By 2020 it aims to have 70 percent of all drinking water sources and 93 percent of urban sources in the safely drinkable category. It sets specific targets for specific regions of the country. The plan foresees using water impact as a major criterion for issuing industrial permits and approving large-scale city plans. The plan is

---

[40] The Lantau Group, "UHV Lines: Shaping the Future of China's Power Landscape," January 2016, p. 1. The Lantau Group's valuable publications are on www.lantaugroup.com/pages/publications/presentations_1.php.

[41] For summaries, see China Water Risk, "New 'Water Ten Plan' to Safeguard China's Waters," http://chinawaterrisk.org/notices/new-water-ten-plan-to-safeguard-chinas-waters/; and Liu Qin, "China Unveils Landmark Plan to Curb Water Pollution," *ChinaDialogue*, April 4, 2016, www.chinadialogue.net/blog/7854-China-unveils-landmark-plan-to-curb-water-pollution/en. The China Water Risk website is a particularly useful source for data on China's water problems and policies.

sufficiently specific that it will be possible to derive targets for specific regions and specific officials and hold them accountable. Because Chinese officials are promoted on the basis of the degree to which they achieve specific targets (see the politics chapter), the country's record in achieving its plans is good, although far from perfect. Sometimes they overachieve, sometimes they miss targets (as occurred with air pollution targets in the 12th five-year plan), but at worst the results usually move very far in the desired direction – a sharp contrast with other countries, such as India, where the government announces a plan to clean up a major river (the Ganges) and nothing at all happens.

At the center, the Ministry's job is easier than in the United States; there is no counterpart of the situation where climate-change deniers dominate the policies of a main political party – highly organized, generously funded by lobbyists, and conducting mass propaganda campaigns to refute scientific consensus and oppose efforts to reduce coal use or otherwise limit climate change. Coal companies and other major polluters and climate-change deniers were significant forces behind the election of President Trump. Science deniers get less opportunity in China. But local resistance in China is fierce, as it is everywhere. As I was writing this chapter, greater Boston, where I live, was experiencing the kind of pushback that important environmental efforts induce everywhere. The US Environmental Protection Agency is issuing standards to stop poisonous dumping into the Charles River, which runs past Harvard, and to clean up existing pollution, while the Municipal Association, the lobbying arm for the region's cities and towns, is demanding weaker standards and long timetables that would postpone, perhaps indefinitely, any serious action. This promises a tough political and legal fight.[42] In China, the center's job of implementing the rules out in the localities is orders of magnitude more difficult given China's six layers of government and the difficulty of monitoring and enforcement in such a vast population.

Further weaknesses come from China's courts, which lack a tradition of engaging with environmental issues and depend on conflicted local officials to enforce their judgments. (The idea that local officials actually must enforce court decisions is only gradually becoming an

---

[42] David Abel, "U.S. Set to Force Cleanup of River," *Boston Globe*, February 22, 2016, pp. A1ff, https://secure.pqarchiver.com/boston-sub/doc/1766947638.html?FMT=FT&FMTS=ABS:FT&type=current&date=Feb+22%2C+2016&author=Abel&2C+David&pub=Boston+Globe&edition=&startpage=A.1&desc=US+set+to+force+cleanup+of+river.

established norm.) Government crackdowns on demonstrators and whistle-blowers limit public participation in environmental campaigns. But recently the government has given substantial powers to 400 environmental tribunals distributed around the country.

Thus the problems are very serious, and the weaknesses of enforcement are very serious. Having said that, China's auto emissions and fuel standards laws have long been stricter than those in the United States, and in the major cities they are enforced (for trucks, not so much). In Beijing, the 2008 Olympics was used as an excuse to spend tens of billions of dollars on environmental improvement – including forced moves of major polluting industries out of the city. In Shanghai, the 2010 Expo served the same purpose. Hebei province, the source of a great deal of Beijing's pollution, is closing 240 out of 400 steel mills at an estimated cost of over a million jobs and 180 billion RMB[43] (a little under US$30 billion) to deal simultaneously with the problems of pollution and overcapacity. In April 2016 the government announced a halt in approval and construction of 200 coal-fired power plants, which would have generated enough power to cover all of the United Kingdom's power needs, and it required the operators of coal-fired plants to pay providers of wind and solar power even if their output is not being used.[44] The government has been experimenting with carbon trading schemes and plans to create a national carbon trading scheme – which would move China far beyond anything that is politically feasible in the United States. The government is subsidizing a vast shift in both rural and urban areas from high-sulfur coal for home heating to low-sulfur coal, gas, and electric heaters. It has even sought to instill environmental consciousness in the population by urging everyone to burn less paper money, paper cars, paper mistresses, and the like in the annual Qing Ming festival to honor ancestors. (Yes, thoughtful Chinese families burn paper mistresses to improve their ancestors' comfort in the afterlife.)

[43] Yu Ning and Liu Xiaojing, "Hebei to Close 60 Percent of Its Steel Mills by 2020," *Caixin Online*, March 3, 2016, http://english.caixin.com/2016-03-09/100918265.html.
[44] Michael Forsythe, "China Curbs Plans for More Coal-Fired Power Plants", *New York Times*, April 25, 2016, www.nytimes.com/2016/04/26/business/energy-environment/china-coal.html.

In June 2016 Beijing announced a plan to clean up soil pollution – still a rough outline without detailed funding and project commitments, but this is the way all the programs start.

China's expenditure on pollution control as a share of its economy is now comparable to that of the major OECD countries – 1.6 percent of GDP in 2013,[45] compared with typical rates of 1.4 to 1.6 percent in the United States, 1.2 to 1.4 percent in Japan, 1.8 percent in South Korea, 0.6 percent in the United Kingdom, 1.3 percent in France, and 1.6 percent in Germany.[46] This is impressive, and demonstrates a seriousness that is not acknowledged in much Western commentary about China, but, given the deep hole China is digging itself out of, the environmental share will probably have to rise higher.

In one area, renewable energy, China has surged far ahead. It is now the world leader in solar, wind, and nuclear energy. In 2015 it invested US$103 billion in renewable energy, compared with US$33 billion by the United States, and committed to spend US$363 billion by 2020.[47]

Given China's commitment to shift to renewable energy, the impasse at the beginning of the Obama administration between the United States and China over long-term greenhouse-gas emissions has been resolved, at least on an interim basis. Initially the United States insisted on commitment to a specific cap. Given the difficulty in forecasting China's economic growth, as compared with developed countries, that rigid approach was impractical. (In retrospect, given reduced prospects for long-term growth, it might have given China an advantage.) In addition, the United States emphasized China's huge contribution to the total emissions while China emphasized that its per capita emissions were far smaller than America's (see Figure 3.4 of carbon dioxide emissions per capita) and that China had a right to become a developed country.

It is noteworthy that this Chinese government, which is highly suspicious of foreign NGOs, has welcomed input from major foreign environmental organizations, including the World Wildlife Fund,

---

[45] Ministry of Environmental Protection, www.mep.gov.cn/gzfw_13107/hjtj/ hjtjnb/201605/U020160604811096703781.pdf.

[46] OECD Environment Directorate, Working Group on Environmental Information and Outlooks, "Pollution Abatement and Control Expenditure in OECD Countries," 2007, www.oecd.org/env/indicators-modelling-outlooks/ 38230860.pdf, p. 33, Table 2.

[47] Andrew Ward, "Wave of Spending Tightens China's Grip on Renewable Energy," *Financial Times*, January 5, 2017, www.ft.com/content/37844fa4-d344-11e6-9341-7393bb2e1b51.

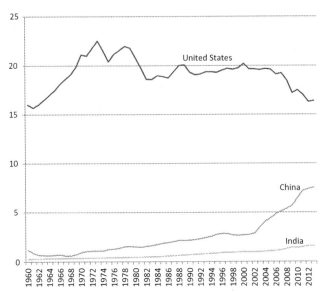

Figure 3.4 Carbon dioxide emissions per capita, metric tons (World Bank data, http://data.worldbank.org/indicator/EN.ATM.CO2E.PC).

Conservation International, and even Greenpeace. That is an indication of seriousness.

China has raised the longevity of its people from the low 40s to the mid 70s in half a century. Given that fact, it is inappropriate to denounce the GDP growth-obsessed strategy for having shortened Chinese lives. Would lives be a little longer if environmental considerations had been given perfect balance? Of course, but critics counseling perfection need to look around their own countries for signs of perfection. Has any country done better at rapidly increasing longevity? No, and the ones with governing structures and goal-setting procedures of the kind favored by the United States (India, Philippines) have done conspicuously worse – on both longevity and the environment. But by this measure, as on others, China now faces a crisis of success. Continuation of the growth-obsessed policy would not add much to longevity and would begin to subtract from past successes. Chinese leaders are beginning to make the appropriate adjustments. The trajectory of their policies has tracked the needs of their people.

China has now agreed to cap emissions by 2030 and to derive 20 percent of its energy from green sources by that time. China is now the world's largest investor in clean energy, investing US$110.5 billion, or about twice as much as the second largest investor, the United States. It has already become the world leader in solar, windmill, and nuclear power, and is a global leader in hydropower. It is replacing as much coal power with natural gas as it can,[48] and it is building coal plants that are 45 percent efficient whereas the older ones are only 27–33 percent efficient – a huge gain.[49] Even relatively conservative US analysts characterize China's goals as ambitious and credit China for catalyzing the 2014 Paris Climate Agreement.[50] Its green progress is inhibited by its urgent need for power to drive its growth now, with coal the only feasible source for much of the needed power, but its past power generation has been so inefficient that it has enormous scope for improvement. It has been taking advantage of the opportunity to improve efficiency (measured in Figure 3.5 by the units of emission required to support a unit of GDP).

In the Paris agreement China promised a reduction of carbon intensity of 40–45 percent from 2025; its internal 13th five-year plan sets a goal of 48 percent.[51] Recently it has been helped by the shift in the structure of its economy away from heavy industry and toward a predominantly services economy, as well as by a slowdown in economic growth. The shift to green energy, necessarily gradual, has been proceeding well. Low-end manufacturing will gradually shift abroad as China moves up-market, creating further opportunities to reduce energy consumption and employ energy more efficiently. In 2015 emissions actually declined.

In sum, China has turned the corner on attitudes toward the environment and is attempting, with some success, to turn the corner on

[48] Andrew Leung, "Can China Reach Its Ambitious Goals for Clean Energy?," November 29, 2014, www.andrewleunginternationalconsultants.com/publications/2014/11/can-china-really-reach-its-ambitious-goals-for-clean-energy.html. This article summarizes the 15th five-year plan's goals.

[49] National Bureau of Asian Research, "The Paris Climate Agreement: Implications for Energy and Environmental Outlooks for the Asia-Pacific," January 22, 2016, www.nbr.org/research/activity.aspx?id=647.

[50] National Bureau of Asian Research, "The Paris Climate Agreement: Implications for Energy and Environmental Outlooks for the Asia-Pacific," January 22, 2016, www.nbr.org/research/activity.aspx?id=647, p. 1: "China not only has announced substantial targets for reducing emissions but has already shown an active commitment to achieve those ambitious goals."

[51] A valuable source on energy and climate issues is "China FAQs: The Network for Climate and Energy Information," www.chinafaqs.org.

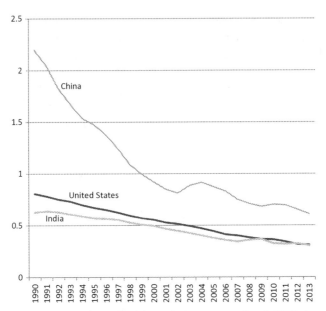

Figure 3.5 Carbon dioxide emissions per unit of GDP (purchasing power parity dollars), metric tons (World Bank data, http://data.worldbank.org/indi cator/EN.ATM.CO2E.PC; Google charts created from World Bank data by Cui Cui Chen).

policy. While the scale of the problems is daunting, the scale of resources China can bring to the problem is impressive, and its ability to articulate and implement difficult policies is unmatched among emerging economies – and perhaps unmatched compared with the developed countries. As with programs designed to enhance economic growth, China's strongest lever for environmental improvement is the evaluation of officials on the basis of their environmental performance.

More broadly, the environmental turnaround will succeed or fail alongside the broader economic reform program. If the central govern- ment can maintain stability and strong leadership over the localities, the environmental cleanup could match what Japan, South Korea, and Taiwan have achieved. Given the magnitude of the tasks, even with a successful effort, the middle of the twenty-first century will still see a great deal of work needing to be done.

The international attitude to China's cleanup program will matter a great deal. Scientific collaboration has thus far been wide-ranging, smooth, and impressive. Economic collaboration has been mixed. The Chinese don't want to pay for ongoing, massive imports of Western technology, and Western companies hold back because they are not willing to risk giving the Chinese opportunities to steal their intellectual property. Sanctions imposed by the United States after June 4, 1989 still irrationally constrain important kinds of environmental collaboration. Much of the Western policy commentary has been hostile and unbalanced. It is common for articles to criticize the Chinese economic growth obsession by pointing to the number of early deaths caused by pollution – while failing to mention that life expectancy has nearly doubled as a result of that obsession. They emphasize (correctly) the negative effects on other countries of China's environmental problems while failing to mention that China is now a leader in cooperating to remedy climate change and other environmental issues.[52] The effect of air pollution on human health is many times worse in India, and India is doing little about it, but in this as in other areas the Western media and policy literature treat India much better, if only by largely ignoring it.

At the end of the Obama administration, the relationship with China over environmental issues was the exact opposite of the anger with which it began.[53] The new warmth reflects both China's heightened environmental awareness and the US administration's new understanding that it is a mistake for Washington to impose a single favored approach on countries with very diverse circumstances. It is a template for rapprochement that would be extraordinarily valuable in other areas. Unfortunately, in the United States the Trump administration

---

[52] See, among many others, Thomas N. Thompson, "Choking on China: The Superpower That Is Poisoning the World," *Foreign Affairs*, April 8, 2013, www.foreignaffairs.com/articles/china/2013-04-08/choking-china and Elizabeth C. Economy, *The River Runs Black: The Environmental Challenge to China's Future*, second edition (Ithaca, NY: Cornell University Press, 2009). Much of the Western commentary on China's environmental policies infringes a basic research ethical standard: if there are two sides to a story, it's okay to have a strong opinion, but you have to mention the available data on both sides of the story. If for instance you hype the number of lives shortened by pollution (caused by what is often portrayed as China's terrible growth model), you have to mention that longevity nearly doubled.

[53] Keith Johnson, "Obama's Climate Envoy: China Will Surprise Us in a Good Way," *Foreign Policy*, April 1, 2016, http://foreignpolicy.com/2016/04/01/obamas-climate-envoy-china-will-surprise-us-in-a-good-way-todd-stern-paris-emissions/.

abdicated US leadership on the environment and made China at least the conceptual leader.

The future of China's environmental improvement will coincide with the success, if success it turns out to be, of China's economic reforms and maintenance of central political authority. For now, it is making rapid progress, but fighting tremendous resistance. In 2016 Beijing experienced tremendous improvement in air quality for much of the year because of such vigorous efforts as the closing of steel plants in neighboring Hebei. But as the end of the year approached, officials became concerned that the environmental strictures meant they would miss their economic targets, jeopardizing bonuses and promotions. They shifted toward maximizing growth and Beijing experienced a major year-end air-quality crisis.

The outcome of this fierce struggle will affect not only China's future but also humanity's. As I write, the intensity of environmental consciousness among China's people and its governing elites gives reason for cautious optimism.

Globalization

Globalization lies at the core of all the Asian miracles. In China's infinitely repeated slogan "reform and opening," the opening part refers not just to allowing trade and investment with foreigners but also a broad embrace of global best practice in manufacturing, education, regulation, management, and many other areas. In this it follows early Japan, which was famous both in the Meiji era (mid nineteenth century) and after World War II for sending delegations abroad to bring back best practice – a British navy, German education, American quality-control ideas, and much else, often refining them to a much higher level than the originals (most notably with quality control). Japan sent large numbers of students abroad; in America's best schools in its best suburbs, Japanese students seemed in the 1970s to consistently produce the best violinists and the best math students. But then Japan turned comparatively inward, with its politicians attributing its successes to unique Japanese cultural institutions. (Virtually none of the institutions cited had anything to do with uniquely Japanese culture, but rather they were emulations of wartime Germany and the USSR.) Japanese students abroad dwindled to numbers less than those from much smaller South Korea and Taiwan (although Japan does send more students to China than the United States). Japan protected many of its big companies from competition at home and abroad, and created standards (for instance for cell phones) to shut out foreign competition. Even at its peak of global competitiveness, Japan had a slate of leading international name brand firms but also a domestic economy riven with local barriers and inefficiency; the government did not reform these in the interest of competitiveness.

China has embraced globalization much more enthusiastically. Although its image in the West comes from Maoist autarky, China is inherently a more diverse and cosmopolitan society than Japan or Korea. South Korea has been overcoming this heritage, even to the extent of currently labeling itself a multicultural society, whereas Japan and, more spectacularly, North Korea have not. In fact, socially China is more like the United States than like Japan and South Korea. Like the United States and Singapore, it is a melting pot of different dialects, cuisines, physical appearances, and cultural traditions – but, unlike India, a melting pot rather than a salad where the component parts retain most of their linguistic and cultural diversity.

Like Japan, China started by copying foreign technologies. (The first Toyota was half Ford parts, half Chevrolet parts, presented with Desoto styling.) Although quite extensive, this was not the most important aspect of globalization. By welcoming foreign investment to a far greater extent than Japan, South Korea, and early-phase Taiwan, China rapidly gained experience with modern management and markets. Prior to reform, it had often imported some of the best technology, but the machinery frequently lay idle or fell into disrepair because there was no experience managing it. When I visited a machine tool factory in Shanghai in 1982, the management was very proud of having imported the world's best. There were three big sets of machines on the factory floor. Two sets were completely idle, the other not doing much. The workers mostly stood around smiling and smoking, not working. The key to success is not buying foreign machines, but welcoming the foreigners who know how to use them and allowing the foreigners to make money so that they will keep coming. Maoist China didn't get this. Reformist China has embraced it and taken it to another level. Xi Jinping may be partially stepping back from these policies.

When I was working on Honda Motors' business strategy for China in the early years of the new century, I spent weeks interviewing

China's regulators and others connected with the car industry. Their common theme was that China could not duplicate the earlier model of building a largely Japanese car or a largely Korean car; in the globalized world of today, to be globally successful a Chinese car would have to have globalized technology, globalized finance, globalized styling. Embrace of that finding is why, when you drive in any major Chinese city, you are never out of sight of Buicks, Volkswagens, and Hyundais. In South Korea and Japan, foreign cars are quite scarce. But China has chosen globalization as a core strategy.

Like Japan before it, but on a much larger scale, China sent teams abroad to study best practice. It copied air transport management from Washington, DC's Federal Aviation Administration, banking regulations from Hong Kong, and capital market rules from Hong Kong and Taiwan. Central banking management took advantage of employees seconded from the Hong Kong Monetary Authority. The deputy chief regulator in many areas was a foreigner or a Hong Kong expat; for instance, Andrew Sheng, a Malaysian who had served as chief capital markets regulator in Hong Kong became Chief Advisor of the China Banking Regulatory Commission, while Laura Cha and Tony Neo, Hong Kong regulators, became successive deputy chairs of the China Securities Regulatory Commission. Foreign coaches were hired to manage some of China's top sports teams. China sends abroad more students than any other country – currently 300,000 to the United States.

Remarkably, China sends many of its vice ministers abroad for a semester of international education, to ensure that they know what is understood to be best practice elsewhere. As noted earlier, at my office in Harvard's Kennedy School, there were always two or three vice ministers in offices across the hall. I met China's current Vice President, Lee Yuanchao, when he was Party Secretary of Nanjing; on a six-week stint at Harvard, he was picking my brain and others' for ideas on how to attract more foreign investment. The Organization Department, which manages personnel for the Chinese government, also sends vice ministers (and many others) to Oxford and other schools. As a thought experiment, imagine the US government sending the deputy secretary of commerce, the deputy secretary of defense, and their counterparts in other departments to Peking University and Tsinghua for a semester to study in Chinese – during or after their children's study abroad there at similar schools. Actually, it is impossible to imagine that happening. Advantage China.

Chinese students are required to take seven years of English to earn a high-school diploma. They must score well in the English part of the comprehensive university entrance exam in order to matriculate at a good college. (Japanese students take six years of English but in most cases do not acquire any useful skill, because it's not taken seriously.)

In high-tech industries, China hires foreign executives and pays international-level salaries. Shanghai not only hires the world's top architects for the buildings that have made it one of the world's two or three most modern cities, but also brought in substantial numbers of US plumbers and construction workers who had skills that were lacking locally. Since 2008 China has implemented a "Thousand Talents" program that lures back Chinese from abroad with senior-level positions, Western-level salaries, and allowances of up to US$150,000.[54]

In these ways and others, China continues to move away from the Japanese model of turning inward. Surprisingly for a continental economy as compared with an island economy, China's trade is a larger share of its economy than Japan's and foreign investment is a larger share. China's banking sector is almost twice as open to foreign institutions as Japan's is. Chinese society mirrors these differences. In fact the percentage of Chinese who see themselves as global citizens is almost double the number of Americans who see themselves as global

---

[54] Contrast this emphasis on doing whatever it takes to get performance with what happens in India. In the 1980s a good friend of mine, an Indian national who was a rising star at IBM's headquarters in Armonk, was invited back to India by the government to get a semiconductor industry started. When he arrived, he found himself slotted into the bureaucracy with layers of less experienced and less talented people over him. The senior bureaucrats resented him, insisting on seniority over talent and on bureaucratic rules over performance; they gave him no scope for initiative. His family was housed in very poor conditions. He was told that the government's only priority for the semiconductor industry was military; they were not interested in civilian development and would not let him pursue civilian projects. After a couple of years he sent me a desperate note wanting out. Shortly afterward, without any assistance from me, he moved to a country where civilian work was considered important and talent was given space for initiative. Such contrasts are why the Chinese system is called meritocratic or performance-oriented and most third-world countries are not. This distinction will become crucial in the discussion of the Chinese governance model in the next chapter. This performance-oriented approach, focused on incentivizing the best people, characterizes all the Asian miracle economies. For an extreme example, study the building of Singapore's Biosphere, where the government searched the world for the best candidate to fill each important position.

citizens.[55] This will emerge as a crucial advantage in coming decades, in comparison with the United States and especially with Russia and Japan, which are far more insular.

An example of China's continuing commitment to globalization is its Belt and Road Initiative (BRI), a strategy for enhancing infrastructure, trade, and investment among 60 countries that lie en route from China to Europe by land and sea. Along with building better infrastructure and seeking common standards, the BRI is an acknowledgment that China's industrial structure must change, that the industries and jobs of the recent past (e.g., making cheap socks) must migrate elsewhere. China stands to benefit by facilitating that process, financing it, building the infrastructure for it, and retaining strong ties to it. This is what US companies do, and what the US government long did, but interest groups behind political parties, especially the Democratic Party, and the Trump administration have benefited from blaming the needed changes on foreigners and impeding them.[56]

Much of China's leadership sees continued globalization as key to economic success and global influence. One scholar, Wang Huiyao, who also spent time at Harvard and Brookings, now runs a government- and enterprise-supported think tank, the Center for China and Globalization, promoting globalization of talent. His theory, which had important high-level support, was that the first phase of globalization was manufacturing, led by Britain, resulting in the rise of the British empire. The second phase of globalization has been finance, led by the United States, resulting in the current preeminent position of the United States in global economics and geopolitics. According to him, the third phase is the globalization of talent and China should lead that phase, resulting eventually in Chinese global leadership.

Many of the recommendations of Wang Huiyao and people like him have become policy, including specific programs to bring huge numbers of foreign students and others to China and to send huge numbers of Chinese students and others abroad.

Having said this, under Xi Jinping the government's attitude toward foreign companies, foreign NGOs, and foreigners in general has

---

[55] Naomi Grimley, "Identity 2016: 'Global Citizenship' Rising, Poll Suggests," BBC, April 28, 2016, www.bbc.com/news/world-36139904#afterFlash.

[56] I have addressed the US aspect of this in "The Great Betrayal," *The International Economy*, Winter 2017, www.international-economy.com/TIE_W17_Overholt.pdf.

become cooler, even though Xi himself continues to give speeches emphasizing how welcome foreign investors are. The government has even been warning Chinese against dating foreigners, since they might be spies. Whether this cooling, together with rising geopolitical tensions, will slow the pace of globalization remains to be seen. Conversely, whether the coming generation's far greater exposure to foreign cultures will enhance globalization and possibly bring liberalizing changes to Chinese society also remains to be seen. Both could happen, on different time scales, and both in fact seem likely.

Overview

This survey of China's major economic and social problems shows that the problems China faces are enormous, that the problems are nonetheless solvable, but that they are solvable only through a vast reform effort that will encounter formidable political resistance. China can mobilize exceptional resources to deal with its exceptionally large problems. Moreover, it has crucial advantages. China's leaders face their economic and social problems forthrightly and they have a national governance system that assigns tasks to officials in a businesslike way, measures their performance, and rewards them appropriately. This is a sharp contrast with most emerging countries and even with many developed countries.

If China can continue to address these mammoth problems as forthrightly and relatively effectively as it has been doing, inequality, corruption, environmental degradation, and globalization will not create political instability or economic crisis. But in each area the intensity of struggle would probably be portrayed better by a great historical novelist than by dry scholarly analysis.

That leaves a crucial question, both for the economic transition and for continued management of the major social issues: will China's political structures be up to the task?

4 | China's Governance Crisis of Success

Maintaining order rather than correcting disorder is the ultimate principle of wisdom. To cure a disease after it has manifested itself is like digging a well when one feels thirsty, or forging a weapon when the war has already begun.

Nei Jing, second century BCE

Some Historical Background

In the West, Chinese communism is still associated with Mao. The death and destruction of the Mao era, following on a century of Chinese disorder, for a time led many to believe that China, and particularly communist China, was inherently unstable. China seemed culturally and ideologically incapable of achieving the unity, stability, and prosperity that some maritime nations on its periphery had accomplished. But that was a misreading. China's history comprises some of the longest, most stable regimes in world history, and Max Weber, in his 1922 work **Economy and Society,** invented the modern concept of "bureaucracy" and analyzed its advantages for efficiency and stability by studying China's traditional expert management systems. Key elements of modern public administration began in China before 221 BCE.

In Malaysia, Thailand, Indonesia, and the Philippines, agrarian revolutionary parties threatened stability in the wake of World War II and decolonization, but in one after another of these countries bureaucratic and relatively technocratic central governments gradually consolidated power, implemented rational economic plans, and chased the agrarian communists into the distant countryside until they nearly vanished. Earlier, China nearly followed this pattern but was diverted by war.

Revolutions in pre-industrial countries virtually always include a peasant uprising. Whether in the French Revolution's *jacquerie* (peasant revolt) or in Southeast Asia, they adopt the same views. If we kill the landlords, we'll all be rich. If we chase out the bloodsucking foreign companies and banks, we'll have all of our country's resources to ourselves and we'll be rich. If we destroy the parasitic urban bureaucracies, we will save all the taxes and share the wealth that would otherwise have been spent on the fine houses and servants of the bureaucrats. Because these movements tend to be anti-organizational and have flawed economic ideas, they generally fail to achieve power and, in the event they do overthrow the government, they persist only if they are coopted by more technocratic urban types.

China started to follow the same pattern but the pattern was interrupted. Two Leninist parties with socialist economic programs, the Guomindang and the Chinese Communist Party, competed for power. Both had charismatic leaders, hierarchical leaderships, a vanguard party, politburos, central committees, and cell structures. Both sought to wed intellectuals and soldiers to an urban working-class base. Both believed a vanguard party necessary to lead and teach their citizenry. More broadly, both were committed to Leninism; Guomindang leader Chiang Kai-shek sent his son, Jiang Jingguo, to Moscow, not to the United States, for college, and there his son, the future leader of Taiwan, became a committed member of the Soviet Communist Party. (In the 1970s I had many dreary sessions in Taipei with leaders of the Asian Peoples Anti-Communist League, who ironically explained, time and time again, the inevitability that a more modern nineteenth-century ideology like Marxism-Leninism would inevitably defeat an obsolete eighteenth-century ideology like Lockean liberalism. That argument was the essence of why Jiang Jingguo got a Soviet education.) Both were committed to socialist economics. Both planned a great land reform. In wartime, socialism – central government control over the economy – is a means to ensure unity and continuity of the material support for the war. All parties converge on socialism, and for the same reason successful wartime parties tend to converge toward Leninism; the centralized control associated with that structure is what the situation requires.

The Guomindang got well-organized earlier than the Communists and consolidated its urban base, chasing the communists into the distant countryside in what was known as the Long March, just as later happened to agrarian communists in Thailand, the Philippines, Malaysia, and Indonesia. But then Japan invaded and conquered the main cities. Bereft of its shattered urban base, the Guomindang became dependent on warlords and landlords, and bore the brunt of the fight against the Japanese. The Guomindang took more than 90 percent of the casualties in the Anti-Japanese War.[1] Mao's Communists in effect hid behind a Japanese shield and restored their shattered organization, then ultimately triumphed with a tremendous boost of military materiel from Stalin's Soviet Union.[2]

In the United States these conflicts were interpreted in moralistic ideological terms. Until his defeat, Chiang Kai-shek was widely portrayed as the hero of democracy, an irony that the old Leninist must have wryly enjoyed. After the Maoists had won, the story became for a while that the communists were inherently more virtuous and the Guomindang inherently more corrupt from the beginning. Accounts that emphasize the Guomindang's dependence on criminal gangs[3] often neglect to emphasize that the Communists often depended on similar gangs, sometimes the same gangs. (Such gangs still operate, particularly in Chongqing and Sichuan. Triad gangs operate across the border into Hong Kong, robbing, kidnapping, and selling drugs with considerable impunity.[4]) Chiang and the Guomindang had to function

---

[1] The best account of Chiang Kai-shek and the Guomindang's role in the war is Jay Taylor, *The Generalissimo: Chiang Kai-shek and the Struggle for Modern China* (Cambridge, MA: Harvard University Press, 2009).

[2] The best general history of modern China and its foreign relations is Odd Arne Westad, *Restless Empire: China and the West Since 1750* (New York: Basic Books, 2012). On this particular point of the Japanese role, although there is a great deal of more recent scholarship, I strongly recommend the China chapter of Barrington Moore, Jr., *The Social Origins of Dictatorship and Democracy: Lord and Peasant in the Making of the Modern World* (Boston, MA: Beacon Press, 1966). Moore's painstaking efforts to locate the origins of modern political systems in deep characteristics of the society is one of the most thoughtful, deeply researched, and provocative analyses ever, whether one agrees with him or not. The China chapter is particularly interesting because everything in his framework leads him to dig and dig for deep social explanations of the Communist victory. In the end, his intellectual honesty leads him to the conclusion that this one can't be explained by deep sociological understanding; the Japanese invasion was decisive.

[3] See for instance Sterling Seagrave, *The Soong Dynasty* (London: Sidgwick & Jackson, 1985).

[4] Here as elsewhere I write with some personal experience. I had to learn about Chinese gangs. In 1994 one of the nastier gangs tried to kidnap a member of my family. They stopped our car, made an unsuccessful attempt to kidnap my wife, then came into my home, held us at gunpoint, and ransacked the house looking for valuables. Failing to kidnap us (never go with a kidnapper no matter how much they threaten) or find much of value, they kidnapped my wealthier next-door neighbor and his wife. This made front-page headlines in the *South China*

within a social and geopolitical context that provided only bad options. The reality was that the huge Guomindang casualties of the Chinese international and civil wars, and the death and destruction of three decades of Maoist agrarian populism, were the Imperial Japanese Army's most enduring legacy.

Mao spent the last decade of his life, 1966–1976, in a desperate struggle against the bureaucratized, technocratic management that was the ultimate enemy of his bloody-minded agrarian populism. This was the culmination of 27 years in which the technocrats built China's infrastructure and education, and made policy based on expert knowledge (1952–1958, 1962–1965), alternating with Maoist agrarian ideological nonsense (the Great Leap Forward 1958–1961, the Cultural Revolution 1966–1976, with several years of violent disorder fading after a few years into more technocratic management). Mao needed the technocrats like Zhou Enlai and Deng Xiaoping to rescue his economy from periodic disaster, so he kept them around, even in high positions, but then launched campaigns to disgrace and disempower them. Fearful that their influence would outlive his, he jailed his able president Liu Shaochi, letting him rot to death, and even denied his faithful prime minister, Zhou Enlai, a great technocrat who came to a delicate but faithful accommodation with his ideological master, treatment for his terminal cancer.

There is enormous continuity in the emergence of a Chinese technocratic elite, founded by Sun Yat-sen but tragically divided into two factions, Guomindang and Communist. It is of course possible to make a long list of differences, but when one compares them with other governments, particularly governments outside the Asian miracle group, what is striking are the commonalities. The themes include central control, socialist ownership, orderly bureaucratic procedure, careful planning, meritocracy, science, engineering, pragmatism, nationalism, egalitarian ideals, and a vanguard party. Many of the

Morning Post, which, however, in the manner common at the time, made up most of the details since neither my family nor the neighbor or the police would give them any information. A year later the gunmen killed some police officers during a restaurant robbery and were subsequently caught with grenades, guns, and the kitchen knife they had stolen from my dining table. One of their fingerprints matched the print on my car window. My neighbor and landlord, who was otherwise known as a very tough character, was too intimidated to testify, but my testimony and my wife's, together with police evidence, led to a rare conviction and the gang members were jailed for 14 years.

differences are situational, not deep differences of ideology. The Guo-mindang intended to do a land reform, but once its urban base had been shattered and it was wholly dependent on landlords and warlords for survival the situation precluded that. In the 1970s I had a long conversation with the official who planned Taiwan's land reform. Chiang Kai-shek had tasked him with planning a land reform on the mainland, but then the Japanese invaded. He made a living as a doctor, a professor, and a university administrator and then, he said, finally on Taiwan he was able to unroll his old plans and implement most of them.

Likewise, after dealing in great detail with Taiwan's economic plan-ners in the 1970s, I found myself experiencing déjà vu when later I had dealings with mainland Chinese planners. Three Harvard professors have even noted that, at the beginning of the last century, Sun Yat-sen, the revolutionary founder of post-imperial China, sketched out key road networks and key infrastructure points like the Three Gorges Dam that the China's Communist Party reformers have been building generations later.[5] Chiang Kai-shek's infrastructure building bridged the great technocrats Sun Yat-sen and Deng Xiaoping.

I begin this chapter with these thoughts because it has not been long since the ideological caricatures of the two great modern Chinese movements were popular, and it has not been long since some scholars were asserting, on the basis of the experience of Maoism, that China is inherently divided and unstable.[6] If you immerse yourself in the details of Chinese political struggles, you become obsessed with the differ-ences between the two great revolutionary parties. If you spend your time in the rest of the region, or the rest of the world, the commonal-ities and continuities overwhelm. Mao was a diversion – as if the *jacqueries* (peasant revolts) of the French revolution had taken over for a generation because of a foreign invasion.

---

[5] Regina M. Abrami, William C. Kirby, and F. Warren McFarlan, *Can China Lead?: Reaching the Limits of Power and Growth* (Brighton, MA: Harvard Business Review Press, 2014).

[6] The most prominent advocate of the view that China was unstable and coming apart was the late Gerald Segal, who led Asian studies at the Institute of International Strategic Studies. See, among many other texts, "China's Changing Shape," *Foreign Affairs*, May/June 1994, www.foreignaffairs.com/articles/china/1994-05-01/china-s-changing-shape. "Regionalism," he said, "especially in its foreign and security policy context, soon raises the sensitive question of the integrity of the modern Chinese state."

The reformers have spent a generation creating a more, albeit imperfectly, institutionalized system. They started by putting age limits on officials. No longer would China's fate hang on the whims of an aged, sometimes frivolously destructive, leader like Mao. For a while China was actually governed by the "eight immortals," aging revolutionaries who were more important than the nominal top leaders, but with each generation the leaders have become younger and more educated, and the nominal leaders have been the actual leaders. They have built orderly bureaucracies and subordinated the military to civilian rule (a powerful lobby, as in the United States, but under civilian control). They have raised the professional standard of officials, first by reestablishing the use of objective examinations and later by establishing professional assessment and promotion procedures (but see the caveats below). They have systematically built a system of rule by law – not rule *of* law of the kind Westerners venerate, but nonetheless an increasingly systematic, increasingly professionalized system that is the antithesis of Maoism.

Gradually, because of the needs of the economy as led in many cases by the requirements of foreign business, there has been an increase in transparency, accountability, legality, and responsiveness. By comparison with what these qualities mean in the advanced industrial democracies, the results remain unsatisfactory, and indeed many Western commentators will respond with derisory language to the use of those terms in the Chinese context. But, compared with where it started in 1978, the Chinese government and Party have traveled a very long way along those dimensions. Xi Jinping has committed verbally to decisive further progress, but so far in his administration there has been as much backsliding as progress.

The transformation of competence is as startling as the transformation from the one-pants family to today's family sitting on a sofa watching one of its televisions. When I first visited Beijing in 1982, I called on the head of the international department of Bank of China (at the time the central bank) and proffered my bank's sophisticated services. He listened for a few minutes about derivatives and such, and then told me that what would be really helpful to them would be information about how to cash a check when one of their officers goes to New York. Not so many years later I began attending annual United States–China financial conferences organized by Hal Scott of Harvard Law School. The head of China's central bank, Zhou Xiaochuan, a first-class mind who understood global markets, would come to the ones held in Beijing and deliver a 40-minute extemporaneous speech in English, then answer questions for a similar period, from some of the world's leading scholars and practitioners, brilliantly, in English. No leading Western central bank governor could pull off such a tour de force, in Chinese or probably English either. They would regard the risk of a misstep as too serious.

The transformation of China's diplomatic corps is similarly emblematic. At one point in the Cultural Revolution, Mao recalled all of China's ambassadors but one. Expertise and connections with foreigners were then held in contempt, and the educational and training foundation of China's diplomatic corps was destroyed. With this legacy, in the first decade or so of reform many of China's top diplomats often came across as clumsy, bureaucratic, ideological, certainly not up to their Western counterparts. One ambassador to Washington had to have his significant presentations ghosted by a Chinese grad student at an Ivy League school. Today most are polished professionals who compare favorably with those of any other country. In fact, as the US Congress has tightened budget constraints on the US State Department, and as political patronage has continually increased the number of unskilled US ambassadors, Chinese diplomats are increasingly often better trained than their US counterparts.[7]

Stability through Incrementalism

After more than a century of severe instability Chinese leaders have given high priority to maintaining overall stability in the midst of extraordinary change. Some Western writers see this emphasis on stability as neurotic, but, given China's century of division before

---

[7] This statement may raise eyebrows. In a not particularly unusual example, Obama's two ambassadors to Japan, America's most important ally, were a political fund raiser and a political clan leader, neither of whom knew much about either Japan or diplomacy. Counterpart appointments would have happened in Mao's China, but not China today. In the past, there were often non-career ambassadors, but to a country like Japan they were the likes of Japan expert Edwin O. Reischauer and former Senate Majority Leader Mike Mansfield. While US professional foreign service officers continue to be outstanding in many dimensions, their non-language training has gradually been curtailed over many years so that it is now a fraction of what they used to receive and a tiny fraction of what their military counterparts receive.

1949, it would be unreasonable to expect anything else. China's technocrats have sought to preserve stability in the midst of some of history's most rapid changes. They have done so through efforts to centralize power and to destroy organized opposition, but these common strategies have been successful through carefully crafted incrementalism.

One crucial technique, mentioned in the first chapter, might be called the "one–two" gambit. A historic, and ideologically unlikely deal, between Lady Margaret Thatcher and Deng Xiaoping over Hong Kong was achieved by saying that China had "one country, two systems." For all the problems, which are accumulating, that deal has kept Hong Kong prosperous and relatively free and avoided a geopolitical clash. In the economy, the transition from state control to market pricing and market management was handled by "one sector, two systems" – for instance a baseline amount of grain was turned over to the state at the old fixed prices and the rest sold on the market, then the market was gradually allowed to become dominant. During a period of gradual transition there was one currency, two systems (the official rate and the swap rate). There was pervasive use of "one company, two systems." As economist Lawrence Lau and his colleagues[8] have shown, this avoided shocks and instability but, since marginal pricing was done by the market, it was remarkably efficient.

Ideological transitions were made in the same way. From 1994 on China called itself a "socialist market economy," thereby avoiding a sharp break with the ideology of socialism. Although it sounded like an oxymoron to many Western scholars, the leaders successfully communicated to the public that the regime intended to retain socialist values while seeking market efficiencies. At the time, Chinese scholars assured us foreigners that the operative part was "market," and that has indeed been the main direction in which economic policy has moved, including lately with the 2013 call for market dominance in the allocation of resources. (Actual progress during the current Chinese administration in market allocation of resources remains to be seen.)

This careful concern for stability and continuity in the midst of disconcerting rates of social change has enabled transformation

---

[8] Lawrence J. Lau, Yingyi Qian, and Gerard Roland, "Reform without Losers: An Interpretation of China's Dual-Track Approach to Transition," *Journal of Political Economy* 108(1), 2000, pp. 120–143.

without shock or total disillusionment. It has been absolutely central both to leadership cohesion and to a reasonably stable relationship between leadership and led. The political counterpart of "socialist market economy" was the shift from Maoist class struggle to technocratic, middle-class cohesion. The Maoist theory, written into the constitution, said that the Party represented the workers, peasants, and soldiers, and that the core political process was class struggle. That was not just Maoist theory; that was how politics was conducted. The ideology and the reality were anti-elitist and divisive.

Under the reformists, building the economy required expert leadership and middle-class-style harmony, not rule by the bottom part of society through eternal struggle against the top. So Jiang Zemin articulated the Three Represents: the Party represents advanced culture, advanced technology, and the shared interests of the people. In other words: the elitism of expertise rather than rule from the bottom; shared interests rather than class struggle; and the ideology of middle-class harmony. This was a monumental change in the ideas around which politics was organized and in the new reality of Chinese politics; it was accompanied by concrete changes like admitting business leaders to the upper echelons of the Party.[9] Careful formulations of this kind attracted ridicule among many Western scholars, but they steered a gigantic country with a gigantic population into the modern world by providing a vision that communicated the essence of transformational change without repudiating the past.

Whether they were marketizing food prices, nudging the currency toward realistic levels, gradually building the complex institutions that undergird a market economy, or explaining that the Party would have a lot more rich business executives and proportionately fewer peasants, this emphasis on stability and on articulating a clear, reassuring message brought China a combination of extraordinarily rapid change and underlying continuity. Change occurred in a way that advanced the well-being of every social group. The Party insisted on having an explicit strategic understanding of where China was and where it was going, and on communicating this to a mass public through precisely honed slogans.

---

[9] Not least it was an explicit rejection not just of Maoism but of Karl Marx's core argument that class antagonisms must inexorably worsen; Marx failed to foresee the rise of the middle class and its concomitant, the welfare state. This made the Three Represents a fundamental ideological break point.

The contrast with the shock therapy that Russia accepted, following Western advice, could not be greater. Change was instant. Russia was knocked into a prolonged depression, with GDP declining by 40 percent. People lost their homes and their pensions. Malnourishment became widespread. An old way of life was jettisoned overnight and nobody knew how the new one was supposed to work. Socialist institutions were destroyed, but none of the integuments of a market economy had been constructed. The country's industrial assets were distributed to the public as share certificates, but Russia had none of the accountants or communications systems or legal structures or compliance procedures or public education about stocks and bonds that make markets work. Since there were only a few people who understood the system, and very few who knew how to value the shares they had been given, most assets quickly fell under the control of a handful of billionaires. The principal consequence of this shock therapy was that Western democracy and capitalism came across as a catastrophe for large parts of the population, who understandably demanded a leader who would bring order and stop the depredations of the billionaires. At the time, it was politically unacceptable in the West to suggest that the Asia Model of rapid incrementalism, with a primary focus on universal economic improvement, on carefully but swiftly building the institutions of a market economy, works better.

The West still tends to believe in shock therapy, even more in politics than in economics, and the world has recently been littered with examples of how that doesn't work.

The GE Model: Institutionalizing the Obsession with Economic Growth

The core of the Asia Model in its mobilization phase is the obsession with economic growth, so governance institutions have to be crafted for that purpose. The core idea of governance focused on economic performance is to recruit highly qualified people, to give them very strong incentives to perform, and to embed them within institutions that give rein to their capabilities. Although the basics of rule by the most qualified were established in China before 221 BCE, the best analogy for the way the Asian miracle economies achieve their single-minded purpose is the governance of the large Western corporation.

When the mobilization phase is over, the emphasis on competent performance remains.

In a company like General Electric (GE), employees are recruited on the basis of their educational qualifications supplemented by interviews. Social and political connections help, but the candidates have to be highly qualified. They start low down in the organization and each year are assigned a set of very specific tasks to perform. If they succeed, they are given a bonus and promoted to a job that has bigger challenges, often in a different geographic or functional area with different kinds of challenges. They are always in a competitive environment; they are being compared with other intelligent, energetic executives at a similar level. The company has a handbook of rules, and a set of informal norms (summarized as the company's culture). They are expected to be loyal to the organization and are penalized if they are constantly sending out their resumes to other firms or saying bad things about the company.

Most of the time, most executives are expected to behave within the rules and within the norms. However, sometimes executives may propose or implement new ways of doing things, even ways that are disruptive to parts of the organization. If they succeed, their careers may rocket ahead of their peers, but if they fail they may find themselves completely outside the organization. This process of testing and promotion is repeated over a lifetime until a small number of executives make it to the C suite (chief executive officer, chief financial officer, and so forth). Unless the top leaders mess up badly, they have a strong voice in the process of selecting their successors.

A company like GE has an advantage in structuring itself efficiently. It is primarily devoted to a single goal, namely making a profit. Because of that, the top officers can be judged against one overarching goal, namely how much money they made for the company or how much the stock went up. Debates over strategy can be cleanly adjudicated by making judgments about which approach will lead to the most profit. Many units can be judged by the same criterion as the top management, namely how much profit they added to the corporate total, and most employees can be judged by whether their diverse tasks and achievements contributed to the bottom line. Subjective judgments, personal factors, and factional alignments all influence particular decisions, but overall the system works because the standards, the goals, and the outcomes are all broadly measurable and broadly enforced.

Effectiveness, innovation, and profitability are driven by competition among executives and competition among units for resources.

This is precisely the model of governance China adopted. There are measures, organized around examinations, for recruiting high-quality candidates. Then each official signs a contract with the next level up to achieve specific objectives. The contracts may specify specific bonuses, as in Western companies and investment banks, but promotions are decided later, as at GE. A mayor may contract to build certain infrastructure and improve education by a certain amount. (Additional details are elaborated below.) Now each mayor is also expected to meet environmental objectives. When it is time for promotion, the mayor will be assessed on meeting the assigned goals and on promoting the overall national objectives, and will sometimes (practice has varied lately) be given what Western human resources people call a 360-degree assessment – all the person's superiors and subordinates are supposed to be interviewed to assess managerial qualities and to check for corruption. The specific findings and conclusions will be stored in a permanent file. If successful, the mayor may be moved from a small place in one province to a bigger city with different problems in another province.

As the mayor moves up, like the counterpart at GE she has considerable latitude in meeting or exceeding the assigned goals. Indeed, if breaking some rules leads consistently to better outcomes, the norm is that the mayor will be rewarded for the outcomes rather than punished for breaking the rules. (The risks and vulnerabilities are real, but probably not too different from those at GE.) Probably the most dramatic instance of this was when, shortly after reform began, peasants in Anhui and Sichuan started taking back their farms from the communes. Local officials tolerated or encouraged that, and the results were so good for the economy that Beijing endorsed the process and spread it nationwide. This latitude can create an opening for corruption,[10] but so far it has been far more important in stimulating creative management. In the case of the commune reform, what the provincial leaders did was absolutely illegal but good for the country. One

---

[10] For an outstanding analysis emphasizing the corruption risk see Mayling Birney, "Decentralization and Veiled Corruption under China's 'Rule of Mandates,'" *World Development* 53, 2014, pp. 55–67.

became prime minister and the other became executive vice premier in Beijing.

Western scholars tend to emphasize the risk of corruption. That risk is real, as one can see everywhere in China, but the risk must be weighed against the benefits of giving officials the space they need to perform under widely varying circumstances. Those benefits may vary with time and circumstance, but in China the net benefits have been enormous.

A personal example may make this less abstract. When I was an investment banker, many things were regulated, as in China, by general principles, such as "Don't steal from the company." Under that rule, on the many occasions when I needed to use the copier for something personal, I used the company copier and then asked what the cost was so that I could pay it back. When I moved to RAND, because of RAND's many contracts with the US government everything was regulated by intricate rules. I returned from a trip to China to find in my mail a tax authorities' demand for paperwork for an audit – due almost immediately. I sent an email saying that I was going to ask my secretary to copy 1,200 pages of records and asked what figures I should use to calculate the value of her time and of 1,200 copies. The reply said that there was no way I could reimburse the cost of my secretary; all of her time had to be charged to a specific contract and there was no contract number to which this could be charged and reimbursed. So I said I would hire a temp and pay for that myself. The reply said that was prohibited because the temp might slip and fall and RAND's insurance would not cover that risk. Various other gambits, such as my making a donation to RAND, were likewise unacceptable. I ended up spending an entire day at Kinko's Copy Center, copying, removing staples, adjusting contrasts … using time worth 10 to 12 times the cost of secretarial time and paper. The advantage of such a detailed rules-based system, as Dr. Mayling Birney emphasizes, is that everything you can do can be measured against some rule. There are many situations in which that's of paramount importance, most notably in rules of military engagement. But it's also why workers in the New York City Subway system can shut the system down by doing a "work to rule," since there are so many rules that enforcing all of them makes it impossible to run the trains. Trying to run China by intricate national rules would destroy all creativity and shut the system down – much worse than a New York subway work to rule.

There are balances in such things, and the balances must be adjusted. But the Chinese results suggest that for most of the reform era they got the balance right. The explosion of corruption under the Hu–Wen administration occurred for other reasons. Excessive rules also foster corruption. At RAND, the personnel head told me, "Next time, Bill, just make the copies and don't tell anyone." In China the rules for starting a company are so intricate and contradictory that the only way to get going is to make a side deal with the Party Secretary.

As at GE, competition occurs not just among executives but also among units. In GE, the financial arm, the jet engines arm, and the medical arm all compete for capital and top management support. The unit that makes more money, or introduces an innovation that is of broad use to the firm, gets more capital and its leadership gets faster promotions. In China, the different provinces, cities, counties, and towns all compete in economic growth and in strategies for achieving that growth. If the central government has not set detailed rules, as is often the case, local officials and governments are free to make their own decisions. The special zone of Shenzhen, north of Hong Kong, has tried innovative governance, including separation of powers, and achieved spectacular growth; even though the center is very skeptical about separation of powers, Shenzhen has been rewarded for its successes.

As at GE, bending the rules doesn't always lead to success. Seeking to displace existing top management leads either to huge success or to huge failure. Toward the end of the Hu–Wen era, the Party Secretary of Chongqing, China's Chicago, was promoting a "Chongqing model" based on populist rhetoric backed up by specific social programs and exceptionally good infrastructure. However, Chongqing's Party Secretary, Bo Xilai, who was beloved of the general public both in Chongqing and in his previous job in Dalian, got too far out of line with the core leadership, and with the rather loose standards of the time for personal behavior, and lost both his job and his freedom. Anyone who reads the **Financial Times** or the **Wall Street Journal** sees this kind of unceremonious job loss happen frequently in large companies, albeit usually without so many lurid details and jail bars.

The Chinese system allows generous leeway for local decisions. If the central government has not decreed specific rules, as in a wide variety of circumstances it has not, local governments and officials are free to make their own decisions. This resembles the US system and is much more conducive to initiative than the contrary approach, common in some of continental Europe like the Netherlands and still prevalent in Indonesia and elsewhere, that everything is prohibited unless it has specifically been permitted. Westerners' image of a socialist system inclines more toward the restrictive Dutch model, or the extreme rigidity of the Soviet Union, but much of the Chinese system is designed, top to bottom, to create space and incentives for entrepreneurship.

The same applies to corporate behavior in China. When I was at Bankers Trust in Hong Kong in the 1980s, our China team was doing complex derivatives in China.[11] There were no rules for derivatives and no legal infrastructure to enforce the contracts. We informed the authorities what we were doing but did not ask permission because if you asked permission you might have to wait for your next incarnation before the answer came. If the business on the whole worked out well for the country, the authorities were supportive. If not, they were, to put it mildly, quite unsupportive. Our China team was very focused on serving the customer, and as a result we were consistently the most profitable foreign bank dealing with China. After leaving Bankers Trust, the head of that China team became a near-billionaire because he had gained the trust of top leaders. Indonesia, on the other hand, had a highly restrictive legal structure and our Indonesia business was run by a transaction-oriented executive (i.e., someone who tries to maximize the profitability of every transaction, in plain language a rip-off artist). That led to catastrophe both for major Indonesian companies and for the bank – prefiguring in 1998 what happened to the larger US banking system ten years later.[12] For me, it was a useful object lesson in how a quite different system from my own country's could be successful. Detailed regulations are not always the answer.

Field Testing New Ideas

China's decentralized geographic competition conveys enormous advantages. Bright ideas can be field tested on sites the size of major

---

[11] I lived in Hong Kong during the years 1985–2001 and 2013–2015.

[12] Bankers Trust became non-viable in 1998 as a result of the kind of counterparty failure that brought down the other major US banks in 2008. Prior to its failure Bankers Trust was the seventh-largest US bank and in some years proportionately the most profitable large US bank.

cities or even the size of major European countries. Then, if they work, they can be spread to the whole country. At the beginning of reform, China tested out more market-oriented policies, and more openness to foreign trade and foreign investment, in a set of Special Economic Zones. The most exciting of those was Shenzhen, north of Hong Kong, which was little more than a collection of rice paddies in 1980 but, because of the openness policies, has become one of the great exporting cities of the world. More recently, moves to liberalize the financial system and foreign investment have focused on a Shanghai Free Trade Zone and two other similar zones.

Not all experiments work. In the 1990s the leadership of Hainan, a large island off the coast, decided to try turning itself into another Hong Kong. They inaugurated free trade policies in the manner of Hong Kong and even considered adopting the Hong Kong dollar as the provincial currency.[13] As it turned out, the quickest way to make money was to import large numbers of cars free of duty and smuggle them into the mainland, so suddenly Hainan's economy became focused on smuggling. Beijing shut that experiment down decisively; Hainan's leaders were fired but not jailed since they had undertaken a plausible experiment. The Hainan experience in turn informed the way contemporary financial liberalization is being done by channeling it through the Shanghai Free Trade Zone; the new "Free Trade Zone" policies are actually national policies, but transactions have to be channeled through trusted institutions in Shanghai so as not to have the intent of the reforms subverted Hainan-style.

Problems within the GE Model

Like a company, an Asian miracle economy has to cope with the reality that any large organization has a lot more problems than a simple

---

[13] RAND's Charles Wolf was the key foreign consultant on the Hainan project, and I (at the time running an investment bank research team in Hong Kong) became involved with him in studying the possibility of Hainan's adopting the Hong Kong dollar, instead of the national renminbi, as the provincial currency. At the time it was popular in the West to caricature China's leaders as a bunch of hopeless, ideological gerontocrats. I can testify from personal experience that they were trying out all sorts of creative ideas that one would not associate with ideological gerontocrats. Picture the reaction in Washington, DC if Hawaii's governor announced an intention to experiment with changing the state's currency to the Japanese yen.

organization chart can convey. There are always factions and personal relations and conflicts of interest and corruption. There are backdoors that people use to circumvent the objective hiring and promotion criteria. Bureaucracies always tend to congeal and lose creativity. Management is a process of continually responding to deviations and bringing the main tendency back to what it is supposed to be. The current anti-corruption campaign, discussed in the previous chapter, is attempting to address the most serious deviation.

The Asian miracle economies other than Japan have been particularly good so far at preventing bureaucratic ossification. Mao's response to it – the Cultural Revolution – was extraordinarily destructive, but his successors have found better ways. Intense competition and flexible rules at most levels have maintained creativity. The Asian miracle economies have all used think tanks to good advantage. In South Korea, the Korea Development Institute, the Korea Education Institute, think tanks of the Foreign Ministry, the military, the intelligence organizations, and many others both provide independent advice and create a flow of talent that can refresh the bureaucracy. Park Chung Hee would personally call up scholars getting Ph.D.s in the United States and ask them to return home to help save their country.[14] The best would go to a think tank like the Korea Development Institute, work for some years on research about the country's most important problems at pay three times the level of an academic, and then move into an appropriate ministry as vice minister, after which, if they were successful, they would become ministers. Similarly, Taiwan and Singapore have think tanks that prod and lead and refresh the bureaucracy, and also contribute directly to decision-making. All these countries highly value expertise; at any given time, Taiwan usually has about as many Ph.D.s in its cabinet as the United States has in a generation's worth of cabinets.

---

[14] Here's one example. My friend Kim Sejin got his Ph.D. in political science from the University of Kentucky and was planning an academic career there. One day he got a phone call from President Park, who asked him why he was wasting his time as a minor US academic when he could be saving his country. Sejin rose through the think tank of the Foreign Ministry and later, as Consul General in New York with an unadvertised more important rank as President Chun's personal representative in the United States, accomplished things that changed the trajectory of his country, before an untimely death from pancreatic cancer. The point is that these techniques for bypassing and refreshing the government bureaucracies are vital to the successes.

China has a vast array of think tanks – the Chinese Academy of Sciences, the Chinese Academy of Social Sciences, the Shanghai Academy of Social Sciences, and many others. The Central Party School functions as both a think tank – a superb one – and a training center for senior leaders. Every region and every functional area have think tanks. As a group these think tanks are required to toe the policy line publicly more than Western think tanks, and everyone acknowledges that this hampers their creativity, but they have many first-rate scholars, and the scholars do often raise difficult questions and advocate radically different policies. In many areas the top leadership gets direct input from think tank and university scholars. For instance, the Institute of Finance and Banking within the Chinese Academy of Social Sciences long had direct input into the big decisions on money supply, interest rates, and exchange rates.[15]

The leadership also reaches out to foreigners. I have mentioned elsewhere in this volume the practice of sending vice ministers and others for training programs at Harvard, Oxford, and other leading universities. That is just the peak of a vast exchange program that sends Chinese officials abroad and brings Western experts to China. Nobel Prize-level economists in the United States can expect to get calls to come and advise the prime minister or to join advisory groups that

---

[15] These points are made from personal experience. At one point in the late 1990s leaders of the Institute of Finance and Banking asked me to give a lecture on financial development and I arrived to find, instead of a room-size audience of mid-level officials, a small group of advisors to the top leaders who had negligible interest in a lecture but were deeply worried about the country's financial situation and grilled me for hours in connection with some urgent decisions. Through that meeting I first learned that these think tank researchers were actually top-level policy advisors. On a very different subject, in 2003, leaders of two think tanks became convinced that China's new leaders were making serious mistakes in policies toward Hong Kong; tensions were becoming severe. They flew to RAND in California and asked my advice on what to do. We put forward an analysis of leadership misunderstandings about Hong Kong and then got the United Front Minister to visit Hong Kong and ease the fears; she was quite effective. Then we got China's Vice President to fly to Shenzhen and invite Hong Kong political leaders across the border for consultations that were mutually educational and reduced tensions. The range of inputs that China's top leaders got (speaking from a decade ago when I had more direct knowledge of such things) was quite remarkable. This is seldom understood in the West, and in fact some leading US scholars have been known to assert that one of the flaws in the Chinese system is that the kinds of meetings I was frequently involved in never happen.

advise the top leaders. Western experts are sometimes even given a role in high-level decision-making groups.

For all the factional infighting, for all the cronyism, and for all the problems of corruption, big problems that must not be understated, the Chinese system has, particularly at the top, a reverence for learning, a hunger for the latest ideas, a cosmopolitan search for best practice, and a system that rewards performance. They end up with the world's most richly experienced cadre of top leaders.

In such a system everything, even corruption, works differently than in most third-world governments. In India, the local official gets ahead by saying no, no, no until a potential investor gives a bribe. If the local economy doesn't grow, that doesn't affect the official very much. In China, if the local official says no, no, no and pockets small bribes and the economy doesn't grow, his or her career is finished. If the official says yes to good projects and the economy grows like crazy, the official gets a big bonus and a big promotion and usually participates in earnings (rakeoffs) from the successful business; when promotion comes, the official gains opportunities to participate in much bigger deals.

Is the GE Model Completely Wrong?

There are controversies among scholars about the extent to which performance criteria actually influence Chinese officials' promotions and behavior. An academic literature based on evidence – overwhelming evidence – that factions and personal networks are important to promotions says that therefore performance criteria are unimportant. The factual finding is true, but the conclusion doesn't follow.

Take the US Treasury Department, probably the most performance-oriented civilian institution in the US government. If you wanted to be Deputy Secretary there in 2001, you needed first of all to be a Republican and second to be part of George W. Bush's conservative Republican faction rather than, for instance, one of the more centrist Republican groups. If you study that decision narrowly, the most important criterion of appointment was factional. But, to be part of the pool of candidates considered, you had to be highly qualified, as demonstrated by a lifetime of performance, and in office you had to perform in order to be eligible for promotion. Competence is usually the prerequisite and in that sense competence is the primary qualification.

Likewise, the US military has very strong performance norms. But every general has his own team and promotes officers that he or she believes will be personally loyal. The bonds among members of platoons, or classmates who were close at West Point, are as intense as any on earth. They hire and promote each other. They like to move as teams. The same happens in the top investment banks; our new general managers at Bankers Trust often made a clean sweep of the existing senior team. *But here is the crucial point: that does not conflict with the necessity that, in order to get a job, retain a job, or be promoted, most have to be highly qualified and to perform.* There are exceptions, there are corrupt deals, but the overall norm is that performance is crucial. Since China is a poor country, there are more exceptions and more corrupt deals, but the norm is that an official must meet the assigned targets or fail.

There is a fundamental difference between the way the US Treasury functions and the way, for instance, Kansas politics functions. Kansas Governor Sam Brownback promises superior economic growth but pursues policies, slashing taxes on the rich indiscriminately, that will obviously lead to a financial squeeze and slower growth. He serves a small coterie of extremely wealthy people who care only about paying less tax and are able through money politics to support his career successfully in any economic scenario short of financial disaster. Contribution to the national economy, not to mention the Kansas economy, is not crucial to his success. If he were judged on contribution to a national growth plan, he could not survive, but in Kansas that is not a criterion for his success.

In China, regardless of faction, Governor Brownback would not fare well because he has a very clear record of not performing on his primary commitment, which is to growth. Most senior US Treasury officials would do very well in China. Anyone who has dealt with senior officials from China's Ministry of Finance or People's Bank of China (PBOC) recognizes that they compare well with their counterparts anywhere in the world. Comparing PBOC Governor Zhou Xiaochuan with Alan Greenspan and Ben Bernanke, I would rank Zhou far ahead of Greenspan and at least on a level with Bernanke. The kind of quality that percolates to the top in China happens only when performance criteria are crucial. As in the United States, this is consistent with factional politics because there are multiple individuals who can perform in any given position, so each faction has competent people.

The same is true of China's other important meritocratic institution, the college entrance exam or gaokao. Cheating, and efforts to cheat, are widespread. There are some "back doors" whereby some applicants are able to circumvent the system. But the gaokao system establishes a meritocratic norm. Students study incredibly hard, putting typical Western student efforts to shame, to prepare for the gaokao. Parents exhaust their savings to buy tutoring for the gaokao. The authorities make extraordinary efforts to limit cheating, even in 2016 using drones to intercept radio transmissions of the answers, banning underwire bras because the wires might hide a receiver, and decreeing a potential seven-year jail term for cheaters.[16] The problems of the system do not invalidate the meritocratic norms. The hard work, the tutoring expense, the desperate efforts to cheat, and the excessive penalties for cheating actually testify to the importance of the system. Anyone who spends time with Chinese officials knows that the official's need to achieve assigned goals generates the same kind of hard work, the same exhaustion of available resources, and the same efforts to cheat and to stop the cheating.

The general reader can skip to the next section now, unless he or she is interested in the weird way academic debates sometimes evolve. Scholars will want to know how these arguments relate to evidence in the academic literature. In most of this book I have deliberately eschewed engagement with academic debates, but this one is particularly important. There is a whole school of US political scientists who argue that merit has nothing to do with promotions in China, that the government is basically a bunch of corrupt political hacks, and that policies are chosen without regard to efficacy.

For the latest literature on factional politics, there is a special issue of the *Journal of East Asian Studies*.[17] Victor Shih's introductory overview is a particularly judicious summary of the overall literature. Shih, along with co-authors, is also co-author of the landmark research article on this subject, published in the most prestigious journal of political science, the ***American Political Science Review***.[18]

---

[16] Javier C. Hernández, "China Threatens Jail Time for College Entrance Exam Cheaters," *New York Times*, June 7, 2016, www.nytimes.com/2016/06/08/world/asia/china-exam-gaokao-university-cheating.html.

[17] *Journal of East Asian Studies*, Volume 16, Special Issue 01, March 2016.

[18] Victor Shih, Christopher Adolph, and Mingxing Liu, "Getting Ahead in the Communist Party: Explaining the Advancement of Central Committee Members

In his prestigious article Shih and his colleagues do a regression analysis showing that, among senior officials, those whose region had the highest economic performance were not necessarily the ones who got the big jobs, but those who got the big jobs were typically members of the top leader's faction. This finding underlies his separate summary of the key point in this literature: "[I]nstead of relying on formal institutions to vet and promote the best possible candidates, senior leaders competed to position their proteges in important positions, regardless of merit (Shih, 2012). The relative positions of factions also determined the trajectories of economic policies and even monetary policies (Shih 2008a; Fewsmith 1994)."

So top officials are chosen, we are told, "regardless of merit"; and policies are chosen regardless of efficacy. But this does not follow at all from the evidence this article musters. It is certainly true that, under a given top leader, a member of his faction is likely to get a top job even when some other official's region may have had better economic performance. If there were any government in the world where that wasn't true, it would be exciting news indeed. But the point is that, just as the Bush administration made a factional choice out of a group of highly qualified officials, the same is generally true in China.

Officials get into a pool of top-level candidates by performing over many years, at many levels (town, city, provincial, national), in multiple provinces, on multiple challenges (growth, education, culture, ...) Out of the pool of high-performing candidates, an individual is chosen using additional criteria, including loyalty to faction and to Party – as in the United States. As in any other organization, the system is imperfect. Just as in other countries or in business organizations, sometimes people are chosen because of bribes, blackmail, sexual favors ... but those are deviations from a performance norm. Neither George W. Bush nor Barack Obama would have qualified for a top-level job in China; they simply lacked the required depth of experience and proven performance.

In the analysis by Shih *et al.*, the performance variables are misspecified. Performance is not properly measured purely in absolute economic growth of the region they served but rather in performance relative to a wide variety of the objectives actually assigned, some of

in China," *American Political Science Review* 106(1), 2012, pp. 166–187 and A1–A47.

which occasionally reduce growth. Even if the assigned objective were solely GDP growth, the appropriate objective would naturally be much higher for Guangdong, a coastal export province with exceptional advantages, than for Guizhou, an impoverished interior province with structural disadvantages. More importantly, assigned objectives are also more nuanced than just gross provincial (or town or city) product growth. The overall evaluation is supposed to cover virtue, professional skills, diligence, achievements, and honesty in governance. Within the "achievements" category, road networks, electricity networks, and schools must be built, and the needs are different in different localities. In addition, performance targets often include local investment, foreign investment, and industrial upgrading. Social stability must be maintained. Officials are given a hierarchy of targets, designated as veto-power targets, hard targets, and soft targets.[19] There is a deliberate policy of assigning successful officials to different areas, where the challenges (i.e., performance targets) are *quite different.*

In the era of economic mobilization, most of the targets were in some way related to economic growth (e.g., building a road is related to economic growth). Today performance targets heavily emphasize social welfare, environmental goals, sound budget management, and the like, some of which are actually inimical to rapid GDP growth. Officially, promotions are supposed to be based 50 percent on faithful implementation of central government policies, 25 percent on the kinds of performance targets just mentioned, and 25 percent on factional affiliations.[20] In 2016 the priority targets for leaders of northeastern provinces focused on the elimination of excess capacity in the coal, iron, and steel industries, an assignment that reduces economic growth. Details and proportions vary, but all of this is a world away from the presumption of Shih *et al.* that the only criterion for promotion is simple GDP growth.

Similarly, at GE the corporate goal is profit, and most goals are related to profit, but the goal of a particular executive might be to increase the efficiency of a turbine by 2 percent. Suppose the turbine expert achieved his goal and was promoted by his team leader who

---

[19] Detailed in Mayling Birney, "Decentralization and Veiled Corruption under China's 'Rule of Mandates,'" *World Development* 53, 2014, pp. 55–67.

[20] Personal communication from an authoritative official.

believed in turbine products in competition with another group that emphasized a different technology. If Shih *et al.* did the same kind of analysis of GE, they would say he was promoted by the turbine faction, regardless of merit, because his team didn't directly produce outsize profits.

These political scientists' database, in other words, measures the wrong thing; it assumes that the objectives assigned to every official are the same. Hu Jintao famously got the top job because he rose to the challenge of maintaining stability in Tibet at a difficult moment. One can view that as a good thing or a bad thing, but he *performed* in his assigned task.

Even if the Shih *et al.* database measured the right thing, the conclusion would be wrong, because what is important for the promotions they analyze is the characteristics of the pool of candidates considered for top jobs, not the individual promotions. China's top leaders are the most experienced, most tested of any top leadership group in the world. A typical official may have started his or her career during the Cultural Revolution, been initially denied a proper education, worked in some horrible state-owned enterprise (SOE) factory, mastered English or economics by listening to foreign radio broadcasts, passed a very competitive exam to get into a university when the universities reopened, got a low-level official job, earned successive promotions to county, city, provincial, and national levels, in different provinces, and dealt with challenges that focused successively on reorganizing a factory, improving education, building a port, smoothly doubling the size of a city, expanding cultural programs, reducing unfair exactions from farmers without wrecking the provincial budget, fixing a rural credit system, managing unrest caused by unfair land seizures, and many other things.

Western readers don't read about the hundreds of thousands of Chinese equivalents of Abe Lincoln rising from log cabin to senior government positions. For the generation that grew up during the Cultural Revolution and just afterward, there is just one eye-watering achievement story after another. However, the stories that make Western headlines are the corruption stories – which are real and important but not the main story.

The Chinese system forces aspiring leaders to clear more hurdles, more varied kinds of hurdles, at more levels than any other system in the world. At every step successes and failures are documented, interviews both with superiors and with subordinates are recorded, the official must participate in an annual appraisal, and the details are retained in national personnel files. I have met, interviewed, and on occasion worked with, hundreds of officials. They are always intensely aware of all the numbers related to their performance. Most mayors, governors, and so forth start off a meeting with a "Brief Introduction," which, despite the name, is typically an interminable river of numbers, mostly related to performance. Like students preparing for the gaokao, they are invariably striving to make their numbers and fearful of failure. Like investment bankers hyping their successes, the fact that they often try to exaggerate the numbers is not evidence that the system is useless, but on the contrary is evidence of how seriously officials take the performance system.

The same kind of argument applies to the finding that policy outcomes are related to factional considerations. Does this mean that competence doesn't matter, that effective policy doesn't matter? Again, of course not. In any organization, on almost any policy, there are divisions of opinion and those divisions often, but not always, reflect factional lines. That is true in the US Federal Reserve, in the State Department, and in the military. Groups around Hillary Clinton were more likely to emphasize military interventions, groups around Obama less so. Short-term outcomes will more frequently reflect the group around the President. But in the United States and China, in contrast with, for instance, Argentina, the opposing lines reflect competent analyses and are adjudicated on the basis of national goals. Most of the policy arguments represent reasonable disagreements among experienced, highly competent leaders, in either the United States or China. If a faction succeeds in winning the policy argument and the policy doesn't work well, typically the policy is changed. In countries where only factional goals count, then one group gets rich and the country goes bust, as in Argentina. In the short term, of course, even in a highly meritocratic system, particular interests do get undue advantages, as the Petroleum Faction did in China and as its counterpart oil industry does in the United States, but in meritocratic systems when such deviations get too large there is a countervailing reaction.

Here it is useful to reflect on another consensus that Shih *et al.* summarize from the political science literature. "[A]lthough factional affiliation had a robust impact on promotions (Shih *et al.*, 2012; Keller,

2014), in actual practice, patrons must work through the formal institutions of cadre evaluation, democratic consultations, and reserve cadres to advance clients (Jia *et al.*, 2014)."

Chinese officials undergo regular appraisals in which their performance – on economic growth, road building, children in school or children graduated, amount of foreign investment, improvement of technologies, enforcement of competition ... is compared with their goals. As in a company, and as with the gaokao, officials work very hard indeed to achieve their goals. They often try to fudge the numbers.[21] They may seek to emphasize loyalty over performance. To get growth they do things like borrowing too much and investing in too many dubious projects. But, as with the gaokao, nobody doubts the importance of the appraisals, which include both quantitative goals and interviews with superiors and subordinates.

The appraisals, along with other material, are kept in two life-long files that follow the official for her entire career. These files are far more detailed than US military performance reviews and civilian personnel and security clearance records. An official who year after year gets poor appraisals has as much chance of getting to the top as a US military officer who gets poor performance reports.

What is the proper way to measure this? The best way would be to find out what goals each official, at various levels, was assigned and then create some kind of index measuring the extent to which officials met their actual goals. Then one could see whether the ones who met their actual goals were the ones promoted. Also, one could poll officials about how important meeting their goals is, and compare this with parallel polls of Indian officials about whether they feel any pressure to

---

[21] Most provinces in China report more growth than the reality can sustain, so that if one adds up all the provincial GDPs one gets a larger number than the national GDP. The National Bureau of Statistics labors to bring these numbers into line with reality. If one adds up the profits each unit in an investment bank claims just before bonus season, the differences from the firm's total profit are even more pronounced. Likewise, if one looks at risk levels reported within Western banks, the reported risks are sometimes very small compared with the actual risk. That is the inevitable consequence of a very strong incentive system. Investment banks have a Credit Department, an Audit Department, and a Credit Audit Department, and the discipline of Generally Accepted Accounting Principles standards to keep the numbers converging toward reality. China's national statisticians have a bigger problem, and auditing institutions are at an earlier level of development, but the problems do not mean that the growth is fictional or that the system is not achieving its core purpose.

meet particular goals related to national needs. One could do deep interviews to discover why Chinese officials say yes to foreign investments and to business projects whereas their Indian counterparts usually say no. One could track the performance of officials over the course of their careers and compare substantial samples of those who rose to the top with those who didn't. One could look at quantitative indicators of performance, such as whether China builds a lot more roads than India, and explore alternative explanations as to why, throughout the reform period, China has generally built more first-class roads in a month than India has built since independence in 1947.

Another component to Shih *et al.*'s argument about Chinese leadership weaknesses is that, because it is an authoritarian system, it weeds out competent leaders in favor of loyal leaders. They argue that, facing factionalism or risks of loss of power, "autocrats find ways to channel resources to their supporters, including promoting them to senior positions." But that is exactly what happens in democratic systems. That and related arguments apply to any Democrat or Republican president in US history and indeed to all but a handful of exceptionally secure leaders anywhere. That is the perfect description of why (democratic) Japanese cabinets include the interesting, frequently incompetent, characters they have. It is the perfect description of why Secretary of State Clinton appointed undeniably incompetent ambassadors to Japan and elsewhere – namely to build a financial and political base for a presidential candidacy. Trump administration appointments are an even more vivid example; the White House and cabinet filled with family and early supporters, including many who lacked credentials or competence. The behavior is universal coalition building and might even be more common in democracies, where a broader base of support is necessary in order to govern. Shih *et al.* contrast this need to build a loyal coalition with what they assert is a necessity to have a fully unified administration (i.e., one completely devoid of factions) in order for decisions to have a long-term time horizon. There is of course no political administration of any kind anywhere in the world that is unified in this way.

Such an impossible factionless ideal is in no way prerequisite to a long-term time horizon, and I know of no one familiar with modern China who would deny the long-term time horizon of its leaders in comparison with most others and especially with leaders of democracies, who are always worrying about an upcoming election – in the US case a Congressional election every two years. Deng Xiaoping's "One country, two systems" formula for Hong Kong and Taiwan was a half-century plan – in this case one that is working for economics and personal freedom but not for political structure. Xi Jinping's Belt and Road Initiative looks ahead half a century. China has a 50-year environmental plan. The country's infrastructure plans and projections of the economic structure look out many years and have typically been implemented with great success. The same is true of the other Asian miracle economies during their authoritarian periods. Taiwan had ambitious 1-year, 3-year, 5-year, 10-year, and 30-year economic plans, and usually outperformed on all of them. Long-term plans, and success in implementing them, are pervasive in authoritarian-era Asian miracle economies. Even if you just study why South Korea has been able to produce world-class violinists, you will find the government created a think tank on building the arts, then systematically implemented the results of the think tank's findings over many years until the system bore world-class fruit. Similarly, Singapore's industrial policies and its recent long-term biotech plans, based around the creation of Biosphere, have a perspective of decades and have typically been successful.

How is it that a political science literature reaches a conclusion that anyone who has ever read a serious article about economic management in the Asian miracle countries knows to be false? The Shih *et al.* article draws on a literature that generalizes about "authoritarian systems" as a group, in contrast with democratic systems. In other words, it compares two categories of regimes. One comprises the democracies, arguably dominated, despite their differences, by a reasonably coherent group of educated, industrialized middle-class societies but nonetheless including systems that behave very differently from each other – for instance, US middle-class electoral competition, Japan's dominant-party system, the Philippines' elitist extraction of resources from the lower classes. The other, autocracies, combines theocracies (e.g., Iran), totalitarian systems (e.g., North Korea), African tribal kleptocracies (e.g., Republic of Congo), kingdoms (e.g., Saudi Arabia), Latin American caudillos (e.g., Venezuela), military dictatorships, failed states (e.g., Somalia), disintegrating empires (e.g., the former Soviet Union), and the earlier Asian mobilization systems into one category. Generalizations about "typical" behavior in these other systems are then used to draw inferences about the pressures degrading Chinese meritocracy. Because the overwhelming majority of these systems are from underperforming Latin American, African, and Middle Eastern cases, they swamp the characteristics of the Asian miracle economies. The inference that average characteristics of the former group imply particular characteristics of China is based on nothing but Manichean ideological bias.

One might just as well argue that, because the former tend to be slow-growing, the Asian miracle economies must be slow growing too. Such a conclusion would be no less inconsistent with the facts than this political science literature.

One can "prove" almost anything by lumping together dissimilar things in the fashion of this category of "authoritarian systems." This kind of argument has been used to demonstrate fallaciously that democracies grow faster than non-democracies (since some failed states, countries afflicted by civil wars, and other slow-growing places are part of the mix in the non-democracies). It can be used with less political correctness, for instance, to argue that American women are more beautiful than non-American women, since the category of non-American women includes more than a billion people who are malnourished. The professor who uses such a method to make the democracy argument gets big grants. The one who makes the American-women argument would (justifiably) never work again. The only difference is not in the validity of the method but in the degree of political correctness. Virtually all such arguments fail when examined more closely. It would make just as much sense for a physicist, enamored of the many valuable qualities of aluminum, to write learned papers contrasting the qualities of aluminum and non-aluminum elements and from those papers argue that uranium must be a dull, mid-weight material of no particular use.

In other words, this political science argument generalizes from the experience of African kleptocracies and Latin American caudillos and concludes that China and other Asian miracle economies can't make long-term plans even though long-term plans, usually implemented with success so far, are pervasive in them and indeed one of their most noteworthy distinguishing features.

The Chinese system has factions like every other political system, including the United States. It has a promotion system that emphasizes performance, like the United States but more explicitly and systematically. Its serious flaws make it a profoundly imperfect system, as even the highest-level Chinese officials acknowledge. This is a third-world country. Some officials exaggerate their performance. There are many cases of officials who do not undertake the required public surveys. Some department heads fake the evaluations. Bosses and subordinates scratch each other's backs. Sometimes the appraisals inappropriately overweight some factors at the expense of others. Sometimes the evaluations are ignored. Moreover, on top of existing flaws, the Xi administration has weakened the system of performance appraisals and promotions. But, like the gaokao, the system creates a norm of performance aligned with national policy. It encourages hard work, competition, and creativity. Anyone who has dealt with officials from a variety of countries knows that Chinese officials, like their counterparts in the other Asian miracle economies, are constantly thinking about their targets and working very hard to achieve them. That behavior is not typical of officials of comparable rank in India or the Philippines.

The data that purport to show that Chinese officials are selected "regardless of merit" show no such thing. Anyone who has dealt with senior Chinese officials and with their counterparts from other countries knows that the Chinese are mostly very impressive. I have dealt with officials from dozens of countries, and I have dealt with Chinese officials at every level from town up to prime minister and president. At every level they are determined to achieve specific leadership-defined goals and they're fearful of the consequences if they do not. Even the prime minister's annual work report is a detailed account of the extent to which his government has met quantitative targets in myriad areas. Most other countries' officials do not feel the same performance pressure, as anyone who has spent time in India or the Philippines can testify.[22] That is why Chinese roads get built mostly to high standards, and Indian roads do not.

---

[22] In this discussion "merit" means ability and willingness to get a job done. The question is whether jobs and rewards go to people who can and do perform. Shih uses it in the narrow sense of raising a unit's economic growth. I use it in a broader sense of getting assigned tasks done. It means that, as in GE or any other performance-based institution, the typical person or team gets promoted, demoted, or fired on the basis of achieving assigned tasks. As in any Western company, perceptions of loyalty factor into every assessment of performance. A quite different definition of meritocracy is equality of opportunity across society. Does the poor farm kid from Anhui have equal opportunity compared with the rich kid from Beijing? On that score China, like the United States, scores

The situation these US political scientists describe characterizes Argentina or Zimbabwe; it has no resemblance to China. While it is the central thesis of this book that China is experiencing a profound economic and political crisis, it is not helpful to our understanding, or to Western policy, to obscure the system's strengths, which include above all its performance-oriented management. Similar strength has been, after all, one of the reasons why post-transition Taiwan and post-1979 crisis South Korea have become such resilient democracies. During their early rapid economic rise, the failure of Western media and scholars to recognize their underlying governance strength was the central reason why so many US officials and politicians advocated abandoning South Korea on the fallacious grounds that it might be another South Vietnam. (South Vietnam conspicuously lacked those strengths.) Getting this wrong can lead to policy tragedy.

Views of the China Model

While there is an unpublished economist counterpart of the political science fallacy described above,[23] economists as a discipline have more effectively articulated the efficiencies of the Chinese system. The central government delegates most social functions to the provinces, which spend 70 percent of total government spending, with 55 percent spent below the provincial level. The central government maintains sovereignty, controls key national functions such as monetary policy, controls appointments of key officials, sets standards, establishes a coherent national organization and personnel system, and keeps the

---

badly, despite a history of belief in egalitarian opportunity. See Mark Elliott, "The Real China Model," *New York Times*, November 13, 2012, www.nytimes.com/2012/11/14/opinion/the-real-china-model.html.

[23] Professor Chang-Tai Hsieh, in a lecture given at Harvard in the spring of 2016, presented an argument complementary to the political science school criticized above. He explains China's economic growth solely through opportunities for corruption. Out of a variety of proffered deals, officials choose companies that they will shepherd through the impossible regulatory tangle. The officials help those companies to make money, and siphon off some of the wealth for themselves. That analysis cannot explain why the officials are competent and motivated to choose so many companies that succeed, why they work so hard (unlike their Indian counterparts) to bring in new companies rather than just squeezing old ones, and why China's supportive infrastructure and education have come to be so successful and supportive of profitable business.

country headed in the desired direction, namely economic reform in the service of economic growth.

The decentralization puts the burden of accountability for social services and local infrastructure on local officials, encourages local initiative, allows local field testing of new ideas, makes reforms more politically palatable because they have been tested successfully in one or more localities, and enables central leaders to encourage experimentation without having to take responsibility for failures. Xu Chenggang calls it "regionally decentralized authoritarianism," characterizes it as "a local experiment-based collective central decision making process," and finds that "Indeed, almost all successful reforms in the past three decades were introduced through local experiments."[24]

Xu accurately characterizes the competition among local governments at each level as occurring in a tournament-like atmosphere. Anyone who has dealt with Chinese officials has experienced this competitive spirit. In smaller, more homogeneous miracle economies, the competition was focused on companies and sectors rather than geographic units, but the effect was the same. In South Korea, the tournament-like atmosphere was created by having a dozen chaebol (huge conglomerates) competing, mostly in the same industries, within a limited domestic market. As with Chinese local governments, they competed not only against each other but also against very high targets set by the central leadership. In Japan, similar results were obtained in the car industry, where six major automobile companies competed within a relatively limited market as compared with three companies in the much larger US market.

As Xu notes, this broad Chinese system dates back to the Qin dynasty (third century BCE) and is largely responsible for the long stability of the most prominent Chinese dynasties.

The system has weaknesses, including weak rule of law, giving local leaders space for corruption, enabling local protectionism, risking loss

---

[24] Chenggang Xu, "The Fundamental Institutions of China's Reforms and Development," *Journal of Economic Literature* 49(4), 2011, pp. 1076–1151, www.aeaweb.org/articles.php?doi=10.1257/jel.49.4.1076. The Fung Global Institute report on the city of Foshan illustrates the model in detail: Geng Xiao, Zhang Yansheng, Law Cheung Kwok, and Dominic Meagher, "China's Evolving Growth Model: The Foshan Story," May 11, 2015, www.asiaglobalinstitute .hku.hk/en/chinas-evolving-growth-model-foshan-story/.

of central control, and focusing on one goal to the exclusion of other important values. I will return to those problems shortly.

Some political scientists have also looked at the model in similar ways. Daniel Bell has sought to characterize a general Confucian model of governance potentially applicable everywhere.[25] He focuses on the need to choose the best people as leaders while having some way to gain the assent of the governed. He takes as given the reality that in all the Asian miracle economies governments are evaluated by their people on the basis of substantive performance, not procedural correctness; if having proper elections in India leads to more babies dying and fewer people becoming literate, that would be unacceptable in China notwithstanding proper electoral procedure. He recommends a reformed system for China of "democracy at the bottom, experimentation in the middle, and meritocracy at the top." That general formula is partly a broad-brush characterization of the system now and partly a framework on which he recommends reforms to make China more meritocratic and also more democratically legitimate than it is today.

Bell arrives at this characterization by applying philosophical arguments about the weaknesses of Western democracy and the potential strengths of a government with a leadership chosen for substantive performance rather than just electoral procedure. He argues in favor of criteria like the Chinese examination system for ensuring that officials are competent, in addition to efforts to select officials with emotional intelligence. He argues that, regardless of its flaws, China's promotion system for officials was the primary reason why China's "poverty rate fell from 85 percent to 15 percent between 1981 and 2005, equivalent to 600 million people being lifted out of poverty." Although he refers to economic accomplishments, Bell's analysis proceeds without any reference to the economic literature; however, his analysis fits the economists' analysis of why China's economic performance is superior.

The criticisms that have been leveled at this model take two forms. One is that it does not fit China. The actual working of the Chinese system is too corrupt, there are too many backdoors to the personnel

[25] Daniel A. Bell, *The China Model: Political Meritocracy and the Limits of Democracy* (Princeton, NJ: Princeton University Press, 2015).

recruitment system, and so forth. The second is that it has had all sorts of failings, particularly regarding the environment.[26]

The first criticism is unbalanced, the second accurate but misstated. In any system, there are large deviations from the ideal type. If you are a foreigner reading about US democracy as described by Westerners sympathetic to the system, you have to note some harsh contrasts between the reality and the ideal type. The dominance of money politics is not at all what the founders had in mind, nor what the democratic ideal specifies. Virtually every Congressional district is gerrymandered to ensure that the incumbent is likely to be reelected. One major party seeks to win by making it difficult for poor people and minorities to register to vote or to actually vote (deliberately distant polling stations, long lines ...). The degree of corruption below the national level is often extraordinary. (I live in Boston, and some readers may have read recent headlines from Chicago.) The incarceration of more people than any other country in the world, heavily black males, does not fit the ideals of freedom. The candidates thrown up during the primary campaigns for election in 2016 were mostly inexperienced, ideological, or unprincipled people – not the sort of people that one would want running a nuclear weapons state. The inadequacies of the system have led youth and much of the middle class to revolt against the establishment (via the Trump and Sanders campaigns in 2016). And much else is wrong. But for all the enormous problems the system has served its core purpose well for two centuries, aggregating complex interests into a government with great legitimacy and choosing administrations in a way that mostly preserves the peace in a very diverse society, maintains a high degree of personal freedom, and has so far built extraordinary prosperity. For all its flaws it achieves the main purposes it was designed to accomplish to a degree that no alternative system has achieved.

Similarly, if you read about investment banks, you read, accurately, that their shenanigans were a core cause of the Global Financial Crisis. The extremes to which investment bankers will go to earn huge bonuses are the stuff of (fully justified) righteous outrage and great

---

[26] Andrew J. Nathan makes these points eloquently, "Beijing Bull: The Bogus China Model," *The National Interest*, December 2015, http://nationalinterest.org/feature/beijing-bull-the-bogus-china-model-14107.

humor.[27] But the problems must never obscure the fact that they serve their core purpose, the allocation of capital in the most efficient ways known to human history. That function, successfully performed, is the core of the growth and resilience of modern US capitalism.

Likewise, for all its flaws, including corruption and damage to the environment, the mobilization system that characterizes the early Asian miracle economies, the economies of Singapore under Lee Kwan Yew, South Korea under Park Chung Hee, Taiwan under Chiang Kai-shek and his son, and China under Deng Xiaoping and his immediate successors, performs the core task that it was designed for. No other system in world history has ever lifted so many people out of poverty so quickly and done so for virtually the entire population. No other system in world history has ever extended longevity so much and so quickly, increased the population's health and physical stature so quickly, expanded education and opportunity so widely and quickly, improved farmers' lives so rapidly, or increased workers' wages and working conditions so quickly. The contrast with India and the Philippines, and much of the time Thailand, which have systems of governance that the United States prefers, could hardly be more dramatic. Even when India and the Philippines grow faster, the benefits of income and health do not filter down to the broader population in the same way.

These "miracle" systems all began as leftist, Leninist, and authoritarian. (I will eschew an extended comment on Japan, which was fundamentally different because it was a revival of an educated middle-class society, not the initial creation of one. But its postwar success also depended on the creation of a system where an entrenched elite could impose reforms with only the illusion of risk that it would be displaced by democratic elections, and implementation of the miracle in the crucial years of 1955–1975 entailed enormous corruption and damage to the physical environment.) In these systems, both the economic structure and the political structure are designed to promote economic growth as an absolute priority, meaning a priority at great expense of all other goals.

---

[27] The works of Michael Lewis are the pinnacle of such literature. They are factual and insightful as well as wonderfully written. See particularly *Liar's Poker* (New York: W. W. Norton, 1989) and *The Big Short* (New York: W. W. Norton, 2010).

Notwithstanding the abuses in investment banks, when one visits an investment bank one sees dozens or hundreds of the world's best-trained accountants poring over the accounts of companies in order to recommend which ones to buy, which ones to sell, which ones to merge. Likewise, when one watches the workings of officials in China, at all levels they are trying to achieve the goals set for them in order to get bonuses and get promoted – or, at the top, to go down in history as one of those who saved the nation. Wherever one looks in China, officials are trying to make their numbers. In Foshan, when the promotion system changed to incorporate environmental goals, the capacity of waste-water treatment facilities became greater than the capacity of waste-water transport facilities.[28] That excess happens because of distorted incentives, but the important thing is that, beneath all the distortions and deviations, the incentives are effective.

At Harvard, when I met Lee Yuanchao, currently China's Vice President, he was Party Secretary of Nanjing and had been told to plan a doubling of the size of the city. He was focused on that task and, among other things, wanted advice on how to attract more foreign direct investment to Nanjing. He was not by training an economic planner, and in fact his previous assignment was as China's youngest ever Vice Minister of Culture, but his focus and performance were outstanding. That made him a candidate to be China's top leader; facing exceptional competition and factional problems, he ended up as Vice President. Factional politics played a key role in which job he got, as it would at GE. But every candidate for every top position had to have accomplished important tasks during a career of very broad experience – much broader than the typical US counterparts.

The same thing happens at the provincial level. When Bo Xilai became Party Secretary of Chongqing, he cracked down hard on corrupt gangs, to considerable initial applause,[29] but the crackdown had unintended consequences for his ability to meet his assigned objectives. The crackdown led to a large-scale exodus of "gray money" (i.e., illegally obtained funds) from the city, and it turned out that much of the capital in the city had been gray money. That left him short of

---

[28] This finding came out in a Fung Global Institute seminar on the circular economy.

[29] Later there were credible allegations that he ignored legal procedures and ruthlessly cracked down on political opponents. That is important to understanding his later fall, but tangential to the point of this paragraph.

what he needed to reach his goals, and if he fell short he would not be a serious candidate for the Politburo Standing Committee. That in turn led to desperate compensatory efforts to raise money, including the licensing of 64 private equity funds. As part of a small financial group, I briefly controlled the license for one of those private equity funds.

The mayor of Chongqing, who survived the downfall of Bo Xilai because of his extraordinary competence, is as cosmopolitan and intellectually engaging as anyone I have ever met. Lunch with him was an intellectually uplifting experience. He had previously planned the successful modernization of Shanghai's extraordinary Pudong district (whose modernity no US city equals) and, with Bo Xilai's support, he has accomplished almost equally dramatic modernization. The extraordinary events around Bo Xilai's downfall, and the competence of his people and the reverence with which his economic/managerial performance was regarded by most people in Dalian and Chongqing, are both essential parts of the story of reformist China. The mayor's survival of his boss's downfall, due to sheer competence, is also a crucial part of the story. Both Bo Xilai and Mayor Huang had extraordinary motivation to perform and that performance ethic was responsible, notwithstanding the dramatic political upheaval and corruption that occurred, for the considerable economic and social success that ensued.

Finally, the obsession with economic growth to the exclusion of concern for the environment and other values is not an inherent part of the longer-term China model. As I noted in the first chapter, it is appropriate to call the initial fear-driven, economics-obsessed Asian miracle model a "mobilization system." All the Asian miracle economies have started with a mobilization system obsessively focused on economic growth, then pivoted to concern for the environment, debt, and other issues when, through the brief era of the mobilization system, their people had acquired the basic necessities of a decent existence – food, shelter, health, education – and environmental problems had reached a crescendo. The model is, as Bell notes, the same basic model as governance of the Catholic Church. He might have added that it is the same basic model as the governance of Harvard University – a mostly self-perpetuating elite at the top, with well understood but often not explicitly articulated criteria for quality; a diverse, experimenting, decentralized middle subject to powerful quality controls and meritocratic personnel procedures; and a rambunctious bottom with aspects of democracy and aspects of rebellious demonstrations.

The meritocratic system can continue after the economic mobilization phase is over, beginning to address environmental, debt, and other issues that previously had less priority. Moreover, it is a mistake to assert, as Andrew Nathan does, that environmental problems are functions either of the mobilization system or the ongoing meritocratic system or of specific failings of the Chinese system. As noted in the previous chapter, London's air pollution problem was far worse than Beijing's is. India's air pollution today damages human health far more than China's does – by a multiple.[30]

The key problem with Bell's Confucian model is the same as the problem with the Washington Consensus. The attempt to come up with a single model that fits all societies at all levels of development is doomed to failure. The mobilization system, with its single-minded emphasis on growth, is the most efficient model in history for improving the human condition, but it works only for a very small number of societies and for a very limited period of time even in those. Western democracy is the most effective model yet discovered for expanding human dignity and prosperity in educated middle-class societies. Bell's model does not adequately specify how the top leaders are to be chosen, how the extraordinarily complex conflicting interests of a modern society are to be aggregated, or how unsatisfactory leaders are to be deposed. Likewise, the effort to impose on the poorest societies a model designed for educated, middle-class, modern societies often defeats the goal of creating a government of the people, by the people, for the people – as we shall see below. There is no universal model.

The Democratic Alternative

If the argument that China's governance structure does not lead to superior performance at early stages of economic development is fatuous, the argument that democracy would do better at the earliest stages of development is equally a triumph of faith over facts. No extremely

---

[30] The standard reference is the Yale Environmental Performance Index. In 2012, it published comparative data for China and India. For example, on a scale of 0 to 100, where 0 is the worst impact of air pollution on human health, China scored 46.3 while India scored 3.7. That is not a misprint – 46.3 versus 3.7.

poor county has developed as rapidly and fairly under democracy as the Asian miracle economies under early authoritarian rule.

The outstanding example of a poor country with outstanding democratic institutions was the post-World War II Philippines, and its fate is the template for many others.[31] The United States spent half a century perfecting Philippine democracy. At independence the Philippines scored higher on indices of development than the colonies of every other country. Filipinos had more roads (per 100 square kilometers), communications, literacy, secondary education, newspaper circulation (per 1,000 inhabitants), steel consumption, electricity consumption, and income than other decolonized nations.[32] Only in railroads, understandably for a country of islands, did the Philippine statistics lag. Manila was the hub of Asia for business and for transport, playing the role that Singapore and Hong Kong play today; if an American wanted to visit Hong Kong, Singapore, Malaya, or Thailand, the route lay through Manila's superior facilities.

Before World War II, any Filipino family of substance had a Japanese gardener. When I lived in the Philippines in 1963–1964, every family of substance had an amah from impoverished Hong Kong for housekeeping and child care. To get slightly ahead of my story, by the time I lived in Hong Kong (1985–2001 and 2013–2015) even our secretaries had Philippine maids; whereas the Filipinos had referred to maids by the Cantonese term *amah*, a generation later the Hong Kong Chinese term, and the term in much of more developed Asia, for a housemaid had become *filipina*.

Perhaps even more importantly in American eyes, and proudly in Filipino eyes, the new country had well-established freedom, democracy, and a modern judiciary. The press was vigorously free – no censorship, no intimidation of reporters, multiple views. People said

---

[31] A version of this account of the Philippines, with somewhat different emphasis, was published while this book was under review as William H. Overholt, "Duterte, Democracy, and Defense," Brookings Institution, January 31, 2017, www.brookings.edu/research/duterte-democracy-and-defense/.

[32] See Fred R. von der Mehden, *Politics of the Developing Nations* (Englewood Cliffs, NJ: Prentice-Hall, 1969), pp. 12–18. The author ranks the indices according to the colonial power. Since the United States had only one colony, namely the Philippines, the US column always presents the Philippine numbers. Von der Mehden's indices date from the time of independence of each country; since the Philippines became independent long before the others, his ranking greatly underestimates the superiority of the Philippines.

whatever they thought without fear of government repression. Elections were free, and until the Marcos-distorted election of 1986 there was never doubt that each successive president was the person who had actually won the most votes. With a US-style two-party system, the two parties alternated in power, demonstrating that the process of campaigns and elections actually operated according to democratic principles. Church and state were separate – reversing the situation under colonial Spain. The courts were independent and operated on American adversarial principles, implementing laws that were either inherited from American democracy or passed by a democratically elected Philippine legislature. Particularly noteworthy among newly independent countries was that the military was firmly subordinate to civilian government. This was the ultimate third-world democracy.

As in other poor nations, elections gave the elite an overwhelming advantage. The landlords were well organized and got themselves elected to Congress. The peasants on their lands had no comprehension of how to organize and assert their interests. They voted as their landlords told them to do, until the point where they became so angry that they joined the communist guerrillas or the Muslim guerrillas. The elite was so confidently entrenched (there was none of the fear present in the Asian miracle economies) that it had no incentive to invest in modernizing the country; the income tax was initially the world's lowest, at 4 percent. There was no possibility of land reform. No impoverished democracy – with the partial exception of Costa Rica – has ever done a serious land reform. As in India, there were high-quality subsidized institutions of higher education for the elite (University of the Philippines, the IITs in India), but the outstanding education that was the US legacy steadily deteriorated for the non-elite. As in India, the Philippines developed world-class hospitals for the elite, but medical care for the bottom of society was drastically inferior.

The finest of the democratic institutions bequeathed by the United States to the Philippines was the legal system. It developed furthest and best because it was Filipinized earlier than other parts of the government.[33] A United States governed by lawyers ensured that the Philippine legal profession was highly developed in numbers, in standards of

[33] For a history of the development of Philippine government institutions, see Onofre D. Corpuz, *Bureaucracy in the Philippines* (Manila: Institute of Public Administration, 1957). On the importance of the early Filipinization of the judiciary see p. 164.

admission to the bar, and in public respect. The pinnacle of the profession was the courts, which were independent. The Supreme Court, like its US counterpart, had the (frequently exercised) power to review the decisions of the executive and legislative branches. In short, the judicial system had competence, prestige, and power.

What it could not do was to provide justice. In America's educated middle-class society the citizen at least has some chance of understanding and functioning within the adversarial system and the layers and layers of complex rules and precedents designed to ensure a fair trial. In a society that combined extensive poverty with extreme inequality and limited education, the typical citizen had no ability whatsoever to comprehend what was happening in the legal system or to afford a lawyer who did. Most people were landlords or tenants, and the complexity and cost of the system provided an almost complete monopoly of power to the landlord. At the height of the Communist Huk rebellion, Luis Taruc, the Huk leader, derived much of his personal popularity from his simple efforts to mediate between landlords and tenants,[34] a task the very sophisticated judicial system was incapable of performing. As the Huk challenge reached its zenith, President Ramon Magsaysay, recognizing the inability of the legal system to deliver justice to the majority, got legislation passed to engage the legal department of the army on behalf of the tenant farmers. This redressed the social balance somewhat and changed the tone of relations between government and impoverished citizens – a key initiative contributing to the defeat of the Huks. However, as soon as Magsaysay was gone, and the Huk challenge suppressed, the system reverted to its old imbalance. The law allowed the army lawyers to intervene only in certain varieties of lawsuits, and the landlords quickly learned that they could counter a peasant complaint by bringing counter-charges of a kind that were

---

[34] This comment is based on personal research. I spent the summer of 1967 doing interviews about the Huks. I spent over 30 hours interviewing Taruc in jail, along with Huk leaders who were not in jail, the top military leaders, scholars, reporters, and many others. After Taruc's release from prison he spent much of his time advising tenants on their problems; in the Marcos era he did so as an employee of the Department of Agrarian Reform. I kept in touch with him whenever I was in the Philippines. CIA operative Edward Lansdale, correctly, refers to Taruc as an "idealist." See Edward Lansdale, *In the Midst of Wars* (New York: Harper and Row, 1972), p. 6. Taruc's idealistic reformism did not, however, deter the Huks from many acts of bloody brutality, including terrorist attacks on clerics and church attendees.

outside the purview of the Army Judge Advocate. The elaborate, tortuous, expensive machinery designed in America to prevent any slight infringement of due process actually ensured injustice for the vast majority of the population.

The intricate US system was almost as helpful to criminals as it was to landlords. The US system was designed to protect all the rights of the accused. The principle that someone is innocent until proven guilty translates into a strong preference for the system to err on the side of not risking any conviction of an innocent person, rather than on the side of convicting most guilty people. In a poor country where the police had limited resources and limited training, while much of the judicial system tried to uphold US standards of proof, this meant that it was exceedingly difficult to convict a criminal. Particularly in conjunction with rampant elite corruption, this meant that criminality of all kinds was rampant. It was of course particularly difficult to convict powerful, rich criminals, who could afford lawyers as fine as any in the world to do combat with an impoverished judicial system. The country had an atmosphere of lawlessness.[35] The same comments apply to India.

In India and the Philippines, as well as elsewhere, electoral democracy has empowered an economic elite at the cost of terrible deprivation for the bottom of society. Even when the elite gets organized for growth, the bottom of society often gets few or none of the benefits; the bottom three quintiles of Philippine society today live little better than they did two generations ago.

In the 1950s this perfect third-world democracy had to be rescued by the CIA from a communist movement that had Manila surrounded. In the 1960s, outrage against the inequality, corruption, crime, and general failure of development built up and eventually led to broad public support, particularly from the middle class, for a brilliant but flawed demagogue, Ferdinand Marcos, who promised to follow the outlines of the Asian miracle economies. He imposed martial law in the early 1970s, and promised to impose discipline, effect a land reform, build good infrastructure, create conglomerates like those of South Korea, collect the guns that were even more pervasive in the Philippines than

---

[35] My research assistant sought official crime statistics data, but was told that the information was unavailable unless I paid a bribe. I would have willingly paid a fee, but since the word bribe was used in the conversation I've had to do without the needed data.

in the United States, and reduce crime and inequality. For a while he was famous for building the roads with real cement, and Philippine society filled with real hope. But in the end his "disiplina" (signs saying "Disiplina" were posted everywhere) was a way of disarming his opponents, his initially high-quality infrastructure building petered out, his conglomerates were crony monopolies (over 200 of them) rather than fiercely competitive, his land reform turned into a power play,[36] he emphasized heavy industry rather than labor-intensive industry because it offered more squeeze, and in consequence he accelerated the exploitative decline that he had promised to reverse.

Marcos's chief opponent was Benigno ("Ninoy") Aquino. Ninoy was politically a disciple of South Korea's Park Chung Hee. Like most Asian political leaders, and far more than most, he was eloquent in articulating the values of democracy. But he had been a young journalist in South Korea at the beginning of his career, and in every conversation I had with him he reverted to an awed description of how, at a time when the Philippines was relatively rich, South Koreans were hungry and the country "had no exports." (His words, frequently repeated.) His concrete program for national revival was modeled on Park's. When I asked him what he needed politically to achieve his goals, he said, multiple times on multiple occasions, "Three years of full power." He knew that reforms would have to be imposed. (The Asian miracle economies typically take off into high growth three years after new leadership begins to impose reforms.) He would have been a tough leader, as tough as Marcos, and his toughness would probably have earned opprobrium from the West, but in my judgment he would have followed through and saved his country.[37]

Before Aquino returned to the Philippines he spent over three hours with me and my family explaining why he believed he could return and Marcos would not kill him. He said that killing him would be just like the right-wing Nicaraguan regime's killing a Sandinista publisher. "It would cause a revolution, and I would play a bigger role in Philippine history than I ever would alive. Marcos is smart enough to know that."

[36] For an account of the Marcos land reform, see William H. Overholt, "Land Reform in the Philippines," *Asian Survey* 16(5), 1976, pp. 427–451.
[37] In the interest of full disclosure, I was deeply involved in the events recounted here. Some details are given in the footnotes of my article, "Duterte, Democracy and Defense," Brookings Institution, January 31, 2017, www.brookings.edu/research/duterte-democracy-and-defense/.

When Aquino landed in Manila, Marcos was incapacitated and Aquino was assassinated while deplaning – on the orders of General Fabian Ver. The second pledge to emulate the Asian miracle economies died with him.

A broad coalition won the 1986 election for Aquino's wife, Corazon Aquino, who came to power amid a universal expectation of reform and development. A group centered around Minister of Finance Jaime Ongpin sought to turn the Philippines into the next Asian miracle. I wrote much of the broad strategy. Ongpin searched the world for best practice on everything from bank regulation to civil aviation regulation and sent draft rules and legislation and appointments to President Aquino. In virtually every case, President Aquino's Executive Secretary, Joker Arroyo, rejected the reforms in her name and replaced them with patronage political appointments under rules designed to defeat the purposes of reform. The new civil aviation rules were rejected in favor of an improperly constituted board dominated by three of Joker's cronies. A proposed outstanding appointment to run the Philippine National Bank was replaced by a Joker crony who had just been served the maximum fine for infringing the bank regulations. Land reform was limited because the new president was not about to jeopardize her control of, and profits from, the great family sugar plantation, Hacienda Luisita. Joker Arroyo was trying to reconstitute the Marcos monopoly system using an institution called the Presidential Commission on Good Government. Gradually the reformists were depleted. For instance, the reformist Minister of Transport and Communications was forced to resign because he had fired one of the President's relatives for massively defrauding the national shipping line.

Eventually Ongpin asked me to make one last appeal for reform. Using a subterfuge, because she was surrounded by officials opposed to reform, I outlined what I thought was needed to create a fast-growing economy. She emphatically rejected my appeal and initially refused to address Joker Arroyo's actions, although she subsequently forced his resignation. Ongpin, his identity totally defined by his failed effort to modernize his country, subsequently committed suicide. The third effort at creating a miracle economy in the Philippines died. The cause of death was patronage politics.

There followed a series of corrupt, elitist presidencies, punctuated by the election of Joseph Estrada, a low-class, corrupt, foul-mouthed, womanizing actor whom the national majority saw as a potential antidote to the system's oppressive elitism. An elite coup, endorsed by the United States, overthrew him. The most important charge against him, for which he was threatened with the death penalty, was involvement in a form of illegal gambling called jueteng. As every knowledgeable person in the Philippines knew, the new President, Gloria Macapagal Arroyo, was supported by a family fortune built by her husband as a kingpin of that particular form of gambling in Bulacan Province. Her presidency ended in corrupt disgrace.

The best presidency of modern times was that of Corazon Aquino's son, Benigno Aquino III, who pursued an anti-corruption drive and achieved economic growth rates higher than any other Philippine presidency. But he too was a member of the elite. He refused land reform because it would have affected the Aquino family holdings in Hacienda Luisita. As always, the elite benefited from the growth but the majority of the population continued to live as it had decades earlier. According to one analysis, 40 families captured 76 percent of the growth benefits while 25 million Filipinos continued to earn less than one dollar per day.[38]

The people erupted again in anger and elected a replacement, Rodrigo Duterte, who promised bloodshed and extra-democratic measures. Accused by Human Rights Watch of supporting 700 extra-judicial killings, he said it was more like 17,000 and expressed a wish to make it 100,000. He said he would kill so many criminals that the fish in Manila Bay would all become fat. He calls himself a dictator. He has recommended that disabled people should commit suicide. Within several months of his taking office, there were just under 1,800 extra-judicial killings of alleged drug dealers and users.

Interestingly, his support is strongest among the educated middle class. Joshua Kurlantzick, a liberal, strongly democratic writer for the Council on Foreign Relations, summarizes the problem exactly as a

---

[38] See the data reported by a former planning minister to an Agence France-Press report in "Philippines' Elite Swallow Country's New Wealth," *Philippine Daily Inquirer*, March 3, 2013, http://business.inquirer.net/110413/philippines-elite-swallow-countrys-new-wealth. A more detailed account is Jillian Keenan, "The Grim Reality Behind the Philippines' Economic Growth," *The Atlantic*, May 7, 2013, www.theatlantic.com/international/archive/2013/05/the-grim-reality-behind-the-philippines-economic-growth/275597/. The data on the number of poor can be verified from national accounts. The 40 families number, although credible and from a credible source, needs scholarly verification.

Ferdinand Marcos advocate would have done in 1971: "Duterte's image rests on a popular perception ... that he is a blunt-talking strongman who will be able to resolve longstanding political challenges – corruption, high inequality, business cartels in many sectors, violent crime, the continuing banditry and insurgency in the south – more effectively than politicians who follow democratic norms and institutions."[39] The issues are exactly the ones that brought Marcos to dictatorial power in 1972 and Estrada to power a generation later. Meanwhile, Imelda Marcos has served repeatedly in the national legislature. The second-highest number of votes for Vice President went to Ferdinand ("Bongbong") Marcos, Jr. Duterte promised to move Ferdinand Marcos's body to a heroes' cemetery. To the shock of this writer, who nearly lost his life opposing Marcos, large numbers of middle-class Filipinos now look back to the Marcos years with reverence.

The cycle of extractive democracy seems inexorable, even in the freest, most carefully constructed democracy the United States has ever supported.

Likewise, in Thailand democracy empowered an urban elite who systematically exploited the rural and uneducated poor. These democracies are hideously corrupt without the compensating performance that characterizes the Asian miracle economies. Peasants and subsistence workers can't donate to political campaigns, so all campaign finance comes from bribes and self-financing; the self-financing part is much smaller and is everywhere seen as a financial investment to be recouped with profit once the candidate wins. When, shortly after the

---

[39] Joshua Kurlantzick, "A Turn Toward Authoritarianism in the Philippines?," *Asia Unbound*, May 4, 2016 4:15 pm, www.cfr.org/blog/turn-toward-authoritarianism-philippines. For other details, see Floyd Whaley, "Philippine Presidential Race Decends [sic.] into Sideshow Amid Serious Issues," *New York Times*, May 7, 2016, www.nytimes.com/2016/05/08/world/asia/philippine-presidential-race-devolves-into-sideshows-amid-serious-issues.html?mcubz=0; Miguel Syjuco, "Why Filipinos Are Voting for a New 'Dictator,'" *New York Times*, May 6, 2016, www.nytimes.com/2016/05/07/opinion/why-filipinos-are-voting-for-a-new-dictator.html?mcubz=0; Julio C. Teehankee and Mark R. Thompson, "Duterte and the Politics of Anger in the Philippines," *East Asia Forum*, May 8, 2016, www.eastasiaforum.org/2016/05/08/duterte-and-the-politics-of-anger-in-the-philippines/; Richard Javad Heydarian, "The End of Philippine Democracy?," *Huffington Post*, April 11, 2016, www.huffingtonpost.com/richard-javad-heydarian/the-end-of-philippine-dem_b_9666998.html. Heydarian recommends that the Philippines need more (Western-style) democracy, and that recommendation certainly represents a consensus of Western expert opinion. Faith dominates facts.

Philippine revolution, I briefly advised on a Thai political campaign, the campaign of outstanding leader Air Chief Marshall Siddhi Savetsila, I was shocked to discover that, except for self-financing, there was no campaign finance in any of the campaigns other than bribes – zero. When I suggesting changing the system, the campaign managers went out and spent the entire campaign war chest bribing politicians from other parties so that the meddling American would have no space to persuade the boss to waste his money on a campaign based on policies. More recently Thai politics has been a struggle between a corrupt billionaire who can buy an election and the exploitative urban elite.

In societies at that level of development, Western-style electoral democracy legitimizes, perpetuates, and often enhances ruthless exploitation, corruption, and crime. Institutions – elections and Western-style courts – that in educated middle-class societies ensure a modicum of political influence for the poor have the unintended consequence in these societies of legitimizing further oppression. In tribal societies at that level of development, competitive elections often deepen tribal conflicts. When George W. Bush and Dick Cheney proclaimed victory after holding elections in Iraq and Afghanistan, they celebrated on the assumption that democratic elections would automatically lead to peace, mutual respect, and prosperity. Likewise when Hillary Clinton was celebrating the glories of the Arab Spring. Such failures are rationalized by an assumption that the US-promoted electoral strategy must have been right, just bungled by incompetent individuals or traduced by bad guys. Why the bad guys get such broad support is something the ancient Greeks understood well and articulated clearly, but thinking too much about the cycle of demagoguery and extractive democracy is not a politically correct subject.

This is where the inclusiveness theories of today's most celebrated development economists, Acemoglu and Robinson, go wrong. They are right about the importance of inclusiveness but do not understand the ways the Asian miracle economies deliver inclusive economic and social benefits. They do not understand that a Western electoral system in countries *at this level of development* often becomes a technique for legitimizing economic exclusion of the majority of the population – extractive democracy.

The West's devotion to democracy is based on an ultimate value of human dignity. When a set of procedures systematically disadvantages millions of people, making them prey for wealthy elites, leaving them hungry and illiterate, it does not serve the value of human dignity. It does not create government of the people, by the people, for the people. It legitimizes the opposite. No system has increased human dignity faster, or distributed it more fairly in extraordinarily impoverished societies, than the Asian miracle political economies.

At a higher level of economic development, the story is radically different, with difficult implications for China now that it is well on the way to creating an educated middle-class society. We shall come to that in the next chapter.

The Lessons

Bumping these various theories up against reality, the ultimate lesson is that there is no general model of development applicable to all societies. The Asian miracle model raises human dignity in the poorest societies faster and more broadly than any other model of governance in human history. If they are sincere about human dignity, Western elites have an obligation to acknowledge that and to tailor their actions appropriately. But it only works in societies with an advanced degree of national identity, simple economic structures, and intense fear of the kind experienced by South Korea after the Korean War, Taiwan after the Chinese civil war, Singapore after the traumatic separation from Malaya, and China after a hellish century. Only a handful of countries fulfill these prerequisites.

Laos, Cambodia, and most of the Middle East and Africa are not candidates for the Chinese/Asian miracle model because they lack the shared sense of national identity. India is not a candidate because it lacks the sense of intense common fear. The Philippines is not a candidate because US political interventions have saved it from domestic sources of fear and US military protection has saved it from international sources of fear.

Some will ascribe the differences in countries' performance to culture. While it would be foolish to discount completely the influence of culture, too often culture is the easy residual explanation for phenomena whose structural origin the commentator doesn't understand. Earlier I noted that Chinese and Indian preference for sons over daughters is usually ascribed to culture, whereas its structural roots are that, for survival, agricultural families on the edge of subsistence need every bit of muscle power they can get. When the structure changes, the "culture" gradually – very gradually – changes. Likewise with the cultural explanations of economic development. Some experts who should know better ascribe the success of Confucian societies to the fact that Koreans and Chinese are "hard working." But visitors to Korea before 1961 found Koreans indolent and indifferent to time. Visiting big Chinese SOE factories in 1982 I found a lot more smoking and joking than hard work. When the structure of incentives changed, peasants, industrial workers, and officials all changed their work habits. Filipinos, Malaysians, and Indonesians share a common cultural background; in fact Filipinos migrated from the area that is now Indonesia. Indonesians' economic behavior has been strikingly different under Sukarno, Suharto, and the current democratic regime. The Malaysian economy follows a trajectory like Japan's because the structure of the political economy – a dominant political coalition gradually serving the political establishment more and the country less – is like Japan's. The Philippines performs like a poor Latin American economy not primarily because Spanish culture influenced both places but because the structure of the political economy is similar.

The US/EU model of electoral democracy carries human dignity to the highest level yet achieved by humanity – for economically and socially advanced societies. When applied to impoverished societies with non-elite populations that lack the ability to organize in their own interest, it can bring additional privation, strife, and injustice to the very people that the ideal of equal political rights is supposed to help. Such people are confused and helpless when subjected to a competitive political process and a complex, expensive adversarial judicial process in which they have no capability to uphold their interests.

The political economy of development is more like engineering than like physics. In engineering, it is impossible to create a single model of bridge that will provide transport over every kind of gap for every kind of river, mountain, swamp, and underpass. Having one model of democratic process and courts is like imposing only one kind of bridge for all the geographies of the world. The analogy to physics is the possibility of articulating a more fundamental concept of human dignity and giving it serious empirical content in a particular situation, then trying to build a bridge between the ideal of dignity and the reality of each particular situation.

A policy that attempts to impose the same institutions in every situation is an ideology, an ideology with a pejorative connotation, not a coherent philosophy of human dignity. In most of the Cold War era, Maoist China pursued an ideological policy, trying to impose its ideas on everything in the world, from China to Tanzania to Indonesia to the University of California, Berkeley. In contrast, with its ideology constrained by Cold War realities, the United States pursued a policy of political pragmatism built around economic development. Americans held their noses at the leftist authoritarianism of South Korea, Taiwan, and Singapore, in the interest of geopolitics, but then discovered that they had achieved both geopolitical success and democratic human dignity. The outcome of these polar opposites was an overwhelming triumph for the pragmatic United States and an extraordinary isolation and defeat for an ideological Chinese nation.

The Manichean mentality prevalent in the United States interpreted the democratic success of South Korea and Taiwan as a struggle between good guys and bad guys, but the ultimate democratic success can only be understood as part of a developmental process that built on the earlier regimes' construction of an educated middle-class society. It is a great irony that the most resilient, effective democracies in the developing world are Taiwan and South Korea, because those democracies built on the foundations of middle-class, educated, relatively egalitarian societies created by the Asian miracle approach to political economy. Achieving an educated, middle-class, relatively egalitarian society does not guarantee the triumph of democracy, but it does facilitate the success of democracy once it is tried. It is one of political economy's great ironies that the most reliable path from catastrophic poverty to market capitalism and real democracy leads through an authoritarian, protectionist planned economy. This has been hard for both ideological democrats and free market ideologues to acknowledge and digest.

Of great importance to our geopolitical considerations later is that one of the great myths of the transition of Taiwan and South Korea to successful democracy is that it happened because of US pressure, and therefore the pressures for democratization would not operate in China in the same way. Having been deeply involved in South Korea's transition, and having been a close observer of Taiwan's transition (with considerable inside access), I can testify that the power of US influence in these cases is a conceit, not a reality. The United States did nag both about human rights and democracy. From beginning to end, as when Park Chung Hee launched his coup against the hapless democratic government in May 1961 and President John F. Kennedy ordered Park's troops back to the barracks, South Korean leaders did exactly what they thought was good for their country. In Taiwan, US influence was greatest before it cut off economic aid in the 1960s. After that, it was greater before it severed the alliance and terminated diplomatic recognition in 1979. The transition to democracy came in the 1980s as a result of domestic pressures. What is true is that the US example of democracy was a beacon for leaders looking for a way to stabilize their countries in the midst of rising political complexity and social mobilization. The military and political hostility of the United States makes it less likely that China will follow a similar path, because it makes acceptance of democracy look like a geopolitical defeat under hostile foreign pressure.

Democracy does better at facilitating development than African tribal kleptocracies, Soviet totalitarianism, Middle Eastern theocracies, and Latin American caudillos. Moreover, a democratic election, whatever the long-term aftermath, is often the most peaceful way to resolve a great national crisis that might otherwise lead to civil war. But there are situations where an Asian miracle economy or a benign military dictatorship or a Yugoslav Tito can do much better. Shock therapy in either economic development or political democratization is almost always advocated by the West and rarely successful. Not infrequently, as in post-Soviet Russia, it becomes a form of extreme human rights abuse. None of the successful Western countries developed either their economies or their polities through shock therapy; none would ever tolerate it at home.

After the Cold War, the United States and China switched places, with China adopting a pragmatic foreign policy and the United States becoming far more of an ideological proselytizer. There is a Washington Consensus that disregards all the lessons of Western gradual institutional development and that has often been devastating for a developing economy where it has been tried – and catastrophic economically, socially, and politically for Russia and for several Muslim countries. In contrast, there is no Beijing Consensus, despite some Western political scientists inventing a fictitious one. China learned its lesson from the Maoist years. As Deng said in domestic policy, but also applied to reformist foreign policy, "It doesn't matter whether a cat is black or white as long as it catches mice." After the first years of reform there is not a single instance of China trying to impose its model on any other country. (It does seem to have a soft spot for hapless socialists from Venezuela, Cuba, and Zimbabwe, which waste an inordinate amount of Chinese money, but it never seeks to impose such systems.) The consensus in Beijing is that it is a mistake to try to impose any particular foreign model on a country. This gives China a very substantial foreign policy advantage over the United States, especially in Africa. China's soft power disadvantage, of course, is that most countries do not perceive Chinese domestic politics, particularly now, as uplifting. Most do see democracy as an attractive ultimate goal.

We shall return to the difficult issue of the China model in a more advanced society, but first we need to characterize China's current situation.

5 | China's Political Economy under Xi Jinping

China's political economy has evolved rapidly. Under Deng Xiaoping and Jiang Zemin rapid economic and political reform occurred. Politically, China underwent a revolutionary change from a system characterized by permanent class struggle and an ideal of dictatorship by society's underclasses (workers and peasants) to an ideal of rule by an educational and technological elite in the interests of a harmonious middle-class society. It evolved from an increasingly arbitrary dictatorship under Mao, and mostly wise informal dictatorship under Deng, to a bureaucratic technocracy under collective leadership. Jiang Zemin and Zhu Rongji shared power, and in turn they were accountable to a broader Politburo Standing Committee. The military went from being the ultimate source of power ("Political power grows out of the barrel of a gun" – Mao) to a powerful pressure group that was nonetheless under firm Party control. Popular compliance with government policies, once based on direct control of farmers working in communes and workers in directly controlled enterprises, came to be based much more on support generated by economic improvement; there were still harsh penalties for disobedience, but even in the universities after the early 1990s the government received strong support in response to general improvement of living conditions.

These were not marginal refinements; rather they were transformational political developments. If they had happened suddenly, they would be consistent with most definitions of revolution: drastic change in personnel, institutions, ideas, and policies. The formula of many Western commentators, that China is an example of economic development without political development, is therefore nonsense. (The inaccurate saying is really implicit shorthand for "China hasn't undergone democratic shock therapy." It reflects the Manichean ideological view dominant in the West.)

The various reforms of the Jiang Zemin–Zhu Rongji era saved China's financial system from collapse, ensured central control of the money supply and defeated inflation, cemented the central government's and Party's ability to move generals and fire provincial governors, and limited corruption through the reforms delineated in the previous chapter. The stress of those reforms, particularly the tens of millions of job changes attendant upon state-owned enterprise (SOE) reforms and downsizing of the government, left Chinese society exhausted. So many groups had experienced so much change and anxiety that there was overwhelming demand for different leaders with a different agenda.

In response to the exhaustion, the newly emerging leadership run by provincial bureaucrats chose to focus on harmony rather than stressful marketization, thus letting both market economic and political reform stagnate for a decade (2003–2012). When the new leadership took office in 2003, there was considerable optimism about fundamental political reform. Before Hu Jintao took office, he was President of the Central Party School, and the Central Party School at the end of his tenure was studying different systems from all over the world for their strengths and weaknesses as models for China. Their research looked at Golkar in Indonesia and the Institutional Revolutionary Party (PRI) regime in Mexico as well as European systems and came up with high praise for the democratic socialist systems of Scandinavia. Top analysts proffered three alternative approaches to democratization, including one modeled on the Japanese system of factions within a dominant party, one based on the Taiwan model of gradual democratization from the bottom up with multiple parties, and one closer to the status quo with more elections inside the Party. At a 2001 conference with Central Party School officials, the school's leading political theorist stopped conversation by remarking at one point during a debate about Taiwan, "Well, we hate everything Lee Deng-hui did in cross-Straits relations, but we admire the way he reformed Taiwan's domestic politics." (Lee Deng-hui's presidency was the triumph of real democracy in Taiwan.) Some senior officials even spoke speculatively about a scenario of democratic reform that might someday allow Taiwan's Guomindang Party to win elections in a coastal province like Fujian, the mainland province closest to Taiwan. This obviously did not happen, however. Instead structural political reforms and economic market reforms lagged for a decade.

Governance became sluggish. Hu Jintao had just one vote out of nine, so sometimes decision-making seemed as slow and fuzzy as the US Supreme Court. Jiang Zemin, the previous president, was allowed to stay on for two years as head of the military; he used that position and his influence over many key officials to weaken Hu Jintao and stymie many of his initiatives. According to some Chinese scholars, Hu Jintao himself was impaired by severe diabetes that turned him from what those scholars describe as previously a lively figure into a droning bureaucrat.

As China prepared for a new leadership in 2013, it was clear that the new leadership would face a huge reform deficit. The reforms detailed in the economics chapter entailed a return to great social stress but now in a context of interest groups that were much larger, much more confident, much better organized, and much better funded than they had been under Jiang Zemin and Zhu Rongji. The reforms would undermine the finances and damage the political clout of every major interest group in China.

- Leveling the playing field for SOEs and private enterprises would take away the most important privileges of the SOEs.
- Reduction of SOE overcapacity would involve laying off tens of millions of workers.
- Eliminating the SOEs' special advantages would hurt every major bank in China, because the SOEs were the principal customers of the banks, and money was lent precisely because of their privileges.
- Freeing interest rates meant that interest rates would rise, damaging the financial positions of the highly indebted SOEs and local governments. (Interest rates have officially been freed already, but informal constraints remain.)
- The combination of higher interest rates, requirements to provide social services to rural migrants, and tighter control of off-budget spending would potentially cripple local governments' ability to finance themselves.
- Environmental standards would reduce the profitability of large and small enterprises throughout China and force the closure of many of them.
- Marketizing the price of energy would drastically cut the income of the single most powerful lobby in China, the Petroleum Faction. (Energy prices have largely been freed, a difficult accomplishment made possible by the anti-corruption campaign.)
- Regulating the shadow banking sector properly would cut off funds to many enterprises, potentially bankrupt large numbers, and

potentially damage the finances of large numbers of citizens by curtailing Ponzi schemes and forcing the shadow banks to take responsibility for irresponsible wealth management products.[1]

- Market reforms would drastically reduce the power of Party and government officials.

- China's successful business leaders are terrified. China has been, and probably still is, the best place to make money. However, one can be successful only by doing deals with Party and government figures that make one vulnerable to future factional changes and to the anti-corruption campaign. Most successful business leaders want to get their money and family out of China. The middle class is rapidly following suit.

- The planned military upgrading involved reduction of the military by 300,000 soldiers and raising standards of equipment and training for the rest, which would antagonize many powerful officers. The growth of military budgets has been cut far more than the military leadership had expected.

In other words, if the reforms are all done quickly, they would encounter the simultaneous resistance of every powerful interest group in China. But they need to be done quickly. Growth based on exports and infrastructure investment could no longer drive economic growth. Rapidly rising SOE debts could cause a national crisis if they were not curtailed.

To put this in perspective, here is the position of the Foshan government in the Fung Global Institute study cited earlier. Its debt service (annual principal plus interest payments) exceeded 100 percent of tax revenues. The shortfall was covered by sales of land appropriated mainly from farmers. Under reform, the amount of land sales would have to decrease drastically, interest rates on the debt would rise, and the local government would have to provide social services

---

[1] Wealth management products entail a bank or shadow bank telling the customer that she can lend money directly to a company or group of companies and receive in return interest payments that would be much higher than bank interest payments. This kind of product helps China marketize financial services, and gets money to companies that might not have adequate access to bank loans. However, it also entails risk that the banks may encourage their customers to make loans that can never be paid back. That in turn could trigger social unrest. Regulators are trying hard to create rules that will make shadow banking safe without killing it.

(free education, medical help, pensions, unemployment benefits . . .) for the first time to rural migrants numbering half of the city's total population. Moreover, the new rules and scrutiny were certain to entail drastic reduction of local leaders' ability to undertake off-the-books obligations for projects that could not be fitted into their official budgets. This combination of bad news naturally stimulated tremendous anger and resistance in many localities, notwithstanding central government assurances that somehow they would find a way to turn the localities' bank debts into longer-term bonds with lower interest rates.[2]

Political Restructuring for the New Challenges

Knowing the need to overcome the opposition of nearly every major interest group, the senior leadership decided they needed to reform the entire leadership structure in order to meet the new challenges. Very early, they chose Xi Jinping, a strong personality polar opposite to the less energetic and less assertive Hu Jintao. They streamlined the Politburo Standing Committee, which is China's decision-making body, from nine senior leaders to seven. In choosing members of the leadership team, to make it easier to agree on decisions they eliminated both political extremes: they jailed the populist leader Bo Xilai,[3] and relegated the most determined political reformers, Lee Yuanchao and Wang Yang, to the second tier – in the Politburo but not the Standing Committee. Unlike the concession to his predecessor, Jiang Zemin, they did not allow Hu Jintao to remain as head of the military for two years; in compensation they persuaded Jiang Zemin, Hu's rival, to promise to step back and not exert so much influence over the new leadership. They also created new small leading groups, which coordinate policy among ministries at the highest level, and put Xi Jinping in charge of those. Moreover, Xi Jinping took over responsibility for some small leading groups that had been the responsibility of the Prime Minister.

[2] In August 2014 China amended the law that prohibited all direct borrowing by local governments.

[3] Bo Xilai was a very effective technocrat and is still beloved in Dalian and Chongqing for his many specific economic accomplishments, but he mobilized political support using Maoist slogans and Mao-era cultural campaigns, and pursued more statist, less law-based, and more egalitarian policies than the center of gravity of the national leadership. In addition, he was convicted of corruption and his wife was convicted of murder.

In other words, the new leadership team, with Xi Jinping clearly in charge, was given as much power as possible to act decisively.

The choice of Xi Jinping was intriguing. He had a limited political base, so the calculation seems to have been that the leadership would give him sufficient authority to implement policies against strong resistance but would be able to control him as necessary. It remains to be seen how the second part of that calculation will work out.

Having created a new leadership structure appropriate to the scale of the reform challenges, they launched the anti-corruption campaign. The campaign had two purposes, first to restore the legitimacy of the Communist Party by reducing rampant corruption and second to decimate opposition to the reforms. Not coincidentally, the initial major target of the reforms was Zhou Yongkang, the security chief and leader of the most powerful interest group opposing reform, the Petroleum Faction. Controlled energy prices meant there were billions of dollars to be made arbitraging the difference between market prices and administered prices, so the Petroleum Faction stood to lose extraordinary profits and influence from the reforms.

Western commentators have expended great energy questioning how Xi Jinping managed to grab so much power. The answer is that he did not grab it. He was given it because of the challenges the country faced. In the West, the tendency is to allow whatever reforms will fit through the sieve of the existing leadership and interest group structure – i.e., very limited, slow reforms. In an Asian miracle economy, the imperative is to revise the leadership structure pragmatically in order to fix the ills of the economy. (The Chinese, and some Western scholars, call this performance legitimacy as opposed to process legitimacy.)

While the initial centralization of power was a deliberate collective choice, it may have reached the point of diminishing returns. Xi is General Secretary of the Party, Chairman of the Central Military Commission, President of the country, Leader of the Central Leading Group on Foreign Affairs, Chairman of the Central National Security Commission, Leader of the Central Leading Group for National Defense and Military Reform of the Central Military Commission, Commander-in-Chief of the Joint Battle Command of the People's Liberation Army, Leader of the Central Leading Group on Taiwan Affairs, Leader of the Central Leading Group for Comprehensively Deepening Economic Reforms, Leader of the Central Leading Group for Financial and Economic Affairs, Leader of the Central Leading

Group for Internet Security and Informatization, and Chairman of the Central Commission for Integrated Military and Civilian Development. Each of these roles is highly demanding for any individual, and the costs of centralizing all of them in one person are substantial. Foreign diplomats complain that no discussion can move forward until there is a decision from the very top. Economists fear that crisis decisions, for instance over drastic moves in the stock market, are made without the normal consultation with bureaucratic experts. In other words, the new structure makes some important decisions too slow and others too fast. Scholars of development fear that the emphasis on top-down decision-making is smothering the bottom-up initiatives that have been key to China's growth success.

Moreover, Xi Jinping now refers to himself as the "core" of the leadership, a label that was given to Jiang Zemin when he was leading reform, and as "commander in chief" of the armed forces in addition to chairing the Central Military Commission. He has undermined the position of the prime minister, the role of the State Council (the cabinet), and some of the technocratic infrastructure built up by his predecessors. He has also decreed that criticism of his policies must be severely limited. If one understands that he was given his power, rather than having seized it, one also understands that the institutions that granted power can take it away. Like an executive at a big multinational, he has been given considerable leeway to fulfill his mandate. But China today is not the fragile, malleable institutional structure of Mao Zedong's time. If Xi does not deliver, or if he does too much damage in the course of delivery, he will be cut down. There will be a golden handshake, or a humiliation or worse, but not a return to Maoist personalism. Xi's personal power has damaged institutions like the State Council but not displaced them. He is supreme in the sense that he has ruthlessly eliminated obvious competition, but, at the time of writing, near the end of his first term, he has not yet demonstrated that he can decisively implement his policies.

The New Political and Economic Context

All these changes are occurring in a drastically changed context. While the economic challenges are universally acknowledged to be formidable, the systemic fear that characterized the Deng Xiaoping era and the Jiang Zemin–Zhu Rongji years has since evolved into confidence and even hubris. The simplified politics based on fear had segued into interest group politics on a vast scale. China's once relatively simple economy had become as complex as any economy on earth. The supportive conditions for the mobilization system have long vanished.

Chinese companies trade virtually every product made anywhere. They manufacture half of the world's steel and large proportions of its aluminum and cement. They extract and refine most of the world's rare earths. They use more copper, coal, and many other natural resources than any other economy. They sell more cars than any other country, and their car industry is far more intertwined with foreign car manufacturers than Japan's or South Korea's. They are becoming a leader in electric vehicles. They burn and transform more coal and oil than anyone else, but also are the world's leaders in solar, wind, and nuclear power. They have the world's largest e-commerce companies. Their SOEs demand support to consolidate into global champions, but their more dynamic private companies demand a level playing field. Crucially, Chinese companies have all the conflicts that occur anywhere – miners versus refiners, green energy versus traditional energy, users versus intellectual property holders, retailers versus wholesalers . . . ad infinitum.

As in South Korea and Taiwan, these economic interests were simply too complex to be aggregated and adjudicated by a Beijing bureaucracy. This was the point at which South Korea and Taiwan had to make major economic and governance changes. Shortly after the advent of the new century Chinese academics and leaders started expressing concern that the political power of these huge interests was so great that the center might lose its hard-won control over national policies. In short, the conditions for an Asian miracle economy, an Asian mobilization system, were no longer present. The meritocratic system that makes the Asian miracle economies so different from India and the Philippines could continue if the leadership sustained it. The leaders' legitimacy continued to be dependent on delivering improved living conditions. But the complexity revolution created a new era of both economics and politics.

An obsession with economic growth had created three decades of growth at 10 percent per year, longer than in any of the other miracle economies. This had given the Chinese people longevity, health, shelter, and education, but the single-priority obsession was beginning to have an unacceptable price. The environment was being destroyed, debt was rising to unacceptable levels, and overcapacity and excess inventories were overshadowing the economy. The growth obsession had reached diminishing returns. Henceforth the whole machinery of government, including all the incentives for officials, was going to have to be geared to multiple goals rather than one – another, particularly difficult kind of complexity.

The efficiency of the GE model of governance comes from its focus on one thing, growth, just as GE is primarily focused on one thing, profit. Judging officials in a balanced way, not just on growth but also on proper concern for the environment, prudent management of debt, elimination of local protectionism, fair treatment of private enterprises (even though officials' power and squeeze come from the state-owned sector), and orderly liquidation of excess debt, excess inventories, and overcapacity – all this would present a management challenge of overwhelming complexity even if China were socially and economically homogeneous. In reality, of course, conditions in different areas and different sectors are as variable as those in any place on earth.

All this complexity accumulated to the point where, in 2013, at the Third Plenum, the leadership declared its new central economic theme – market dominance of resource allocation. This was the latest in a series of decisions acknowledging that central control just couldn't manage efficiently – following such watersheds as the dissolution of the communes in the early 1980s and the declaration of a "socialist market economy" in October 1992. That organizing theme of market dominance demonstrated intellectual clarity and intellectual honesty – a sharp contrast with Soviet refusal to address the core problem of socialist inefficiency and an equally sharp contrast with the refusal of both US political parties to address the reality that manufacturing jobs are in a broad decline that will end in their virtual disappearance.

There is another side of the coin of this economic gigantism and complexity: each of the economic concerns is, equally, a political interest group. The political interest groups are now enormous; they have skills, money, diversity, and a scale of organization that was almost unimaginable when reform began. The conflicts of their leaders and spokespersons in the political realm mirror their conflicting economic interests. They form factions and varying alliances, just as they do in Washington, DC. The attenuation of the fear that characterized the earlier, mobilization phase of development liberates these interest groups to push with full energy for their narrower interests.

For ordinary people, the new situation is possibly even more transformative. When they were afraid of social collapse and family starvation, they were willing to put up with extraordinarily stressful measures. Countless families bore with stoicism having husband and wife separated by 1,500 miles for years at a time, having the whole town lose its jobs, and much else, in the hope that they and their children would have a better future. In short, they accepted being jerked around by the GE model the way senior executives do. In the GE model, or the investment banking model, the firm or the country does whatever it needs to do in order to maximize profit or growth. The firm lays people off, moves them around the country or the world, suddenly shifts them to different jobs. So does the country that is being run on the GE model. But executives at GE or at an investment bank are highly compensated, so they can absorb the changes. And, unlike in government, the single-minded focus of the firm on profit is accepted as legitimate.

These conditions are different for Chinese workers and Chinese middle-class families than they are for a senior executive or investment banker. They do not have a large financial cushion. They are frightened by big changes of career or location. They often do not accept having their apartment building ripped down for a factory and its occupants being moved to a distant high-rise apartment. Husbands and wives start to resist being sent to opposite ends of the country. They become aware of the health risks posed by the factory next door. In the West, comparatively tiny and gradual movements lead to the emergence of political movements like those of Bernie Sanders and Donald Trump. The stresses and the emotions run higher in China. And the West's big companies and banks are comparatively quite comfortable and complacent, whereas China's biggest institutions are the principal targets of painful reform.

Not only does frustration at being jerked around make people indignant. They find new things to be frustrated about. Once the basic needs of food, shelter, and health have been more or less satisfied, education becomes crucial – it is extraordinarily important in a Confucian society. Then people start sharing their opinions, including opinions about broader issues they never thought about before, and value their ability to share freely. Some become lawyers, and for many the law becomes a devoted vocation, not just a job. Some become journalists, and for many journalism becomes a devoted vocation, not just a job. After the cultural destruction of the bad years (described below), they start assembling in churches again, and for some the church becomes the center of their lives. Some become scholars and see their value in life as finding and communicating the truth. They are individually powerless and vulnerable, but, if challenged, a significant minority, those who are not just time-servers, begin to react as if their identities are at stake – because they are.

These groups not only become large, but also now have more education. In many cases they have rapidly rising incomes that are newly independent of the government. They can communicate through phones and email and WeChat, and they are now much more articulate in their communication. Working in industry rather than in single-family agriculture, and in large-scale modern industry rather than small-scale handicraft-style industry, they develop organizational and leadership skills. Suddenly society is composed of large, resourceful, highly organized groups. Political management of such a society requires just as much of a sea-change as management of the economy does.

In sum, as fear gives way to confidence, public willingness to accept great sacrifices declines, the willingness of leaders to take great risks declines, and resistance to the costs of reform comes to be led by newly powerful groups. The conditions of the Asian mobilization system are gone. A meritocratic system will still outperform a non-meritocratic system, but even there the residual GE model works only if it is modified to take account of more complex goals and social interests that demand to be heard.

The problem of reforming an economy so that it can continue to grow well in the presence of more highly organized interest groups affects a very broad range of economies, not just the Asian miracle economies. Economists call the slowdown that typically results the "middle-income trap." The economic literature has had considerable difficulty explaining why this happens – for two reasons. It is not an economic problem but rather a political interest group problem. And it is not a middle-income trap; Japan is in a "high-income trap" because big interest groups have immobilized reform at a higher level of income, and the Philippines has been in a low-income trap because its elite blocks the interests of the larger society.

In early-twenty-first-century China, the problem of dealing with the new interest group complexity is particularly intense. Earlier reformist leaders got the balance of centralization and decentralization right. They centralized control of the money supply, control of Party and government appointments, control of the military, and a broad strategy of economic development. They decentralized most farm and enterprise decision-making, responsibility for local social welfare, and decisions on the details of local growth-stimulating policies. By the end of the twentieth century this balance was working reasonably well, notwithstanding key problems such as a disjunction between local social responsibilities and local fund-raising authority. But under Hu Jintao and Wen Jiabao (2003–2013) the uncontrolled metastasis of the Party and government bureaucracies, the financial anomalies as local governments improvised to generate growth with inadequate budget authority, the emergence of vast bubbles (property, resources, industrial production) as the scale and pace of the economy outran the ability of planners to manage it, and the failure of the Hu–Wen government to keep implementing market and political reforms in sync with the economy's development all led to a sense of things spinning out of control.

The Xi administration is desperately trying to get things back under control. In this general enterprise, Xi has vast and deep public support. Likewise, Xi has enormous public support for the notion that economic complexity can be managed only by market allocation of resources. But the key to the future is whether his administration is centralizing the right things and decentralizing the right things, and whether it can actually implement the needed reforms.

The experience of other Asian miracle societies can provide some insights into what works and what doesn't in managing the new interest group environment. Unquestionably market allocation (i.e., decentralization) of resource allocation is the right decision if the government can implement it. In the political area, the balance is more dubious.

The Emergence of Powerful New Social Forces

Moral Vacuum and Religion

The political and social issues around religion provide a case study of some of the issues the Chinese regime faces in the new era. It therefore merits extended commentary. Religion is a powerful force in Chinese society. It has a particularly vital function in helping the Asian miracle societies recover from an era of moral vacuum. In the medium term, partial repression of religion strengthens the power of religious movements and maximizes the political cost to the regime.

The trauma and fear that lay behind the Asian miracle economies has typically destroyed the traditional social structure and much of its ideological or religious rationale. The Korean War and the century of disruptions in China smashed the traditional ruling structures and their Confucian rationales. The thoroughness of the destruction is the counterpart of the fear[4] that leads people to accept government policies that break with tradition and uproot their traditional habits, and even their current livelihoods, in the search for a better future for the society. In China, Mao's Cultural Revolution culminated and caricatured this process. The Cultural Revolution sought to destroy everything old, including much whose loss the entire society now mourns, and to create a new kind of society that turned out to be an old man's foolish fantasy. But the thoroughness with which it destroyed the old structures and discredited the fantasy created widespread public willingness to follow Deng Xiaoping's vision of a social order that was radically different both from old China and from Mao's fantasy.[5]

In each of the Asian miracle societies, economic progress and economic incentives created a new god: money. Rapid growth showed families who had previously worried about hunger, illness, illiteracy, and premature death that they could aspire to watches, televisions, air conditioners, cars, and fashionable clothing and shoes. It launched not just a nouveau riche class but a nouveau riche society. Obsession with money, and underdeveloped regulation, led also to every kind of cheating, scam, and fraud, from adulterated milk to financial Ponzi schemes.

---

[4] To recall a point from the first chapter, fear makes people willing to accept enormous stress from a leader who offers a convincing path to social salvation, but an educated populace is not a sophisticated judge of what policies will actually work. Out of fear the Chinese people followed Mao until the Cultural Revolution disillusioned everyone. That paved the way for Deng, whose strategy actually worked.

[5] See footnote 2 in Chapter 2.

Within a generation this in turn led to a sense of spiritual emptiness together with a revulsion against the lack of morality. There followed a cycle that is familiar from many parts of history: tradition, destruction, emptiness, cults, more traditional religion. One can trace this cycle even on US college campuses in the Vietnam War years: the University of California (Berkeley) had a relatively traditional campus society, but parts of campus society, stressed by the Vietnam War, went through the relatively traditional Free Speech Movement, then the Foul Speech Movement, then Hare Krishna and other cults, then a reversion to an updated version of more standard religions and ideology. Sometimes the government finds it crucial to fill the moral/ethical vacuum, sometimes it happens spontaneously. In Singapore the government decided it needed to promote Confucianism.

Some Westerners have questioned the idea of a period of spiritual emptiness.[6] They would not if they spoke with large numbers of ordinary South Koreans or Chinese or Thais. The current Chinese government acknowledges it and has a strategy for addressing it. Educated Chinese talk frequently of the problem of a society that has some of the worst qualities of many Western investment banks – an obsession with money in the absence of a moral compass.

The triggering aspect is ruthless business dealings, something that happens everywhere but in these societies occurs omnipresently, engendering not just ill-gotten profit but also poisoned food; Chinese desperately seek to import powdered milk that is safe for their babies to drink. But one really understands only when one has the opportunity to speak with people about their family and sex lives. When money is god, all the rules are suspended. Young women who migrate to the coast for manufacturing employment really do increase their social stature and self-confidence over time, but in the process it's quite common to sleep with a temporary boyfriend, not as prostitutes and often not so much for the sex but to save money on shelter in order to

---

[6] This kind of summary overview is necessarily somewhat bloodless. Just as this book was going to press, Ian Johnson's *The Souls of China: The Return of Religion After Mao* (New York: Pantheon Books, 2017) appeared. Johnson conveys a sensitive understanding of both the spiritual emptiness and the eventual filling of it by (mainly) traditional religions, based both on scholarship and on very detailed personal experience.

buy more good clothes and to remit funds back home to proud parents. Husbands and wives often take jobs in distant parts of the country for long stretches of time, to maximize income, and it is not unusual for both to have local partners. (In the Maoist days, such separations were forced by the Party, but they are now voluntary.) When the government sought to curtail a housing bubble by limiting each nuclear family to one purchase, many couples divorced so that they would be able to buy two homes. Everything is monetized: hiring a boyfriend to go home to the village at Chinese New Year to convince the parents that a woman is en route to marriage; hiring strangers as bridesmaids for a wedding; hiring professional mourners for a funeral.

   None of this is unique to China. In Bangkok for a couple of decades it was common for middle-class women – women with families, good homes, and good cars – to provide sexual favors in the afternoon in order to afford genuine Gucci shoes and Chanel dresses. Even on my job I was shocked when my former Harvard undergraduate colleague and future Thai Finance Minister told me that the Bankers Trust office was referred to in the financial community as Bankers Trash because our branch manager had lined up the nurses at a prominent local hospital to provide sexual favors to clients.[7] None of these people needed to sell themselves to live decently. All are living far better than they would have if they had remained under the conditions of a decade earlier or remained in the village. (There were of course many people in each society who still were severely impoverished, but I am not talking about those.)

   After one makes close friends, or after everyone has had a few drinks, a conversation bemoaning China's spiritual and ethical vacuum frequently emerges. The Chinese government recognizes the problem and is taking strong measures to deal with it, but some of those measures are counterproductive.

   In South Korea, the archetypical movement of the cult period, the reaction to the era of spiritual vacuum, was the Unification Church of the Reverend Sun Myung Moon, who claimed to be a Christian messiah. He inspired a vast following outside as well as inside Korea and particularly in the United States. In the 1970s, some parents of my

---

[7] Bankers Trust was proud of being in the forefront of gender equality and won a number of well-deserved prizes for its superior treatment of women. The Bangkok situation was local, temporary, and decisively terminated.

daughter's classmates in New York felt it necessary to hire "de-programmers" to try to rid their children of the powerful influence of the cult. Moonie conferences were sufficiently prestigious, and more importantly well-funded, that multiple Nobel Prize winners would speak at them. Despite South Korea's small size and (at that time) poverty, the Moonies' influence reached farther, deeper, and higher than did that of China's Falun Gong. The movement developed and in turn was funded by Moon's substantial business conglomerate, the Tong-il Group.

Moon was not threatening to the South Korean government. He advocated Korean unification and, despite his anti-communism, was tolerated by the North as well as the South. As South Korea matured into an educated, middle-class society, the cult's attraction faded and the influence of established Christian and Buddhist institutions strengthened. In the Asian Crisis of 1997–1998, Moon's conglomerate collapsed financially along with many of the other leading South Korean conglomerates. The most prominent residue of his business is the right-wing *Washington Times* newspaper in Washington, DC, which has a powerful pro-military, anti-China thrust. In South Korea, Moon's Unification Church continues to exist but is not a substantial social or political influence. What is noteworthy overall is how the waves of powerful sentiments and social movements passed without disrupting the society or polity.

In China the counterpart of the Moonies is Falun Gong, whose theology is organized around a quasi-bible called the Falun Dafa. The Falun Dafa tells us, for instance, that the way to cure cancer is to reach into the body through the fifth dimension and remove the cancer, rather than consulting a doctor. Falun Gong might well have followed the same trajectory as Moon's Unification Church, were it not for key historical and personality differences. China had an early counterpart of Sun Myung Moon, a figure named Hong Xiuquan in the mid nineteenth century who portrayed himself as the younger brother of Jesus Christ. His civil war against the government of the time, the Taiping Rebellion, seriously threatened to overthrow the dynasty of the time and cost China tens of millions of casualties. Any Chinese leader must worry about reprising that catastrophe. At the same time, Falun Gong is very different from both the Taipings and the Moonies in lacking a political and policy agenda, so it would have been possible to treat it as innocuous.

The Chinese Communist Party instinctively seeks to disperse any large organized group that might conceivably challenge its authority. In April 1999, about 10,000 Falun Gong believers demonstrated peacefully outside the Chinese leadership compound, Zhongnanhai, in Beijing, to demand organizational freedom and legal recognition – an unwise move in a communist regime. According to senior figures, Premier Zhu Rongji was inclined to meet with the group and seek an understanding, but Party leader Jiang Zemin insisted on a severe crackdown, which has been under way ever since.

If Park Chung Hee had cracked down on the Moonies, it probably would have strengthened them and turned them into a formidable political force. If Zhu Rongji had been able to negotiate with the Falun Gong adherents, the trajectory of Falun Gong might well have been ultimately innocuous in the manner of the Moonies. In the event, the crackdown appears to have strengthened the movement.

The Chinese Party has had an ambivalent relationship with established religions. During the reform era, they have been granted considerable space, subject to efforts to control their organizations and leadership. The regime insists on the right to appoint Catholic bishops. It has told the Dalai Lama that he is required to reincarnate, a somewhat peculiar demand coming from a secular regime, and it has made clear its intention to control the choice and upbringing of the "reincarnated" figure, as it has with other senior lamas. Notwithstanding the controls, traditional Christianity and Buddhism have flourished. I have gone to Buddhist temples with Party members who pray fervently and are known to their colleagues as strong believers. Many senior officials are attracted by Tibetan Buddhism. President Clinton attended services in a large Christian church in Beijing.

For most of the reform period there has been a vast network of proselytization that is technically illegal but was open and widely tolerated. One friend of mine, a proselytizing Catholic priest, took a job at a Chinese university teaching English in order to gain converts. I asked him before he left whether the university knew his underlying purpose; he said, yes, but to them the more important thing was that the students should learn good English. Two years later, he came to Hong Kong and I took him out for a good meal since he was looking thin and pale. I asked him whether his mission had encountered any problems. He said, "Yes, the food at the university is absolutely terrible." That was his worst problem. He had, at that time, encountered no negative reaction to his proselytization. Protestant proselytization was at that time similarly tolerated.

Such general tolerance has coincided with periodic crackdowns on unofficial churches. The reasons for the crackdowns seem to vary with the specific teachings, the mode of organization, the mood of the time, the location of the church, and the politics and personalities of local officials. The crackdowns have not halted the rapid spread of Christianity and Buddhism, well beyond official numbers, but they have certainly proved sufficient to maintain a siege mentality among a high proportion of Christian believers. Contrary to the intention of the government, that combination of partial tolerance and siege mentality is probably ideal, in the long run, for the spread of believers who will stand up for what they see as their God-given rights.

In recent years this syndrome of partial tolerance and partial siege has taken a particularly intense form in some parts of China. Some local governments have been taking down the crosses from Christian churches or, most recently, putting onerous restrictions on the size and location of crosses. Members of local congregations sometimes resist and are, of course, quite decisively repressed. But this short-run successful repression makes it likely that large numbers of people will meditate on Christianity's rise from the period in ancient Rome when Christians were being thrown to the lions and steel themselves for long-run assertion of their place in society.[8]

Similarly, the current government has prohibited Muslims in Xinjiang from fasting for Ramadan, and forced restaurants to remain open during the fasting period. Moreover, it has begun to silence the mosque loudspeakers used to call Muslims to worship. It is quite easy to understand the spirit of resistance induced. Like the campaign against Christian crosses, and the repression of religious observance and institutions in Tibet, this seems certain to inflame and toughen religious, anti-regime sentiments.

The regime needs to fill the moral vacuum, not just because of the vague emptiness in many people's feelings but also for quite concrete social reasons. My Harvard colleague William Hsiao speaks eloquently of the breakdown of ethics in medicine. The collapse of

---

[8] For a sense of this reaction, see Yu Jie, "China's Christian Future," *First Things*, August 2016 (but accessed online July 14, 2016, 7:00pm EST), www.firstthings.com/article/2016/08/chinas-christian-future.

traditional Confucian, Buddhist, or Korean ethics has coincided with a system where doctors are underpaid and have to supplement their incomes by overprescribing (they get a cut from prescription drug sales, so, as in Japan, doctors overprescribe to the point of absurdity) or by taking supplementary fees under the table – and denying proper service to those who can't afford these supplementary emoluments. Moreover, and this too is emblematic of the new era, Hsiao points out that the medical constituency has asserted nearly complete control over the Health Ministry. One new minister, according to Professor Hsiao, made the mistake of giving an early speech saying that he represented 1.3 billion Chinese people, not just the medical profession; he was forced by his medical constituents to recant publicly. (For comparison, in the United States Congressmen supporting the drug companies or the National Rifle Association must at least pretend that they are serving the national interest.) Observers of US politics will experience déjà vu; the gun lobby and the teachers' unions have the same sort of clout in US politics. But in China it is much more serious. People are much poorer, the consequences of their loss of health care or overpayment for it are much more serious, and some of them have taken to beating or killing their doctors in retribution. We will return to the issue of interest group power shortly. Here the issue is the absence of a moral compass in a profession where that moral compass has more profound significance than it does in any other.

The regime has allowed Christianity and Buddhism to become omnipresent. Temples and churches are everywhere. At the same time, it fears the combination of autonomous organization and passionate revivalism that is the hallmark of religious movements that change society, the ones that really fill the moral vacuum for many people. Compare with the Black Muslim movement in the United States. It frightened traditional US politicians and wide swaths of traditional US society, but in the US context the traditional conservative politicians could not repress the movement; notwithstanding substantial harassment, the Black Muslim movement did a great deal of good for a troubled part of the society. In China, given the history of the Taipings, the fear of organized, passionate religion is stronger, and the full range of repressive instruments is available. The result is partial repression of rapidly expanding movements; this enhances the passions of the partially repressed without filling the need for an ethical context to constrain the greed for gold.

The dilemma for the current Chinese government is profound. It recognizes the problem of the moral vacuum and is addressing it firmly. Its strategy under Xi Jinping is three-pronged: partially repress the major religions; revive Confucianism; and revive Marxist ideology.[9] Judging from the experience of the earlier Asian takeoffs, the partial repression will be successful in the short run but will backfire in the long run. The Confucian revival will enjoy considerable success, because it addresses the need of the Chinese people for an ethic of order and proper behavior and it taps pride in the legacy of a great civilization.

The attempt to revive a relatively primitive version of Marxism will almost certainly fail. Marx's genius at analyzing the societies of his day failed to foresee the emergence of a middle-class society – an emergence that mitigated the social polarization at the core of his analysis, facilitated the rise of the welfare state, and thereby ultimately doomed the political project that he and Lenin supported. The single most important social characteristic of China today is the emergence of a middle-class society, exactly what Marx could not foresee. Under Jiang Zemin, the Three Represents codified into China's ideology the ideals of a middle-class society and repudiated the class-struggle dynamic. China's educated elites understand this, although the non-scholars might not articulate it with great precision. China's students despise having to spend time in dreary classes on Marxism. That part will fail.

In sum, by not responding flexibly in the manner of South Korea, Taiwan, and Singapore, the Chinese government is creating a political problem for itself. The tide back to religion is a powerful tide and it is dangerous to get in front of it by challenging its most respected movements. Similarly, by making competition for Party membership very competitive while requiring potential members to recite empty old Marxist ideas, the Party is perpetuating the problem of amoral opportunism; candidates memorize passages, repeat slogans, and roll their eyes as they seek opportunities for advancement.

[9] For a nuanced study of the Party's "cultural governance," focused on efforts to bolster unity through emphasis on China's great cultural tradition, and to brand the Communist Party as the carrier of that tradition, see Elizabeth J. Perry, "Cultural Governance in Contemporary China: 'Reorienting' Party Propaganda," Harvard Yenching Institute Occasional Paper, 2013, www.harvard-yenching.org/sites/harvard-yenching.org/files/featurefiles/Elizabeth%20Perry_Cultural%20Governance%20in%20Contemporary%20China_0.pdf.

Private Business

Another crucial area is the emergence of large, powerful private business interests. These have, as documented in the economics chapter above, become the key to growth and jobs, hence crucial to the legitimacy of Party rule. But, notwithstanding private businesses' ties to the Party/government and SOEs, the relationship between private business and the Party regime now suffers from both a chronic, worsening tension and an acute alienation.

Chronically, there is enormous tension between the power of the Party Secretary and the interests of the business community. Given the rules, business cannot germinate, grow, and survive without proactive support from town or city or provincial Party Secretary. Without the willingness of the Party Secretary to accelerate decisions and bypass most of the rules, the business can't get land, electricity, environmental permits, construction permits, licenses to do a particular kind of business, and much else. Keeping on the good side of the Party Secretary usually requires making large donations to the Party Secretary's latest project (which may be the enhancement of his or her own wallet but often involves beautification, welfare programs, or improved infrastructure). In an earlier chapter I told the story of the large, modern export business that got shut down for months due to the CEO's slow response to the Party Secretary's demand for a large donation. The more China succeeds, the more hundreds of thousands of business leaders it has with powerful organizations and millions of dollars of resources at their disposal – many of them unhappy over what they see as abuses by Party officials. The anti-corruption campaign addresses only part of this problem, the other part being the Party Secretary's confidence that every business has a responsibility to contribute to the public good, and that he or she, the Party Secretary, is the arbiter of the public good.

A crucial part of reform is to level the playing field between SOEs and the private sector, enhancing the already crucial role of the private sector. Meanwhile the SOEs are weakening because of inefficiency, debt, and overcapacity, and local government is being constrained by debt, so the political influence of the private sector is becoming formidable – and will assert itself if it is too hampered by controls. If the fiscal squeeze eventually leads to a mass privatization of local government assets, as it should in the interest of economic efficiency, then these trends will accelerate.

Moreover, a key finding of the Foshan study cited earlier was that Foshan city's exceptional success derived in part from a decentralized structure that kept the district governments intimately connected to an organized business sector. That imperative to have an organized private sector working closely with the local government directly contradicts the current central government's fear of uncontrolled political organization and interest group power.

A particularly acute problem for this sector is that the anti-corruption campaign has led to numerous disappearances for unexplained reasons. A neighbor or business associate disappears and is not heard from for long periods of time. Nobody knows who took him or why. For fear of inviting attention to themselves, everybody is afraid to ask why. People don't know whether the person was grabbed by an official Party discipline inspection team or by an antagonized local government office or by someone else, and they are afraid to ask. Fear is pervasive, and that encourages short-term compliance, but resentment festers and that creates the risk of explosion in the possibly not too distant future.

As an indicator of private business discontent, the rate of increase of private business investment declined from over 20 percent in late 2013 and early 2014 to 2.1 percent in August 2016 before rebounding modestly, a fall radically disproportionate to the slowing of the economy. Since private business is the predominant source of economic growth and new jobs, this is both economically and politically ominous.

The balance of power between private business and Party secretaries is shifting decisively. One entrepreneur said to me, "In the beginning Alibaba needed the Party Secretary. Now the Party Secretary needs Alibaba." Reality is more complicated than the quip suggests, but the balance is indeed shifting, from central Beijing right down to the villages, and the shift will continue with exponential force as private businesses expand. The caveats enunciated earlier about how "private" Chinese private businesses really are do not negate the shift. If Party Secretaries understand the tide, and channel it rather than fighting it, then in principle the shift could be smooth. But the Xi Jinping administration is trying to reinvigorate Party committees inside enterprises, including even majority private enterprises listed in Hong Kong, to reassert the right of Party committees to influence and approve major policies, and to insist upon the right of the local Party to ensure that business strategies serve what it determines to be the best interest of the Party. An optimistic scenario would see a nearly infinite number of smooth local incremental adaptations. But officials don't necessarily understand the tide, and many or most may see Xi Jinping's policies as a mandate to reassert or expand their traditional authority. The center's attempt to push back the rising tide of private sector power could, in the short run, create payoff incentives that would defeat the anti-corruption campaign, and if carried too far too long could set the stage for a historic upheaval.

Legal System and Demonstrations

The emergence of stronger or better organized or more confident interest groups leads, among many other things, to more demonstrations. Chinese official statistics show 8,700 "mass incidents" in 1993, 32,000 in 1999, and 58,000 in 2003. (A mass incident is a demonstration involving more than 100 people; some involve more than 10,000.) As their number later headed toward 200,000 the government stopped publishing the statistics and began referring to 80,000 to 100,000 per year.[10] Originally they mainly comprised groups of people outraged over the government's taking their rural or urban property for development purposes, often in cahoots with illegal businesses, and sometimes brutally beating people defending their homes. In recent years, environmental issues have caused a high proportion of the mass incidents.[11] In the last few years, labor strikes have broken out in substantial numbers all over China,[12] along with demonstrations by workers losing jobs as a result of SOE reforms. _China Labor Bulletin_ counted 2,774 serious strikes in 2015, with the number rising fast

---

[10] For an early analysis of rising protests, see Murray Scot Tanner, "Chinese Government Responses to Rising Social Unrest," testimony presented to the US–China Economic and Security Review Commission, April 14, 2005, www.uscc.gov/sites/default/files/Tanner_Written%20Testimony.pdf. In 2010 there were mentions of 180,000 mass incidents. Subsequently, no official numbers have been available and informal comments have referred to a mysteriously lower number.

[11] For a report on a government study of the causes of mass incidents, see Hou Liqiang, "Report Identifies Sources of Mass Protests," _China Daily_, April 9, 2014, www.chinadaily.com.cn/china/2014-04/09/content_17415767.htm. See also a report, "Mass Incidents in 2012," www.thechinastory.org/yearbooks/yearbook-2013/chapter-4-under-rule-of-law/mass-incidents-in-2012/.

[12] _China Labor Bulletin_ publishes an online interactive map showing the number and locations of strikes. See http://maps.clb.org.hk/strikes/en.

despite the general political repression.[13] The cumulative rise of demonstrations has been non-linear and has caused the authorities to stop publishing the numbers.

The disaster of June 4, 1989, taught Chinese leaders a difficult lesson. Among other things, to ensure that non-military methods of stability maintenance and crowd control would be available in the future, they created the People's Armed Police (PAP). Premier Zhu Rongji later institutionalized the standard that troops may not shoot the people. The management of protests became relatively sophisticated. Farmers would march on Party headquarters and threaten to burn it down, in order to draw the attention of Beijing to their problems with corrupt local officials and businesses. (Polls consistently indicate that, year after year, people have a high level of trust of the central government but view their local governments even worse than the way Americans view their Congress.) Reacting to a demonstration, a higher level of government will send police, who will arrest the leaders of the demonstration but also arrest the corrupt political and business leaders. The fact that the demonstration leaders will *always* be arrested keeps the threshold of protest high; you only do this if you're so upset that you're willing to sacrifice a few relatives or friends. But the fact that the wrongdoers usually get arrested means that rough justice is done.

In this way, the armed police come to perform a judicial function. They have to perform this function because people don't trust the courts. Americans would normally sue. Chinese don't trust the courts because the local mayor and Party Secretary, who are usually the objects of protest, appoint the local judge and have responsibility for enforcing court judgments; local court judgments are rarely enforced against powerful local officials or executives.

Over the years, the Chinese judicial system has made enormous progress, from a very low base. There is a reasonably coherent body of law, which had previously been absent. Judges are now supposed to have studied the law, which was previously not required. Accused people are supposed to be able to choose lawyers to defend them, although there are still many exceptions and many official threats against lawyers.

[13] "Strikes and Protests by China's Workers Soar to Record Heights in 2015," *China Labor Bulletin*, January 7, 2016, www.clb.org.hk/en/content/strikes-and-protests-china%E2%80%99s-workers-soar-record-heights-2015.

Increasingly officials are expected to enforce court judgments. But practice is inconsistent, and behind every judgment there is a Party commission that has the final say. Reform of the legal system has not kept pace with the need for an objective system, although reforms continue. Xi Jinping has officially banned the practice of local officials kidnapping and incarcerating (in "black jails") local citizens who go to Beijing to petition against injustice. (How much this has been implemented remains uncertain, and the central government is also trying to discourage petitions.) Of enormous importance, he has centralized judicial appointments, so the local Party Secretary and mayor are not supposed to be able to control the job of the local judge anymore. But, notwithstanding all the reforms, and all the promises that rule of law is a priority, environmentalists, laborers, and people being evicted from their homes feel that the rough justice of the streets offers better prospects.

The Chinese leadership has had great difficulty balancing the need for citizen support on many issues with fears of citizen organization and citizen-caused loss of face. It has on multiple occasions caved in to citizen protests against construction of chemical plants, but it has also cracked down hard on many similar protests. It allowed widespread distribution of the video documentary *Under the Dome*, which dramatized not only the extent of pollution but also the extent to which government officials connived with or acceded to illegal polluters, but then it suddenly banned the film. In April 2015 the Ministry of Environmental Protection released devastating data on the extent of air pollution to Greenpeace – a particularly interesting decision because even many democratic governments object to Greenpeace tactics. Earlier in 2015 the government decided to allow NGOs to sue government over severe pollution, but then put severely restrictive conditions on such suits. Likewise, the government often acts on citizen complaints about official corruption but also ruthlessly prosecutes many people who publicly expose corruption.

Despite talk of the rule of law, the progress of that rule has also been slow enough to impede the government's ability to achieve other objectives. Given rising costs, rising local competition, more competitive energy prices at home, and increasingly antagonistic application of Chinese laws to them, foreign businesses increasingly calculate that the cost of coping with complex and un-transparent rules is no longer sufficiently offset by savings in labor costs; hence many are investing their money at home or in a different emerging market rather than in

China. In another crucial constraint, the Chinese government's efforts to make the country's currency, the renminbi, a major international currency can only go so far when the ultimate decision over a dispute is not an objective, independent court, but rather a Party commission that oversees the court. If another country is going to entrust billions of dollars of its assets to Chinese currency for use in the event of a crisis, it wants to know that a dispute will be handled objectively. The complexity revolution is making the costs of a Party-controlled and opaque legal system higher and higher.

Repressive vacillation leaves the government with the worst of both worlds. It does not get the systematic input from citizens that it needs, but it doesn't quash the movements either. They flare up, feel momentarily encouraged, get partially repressed, and fester with resentment while retaining a temporarily silent network.

Labor

In recent years, Chinese wages have risen extremely fast, driven by emerging blue-collar labor shortages and by a government mandate that during the 12th five-year plan (2011–2105) the minimum wage in each area should rise at least 13.1 percent per year. In leading coastal provinces, wages often did indeed double in five years. In some cases, particularly ones involving big foreign firms, the government openly supported strikes to drive wages up, but that forbearance or encouragement was short-lived. Despite rapidly rising wages and rapidly improving conditions, the incidence of labor unrest has risen and it has spread nationally. A map provided by the Hong Kong-based **China Labor Bulletin** shows a very large number of strikes despite the current repressive atmosphere.[14]

Education

As befits a Confucian society, no sector has expanded faster than education – in scale, quality, and globalization. Because the education of leaders requires it, students at the best universities have been given exceptional latitude to explore different ideas, and they still are given

---

[14] See http://maps.clb.org.hk/strikes/en. Also note the citations in the previous section.

exceptional freedom to use the internet in ways prohibited to most of the rest of their society. China's leading scholars are proud members of a global profession and identify with global professional standards. They appear, and are respected, at great universities and think tanks throughout the world. They win high international positions, such as Justin Lin Yifu's recent position as Senior Vice President and Chief Economist of the World Bank, on merit.

For nearly two decades the relationship between Chinese political leaders and Chinese academia has been remarkably constructive. That relationship reached a very low point in June 1989, and intense anger lingered for several years afterward, but for most of the subsequent years most university faculty and students have been supportive of the government. The government was doing good things for the country, they felt, and despite many complaints they believed that it deserved their support.

This is extraordinarily unusual in a developing country. Everywhere there are tests of strength between unhappy students on the one hand and governments on the other. Disruptive demonstrations in Taipei 1947, Kwangju, South Korea 1980, Bangkok 1976 and 1992, and so forth, are endemic in rapidly developing countries. For instance, in South Korea, students have opposed the government continuously since the late nineteenth century. They demonstrated against the obsolete emperor system, then against Japanese colonialism, then against 1950s militarism, then against weak democratic government in 1960–1961, then against Park Chung Hee's subsequent repressive dictatorship, and so forth. What is unusual is a supportive relationship such as the one that evolved in China. So the support given by Chinese academia to the regime for a decade and a half is exceptional. It belies the arguments of those Western scholars who assert that Chinese stability has been built primarily or solely on efficient repression.

That support continued into the beginning of the Xi Jinping era. There is broad, albeit diffuse, support for the planned economic reforms and the campaign against corruption. Support among youth for the ongoing anti-corruption campaign remains strong. However, more recently deans, faculty members, and some of the students are beginning to ask difficult questions. When are the reforms going to take hold? Why is such harsh repression necessary? Everyone is somewhat afraid. "We can't do the things we used to do, and we can't say the things we used to say." If the anti-corruption campaign and the economic reforms do not seem to be accomplishing their stated purpose, permanently, the broad public support could evaporate overnight. Ongoing sacrifice of the support of the scholarly community of teachers and students is a huge loss for the administration.

While students remain overtly quiescent, there are signs of changing attitudes. From the time of the May 4th Movement a century ago (1919), Chinese students have used anti-Japanese demonstrations as a way to demonstrate against aspects of their own government. Some of the fervent anti-Japanese demonstrations that periodically occur, and much of the internet nationalism, have this mixed quality of asserting China's national interests and implicitly criticizing the Chinese government. Party leaders crack down on anti-Japanese demonstrations at some point, and they rightly fear the internet nationalism. They try to appease the nationalism by taking tough international stands, for instance on maritime conflicts, but that does not address the underlying discontents. There is a similarity to developments in the United States, where discontented white workers support Trump's nationalism as part of a protest against being neglected by the establishment. The vehemence of internet nationalism is thus a useful barometer of stresses in Chinese domestic politics.

Journalism and the Media

Over the last generation a cadre of highly principled (in the Western sense) professional journalists has arisen in China. They feel strongly about getting the truth out. They look to their peers around the world for techniques and standards.[15] They constantly push the boundaries. Led by **Caixin**, which has acquired an ability to communicate vital realities without being shut down, and by a host of other publications that push the boundaries in various ways, a highly professional subgroup of Chinese journalists manages to address the basic issues with considerable breadth and accuracy. In numbers they are overwhelmed by those who have jobs rather than vocations, but those with vocations are more influential. The boundaries of the politically acceptable have contracted sharply under the Xi Jinping administration, which has emphasized a traditional communist approach that journalism,

---

[15] I wrote this from personal experience, but the point has just been documented in a way I could never have done in a new book: Jonathan Hassid, *China's Unruly Journalists: How Committed Professionals Are Changing the People's Republic* (London: Routledge, 2016).

education and the arts must serve the Party, but real journalism is alive in a way that it never was in Mao's day or under the old Soviet Union. The internet has created a large community of shared information, including, among a diverse educated elite, information that is often nuanced and highly informed. Against this, the regime has developed remarkable technical tools to manage the spread of internet information and opinion. A Great Firewall blocks many sites and makes it impossible for most citizens to, for instance, use Google. The government has even banned foreign companies, including Apple, from selling downloaded music, movies, and books. To manage the flow of conversation on WeChat and Weibo (China's more sophisticated versions of Twitter, Facebook, WhatsApp, and integrated email) the government has a technically advanced system, so sophisticated that the US National Security Agency must admire it, to monitor the flow of words and thoughts. Under the Golden Shield Project, when a trending subject takes a turn that propaganda officials find objectionable, they can for instance block all internet traffic containing a specific phrase. They don't have to read individual emails or conversations; they can quiet a whole wave. They supplement this ability by employing members of the "50-Cent Army," who create their own waves of pro-government thoughts in return for small payments. On geopolitical subjects, this seems to work reasonably well. On many domestic subjects, cynicism is high among educated people, who typically have multiple alternative sources.

Large segments of Chinese society accept the censorship as a valid function of government. When the educated elite feels that great things are being done to improve China's stature and the Chinese people's welfare, a substantial proportion will accept the tradeoff. But the tension between strict censorship and some disinformation on the one hand, and the creation of a large educated elite, including government/Party officials, university teachers, students at elite universities, business leaders, and vast swaths of the population who can figure out how to circumvent the censors on the other, can quickly become problematic if there is disillusionment about the pace or direction of reforms.

Government Interest Groups

The SOEs, Party units, military units, and government units are likewise now powerful pressure groups that pursue their own interests, including blocking reform. Some of these units are the size of small countries. The Party has many more members than Germany has citizens. The interest groups are large, well-informed, and well-organized.

In sum, economic development has fostered the rise of powerful interests, religious, economic, professional, and governmental, that create an entirely different political environment than in the early days of reform. These changes are just as factual and important as the changes in the structure of the economy, and they will have to be addressed.

The Turning Point

So China has come to a turning point. The interest groups are now exceptionally large and powerful. The economic reforms fundamentally challenge the interests of every one of the most powerful groups in Chinese society. The anti-corruption campaign is also taking on all those groups simultaneously. While this is happening, the major professional and religious groups are being repressed and the mood in the private sector is quite negative. The wealthy and the upper middle class are trying to get their wealth out of China; many are trying to get their families out too. Moreover, as noted earlier, the government has antagonized foreign business at a time when technological upgrading and new investment are particularly needed. And it has chosen this moment in history to challenge China's maritime neighbors and the US Navy. All this is happening at a time of financial fragility.

For the leadership, this could hardly be a more risky strategy. Mustafa Kemal Atatürk of Turkey, who sequentially took on limited opposition, defeated it, and then pivoted to take on other groups, is the archetype of sophisticated political reform strategy. In contrast, during the late 1970s the Shah of Iran took on all major interest groups simultaneously, as did the Polish government of 1980; in both cases that led to regime collapse. Although top leaders united at the beginning of Xi's administration around the ideas of economic reform and an anti-corruption campaign, usually the first rule of politics or life is that one should never take on all powerful groups at the same time.

We can appraise the Xi administration's situation and likely outcomes by looking at what the other Asian miracle societies did at comparable turning points.

Asian Miracle Responses to the New Era

Each of the Asian miracle economies has eventually reached this point where the conditions of the mobilization system no longer apply. Fear gives way to confidence or even hubris. Economic simplicity gives way to economic complexity. Political simplicity gives way to political complexity. How have the others responded?

Importantly, none has collapsed. In the mid 1970s, sound Western opinion believed that Taiwan and South Korea would collapse because their lack of democracy and human rights would lead to collapse. The US media commentary on South Korea in 1976 provides a model of how not to understand the Asian miracle systems.[16] Prosperity, employment inclusiveness, and asset inclusiveness provide ballast to these societies; their citizens are determined to retain the benefits they have attained. But they were all forced to evolve in a shape-shifting manner.

Japan, as I have noted, was rejuvenating an industrial society with an educated middle class, not building one from scratch, so it had a relatively straightforward task. It implemented rapid reforms and implemented best practice based on global experience for the first two decades, 1955–1975. Then, flush with confidence that its economic management was inherently superior, it turned inward and allowed the biggest interest groups (retail, agriculture, construction, property, and banking) to dominate the government. Economic growth rates collapsed within a few years after 1975 and have remained relatively stagnant ever since. (An aging demographic has been an important part of the low growth, but does not explain why Japan's productivity has remained only 70 percent of US productivity and why in sectors like cell phones, where Japanese products were the best in the world, Japan has been surpassed by South Korea and China as well as the United States.) Given the dominance of the Liberal Democratic Party (LDP) and the comfortable prosperity of the population, it has not faced overthrow, although for a long time the public expelled the prime minister from office about once a year.

---

[16] Typical was the *New York Times* coverage of South Korea in 1976, with news and editorials about instability almost weekly, with reportage about economic growth confined to a few column inches for the year and no coverage of improved living standards. Its coverage of China after the turn of the century has been much more balanced.

Politically, Japan's dominant party maintained a near-monopoly on financing and organizational talent, along with strong control of information and the judicial system. (Judges need to follow the LDP line in general although nobody dictates individual judgments, and 99.8 percent of those arrested are convicted, usually confessing after treatment that would be considered human rights abuse in the United States or Europe.) The current Abe government is tightening control of information, asserting the right to shut down any broadcast station that the government judges to be "biased," and increasing government control of universities' management and curricula. (China of course exercises incomparably greater control over information, the judiciary, and universities.) Its "reinterpretation" of the Constitution, applauded by the US military, in order to expand the role of the military, is held by many experts to be unconstitutional and is opposed by a strong majority of the public. It holds elections, which mostly shuffle the factions within the LDP.

The public grumpily accepts this; voters are apathetic, not revolutionary. Japan's brief experiences of opposition government have made the LDP seem like the least bad option. Now Abe seeks to rewrite Japan's constitution in ways that would make it more authoritarian, base it on allegedly unique ethnic characteristics rather than universal values, and potentially undercut the rule of law.[17] The system works, although there is a gradually rising risk of financial collapse that could bring the whole system down. Barring that, the Japanese system copes with modern interest group complexity while maintaining a dominant-party system, at the cost of economic stagnation. This is stable at Japan's extremely prosperous level of development, but the Chinese people would almost certainly not accept it at an income level about one-third of Japan's.

Taiwan had its economy dominated by about 40 large Party-owned conglomerates, the counterparts of Chinese SOEs. These became

[17] See Keigo Komamura, "The Unbearable Lightness of Our Constitution," *Asia Unbound*, a blog of the New York Council on Foreign Relations, August 17, 2016, http://blogs.cfr.org/asia/2016/08/17/the-unbearable-lightness-of-our-constitution/. Abe's personality and approach to politics bear striking resemblances to Xi Jinping, being characterized by authoritarianism, disrespect for historical truth, a grasping search for control that overrides law and tradition, a princeling's sense of entitlement, and inability to empathize with the reactions of other peoples. The similarities are usually obscured by the different environments they operate in, with very different constraints.

sluggish, like their current Chinese counterparts, and were gradually surpassed by a remarkable collection of private enterprises (TSMC, Hon Hai, Acer, Gigabyte ...) that emerged from a base of 200,000 Taiwanese trading companies. The Guomindang naturally favored its conglomerates and, fearful that size would bring political power, initially tried to keep the Taiwanese enterprises small. But economic performance was the only sustainable source of political support, so gradually it accommodated the rise of the Taiwanese enterprises. The big Guomindang conglomerates went into financial crisis in 1990 and, although the government bailed them out to varying degrees, they are a footnote to today's Taiwan economy, not the main story, because the private Taiwanese companies' superior growth overshadowed them. President Tsai Ing-wen (of the Democratic Progressive Party, DPP, the main opposition to the Guomindang) will further dismantle the conglomerates. The parallel with what has happened in China a generation later is remarkable, but the Xi administration is trying to push back the tide by reasserting the importance of the SOEs and of Party control over them.

Likewise, Taiwan was a tough Leninist dictatorship. Chiang Kai-shek was not as bloody in his initial crackdowns as Mao, but a massacre of Taiwanese protestors in 1947 killed somewhere between 18 and 60 times as many people as June 4, 1989 in China.[18] Chiang's son, Jiang Jingguo, educated in Moscow as we have noted, was a member of the Soviet Communist Party and was a particularly tough chief of security for his father. Taiwanese dissidents were likely to be taken to Green Island and shot, whereas mainland dissidents were more likely to be left to rot in jail. But Taiwan is a small place, and father and son were in touch with local realities. In the late 1960s the government became more technocratic – the counterpart of Deng's technocratic revolution on the mainland more than a decade later – and by the mid 1970s technocrats dominated the government. At the end of the 1960s local elections were extended up to the center. The Party accepted that it should be formally separated from the government, a decision that came proportionately later on the mainland. On December 10, 1979, a major confrontation over human rights called the Kaohsiung Incident

---

[18] Chiang Kai-shek personally moved to Taiwan later, but his colleagues were in control in Taiwan and he was fully in charge of major Guomindang decisions in 1947, including those in Taiwan.

provided a wake-up call regarding the strength behind dissident Tai-wanese public opinion.

The early 1980s saw clear recognition of a new relationship between the government and the determined opposition. Chan Lien, then a professor of political science and later chairman of the Guomindang Party, spent an afternoon explaining the government's new thinking to me. It was important, he said, to keep the opposition illegal in order to maintain social order. At the same time, it was important to allow them to organize so that the government would have an interlocutor to negotiate with. Having them organized made deals possible and reduced conflict. Keeping them technically illegal gave the government a club in case it was needed. This was a pragmatic decision, not based on ideology, not based on foreign pressure, but based on a very tough leader's pragmatic recognition of the most efficient way to solve problems.

The succeeding steps toward what became a very resilient democracy occurred through the same pragmatic progress – at about the time Deng Xiaoping was telling mainlanders that it's not important whether the cat is black or white, only that it catches mice. Practical men (the decision-makers were all men at the time) were making practical decisions. It is crucial to recognize how this happens – not through ideological conversion or foreign browbeating but through pragmatic leaders trying to make their cats catch mice.

In 1980 a new election law made elections fairer. By 1981 non-Guomindang candidates received 44 percent of votes. By 1983 the Guomindang had transformed itself from a "mainlander" party to an inclusive party, with 11.4 percent of the population as members and 70 percent of those Taiwanese. Polls of Party opinion, rather than top-down decisions, became key to nomination of local candidates for the first time. In 1986 Jiang Jingguo announced the formation of a committee to study political reform, in 1987 martial law was lifted, and in 1988 for the first time nominees for the Central Committee were elected rather than being selected by the party chairman. In 1991 the repressive "Temporary Provisions for the Period of Mobilization and Suppression of Communist Rebellion" were lifted, and subsequent changes to the island's constitution made politics more democratic. In 2001 the opposition DPP won the presidency for the first time. All this, except the last few years preceding full democracy, was orchestrated by the formerly tough, hardline security chief who had been educated as a communist and joined the Soviet Communist Party. The transition from a more corrupt regime than China today, and from an initially more repressive regime than China today, had been accomplished without bloodshed, without disruptive shock therapy, and without economic damage.

South Korea had the roughest transition, but bloodshed and economic disruption were still quite limited. The Park Chung Hee government supported a dozen giant conglomerates (chaebol), which mostly competed in the same businesses – starting with cheap textiles, radios, and TVs, and working up to computers and cars, while also building infrastructure and military-related industries (steel, chemicals, shipbuilding) – an industrial structure very much like China's a decade or two later. The chaebol were private in ownership but tightly state-led. As in Japan, the government was supported financially by huge slush funds from the big companies.

This system provided 10 percent annual growth and rough, but increasingly authoritarian, stability, until 1979. At that point the complexity revolution kicked in. Park's economic policies led to extremely high inflation (clocked at 40 percent at the time, although the figures have since been smoothed) and extremely high debt. On the political side, increasing discontent with Park's repression led to a cycle of rising student demonstrations and increasingly organized opposition from Christian churches, labor unions, and above all students. A huge student demonstration was planned for October 1979 and Park's advisors split about the proper response to it. His bodyguards favored using sharpshooters to shoot the student leaders. The Korean CIA (KCIA), whose head was the second-most-powerful government official and very close to Park, argued that the only response that would maintain stability was democratic and human rights concessions. Park decided in favor of the bodyguards. In response, on the basis of a very detailed analysis of the social consequences,[19] the head of the KCIA invited

---

[19] The official investigation of the assassination was inconclusive and remains controversial. The interpretation here is based on personal experience, because I inadvertently acquired an observer's seat at the edge of the table. I wrote a Hudson Institute paper about what I am now calling the complexity revolution and argued that the economic and political system would have to change. Suddenly I was deluged with requests for copies of the paper and for lectures at Korean think tanks. I did not know at the time that the think tanks were KCIA fronts. Later, after the assassination, the US general commanding I Corps on the Demilitarized Zone told me that the KCIA chief had come to him time after time

Park to dinner with two "sing-song girls" and shot the President in the head. He did not attempt to take power. He did not attempt to flee. He did not deny what he had done. Subsequently South Korea had a very bumpy transition to democracy over a nine-year period, but, after a gradual increase in political competition and a dramatic dismantling of the huge slush funds that had supported the ruling generals, eventually became perhaps the most stable democracy in the developing world.

The chaebol survived in their politically supported form until the Asian Crisis of 1997–1998, when many of them, including most dramatically Daewoo with over US$50 billion of debts, came crashing down and took the Korean banks with them. Kim Dae Jung, the great opponent of Park, saved the economy by supervising a vast reform of the chaebol and the banking system – a reform parallel in some ways to the reforms China's SOEs and banks need today. The reform of Korea's chaebol and the overshadowing of Taiwan's SOEs by a truly private sector constitute the only plausible models for China's economy to continue strong growth.

Park's choice of maximum repression of the new forces contrasts sharply with Jiang Jingguo's incremental accommodation of those forces. However, both systems made relatively smooth transitions, meaning considerable administrative continuity and an absence of huge upheavals with mass casualties, to democratic government.

In **Singapore** as in China before 1949, the regime began as a struggle between two Leninist parties, the Communist Party and the People's Action Party (PAP) of Lee Kwan Yew. The PAP maintained a hierarchical structure and, symbolically, for many years required party members to call each other "Comrade." Singapore held elections, with opposition parties, but, as in Japan, the PAP had superior financing, organization, and technocracy and maintained control of

after time to discuss how democracy worked and whether a smooth transition was possible. Neither of us had guessed what the KCIA chief would eventually do. The KCIA chief and his organization had concluded that shooting the student leaders would leave the country in chaos and that democratic concessions were the only way to save the country. He assassinated his friend and mentor, and accepted the consequences for himself, out of patriotic duty. Like Park, all he cared about was saving his country. Park never made a lot of money, always maintained the strictest personal discipline, and, along with his friend/protégé at the KCIA, sacrificed his life for his country. It was a tribute to Park that he chose key subordinates who, like himself, would make the ultimate sacrifice for their country.

patronage. Criticism of the PAP or its leader was deterred by the vigorous use of libel suits. Untoward comment on Singapore, its policies, or its leader quickly led to large fines, jail time, or administrative decisions that deprived the offending person or organization of economic opportunities. I was for a while the target of such policies. I published a bank research paper and gave a speech showing that it was not true that Hong Kong people and businesses were migrating en masse to Singapore. The numbers I used were undisputed and in fact the most important ones (that over a four-year period fewer than 10 people per year had migrated from Hong Kong to Singapore) came from a Lee Kwan Yew National Day speech. Nonetheless, my research interfered with a Singaporean campaign to create a stampede from Hong Kong, and the Monetary Authority of Singapore made vigorous efforts to get me fired, demanding of my chairman in New York to know why he was "harboring an anti-Singapore economist." These folks played rough.

The Singaporean government retained a remarkable degree of state ownership and control of the economy while, as noted earlier, giving rein to independent boards. It got the benefits of government ownership, namely influence and funding, while obtaining the benefits of market competition. As noted earlier, Singapore Airlines, possibly the world's best airline, symbolizes the country's success in combining state ownership with market efficiency. The PAP guided the structure of the economy by selecting industries and heavily subsidizing them. Like a multinational corporation it looked all over the world for best practice and best corporate leadership. Readers who are interested can trace the decision to become a biotech hub, the subsidized building of Biosphere, and the hiring of distinguished leadership from Europe and elsewhere. Within Singapore, the most talented people are nurtured from elementary school, given full scholarships to prestigious universities abroad, and required to work for the government for several years to repay their scholarships. As they advance in the government, they are rigorously vetted to ensure good work and to avoid corruption. When they become ministers, a junior minister makes about US $700,000 and the prime minister about US$1.7 million, plus one to three corporate board seats, each paying about US$1 million per year. Corruption is insignificant.

This system has worked much longer in Singapore than in the other Asian miracle economies, because Singapore is so small. The government can fine-tune patronage down to the city block. It could issue an ordinance against chewing gum or against peeing in the elevator (there was a campaign on that subject at one point) and, if you chewed gum or peed in the elevator, the government would know. The system has been a beloved model for some Chinese leaders, especially Li Peng, but it is hard to scale up to Chinese, or even to South Korean, levels. In recent years, the leadership has been forced to begin modifying its approach, conceding more seats to the opposition and responding to major riots over the importing of talent from abroad. Even in Singapore the GE model has its limits.

China's Complexity Revolution and the New Repression

China now faces the same complexity revolution – dissipating fear, emergent hubris, economic complexity, political complexity – that all the others have faced. China has reached a level of development, and hence of complexity, that in the other Asian miracle economies forced fundamental changes in the way both the economy and politics were managed. On the economic side, China has accepted that economic complexity requires a move to market-dominated allocation of resources, thought through a brilliant plan, vetted that plan with brilliant economic analysts from all over the world as well as China, and published it transparently. But politics has so far inhibited rapid implementation.

On the political side, there has, so far as an outside observer can tell, been no such top leadership analysis of the implications of the political complexity revolution and certainly no agreed plan other than repression. The anti-corruption campaign has hit potential opponents of reform, starting with Zhou Yongkang and key military chiefs, quite hard, but has not yet institutionalized the process sufficiently to provide confidence about the future. Recently the campaign has hit particularly hard at the supporters of previous leaders Jiang Zemin and Hu Jintao (in the latter case accompanied by a decision to "reform" the Communist Youth League, the foundation of Hu's power). And widespread fear for personal position in the face of the anti-corruption campaign has at least temporarily paralyzed the reform program.

As noted earlier, the political strategy for economic reform involves taking on every major interest group simultaneously, an exceedingly risky strategy.

The Ten Great Paradoxes

Moreover, the government confronts a number of paradoxes.

- To implement environmental cleanup, the government needs the support of a mobilized public, but it fears the emergence of too many whistle-blowers or too much popular organization.
- To institutionalize the anti-corruption campaign the government likewise needs the support of public whistle-blowers and popular organization, but it fears and suppresses them.
- To make the SOEs efficient, as the big government-connected firms became in Singapore and South Korea, the Party needs to step back and make them autonomous, but the administration has vowed to strengthen Party supervision of them, with a powerful faction insisting that supervision includes making strategic decisions for each firm.
- To take domestic and foreign business to the next level, and to make China's currency an important global reserve currency, China needs to strengthen the rule of law, but the administration has vowed to strengthen Party supervision of the judicial system.
- To move Chinese manufacturing up-market China needs to accelerate investment by the world's most advanced firms, but the administration has antagonized foreign business, especially Japanese business, which has been a particularly important source of advanced technology. In 2016 foreign direct investment declined slightly from the previous year, breaking a long record of continuous increases.
- China's economic success is tied to globalization, its rising leaders benefit from exposure abroad more than those of any other major country, and some of its leaders see it gaining global leadership through superior globalization of talent, but China's current administration is trying to curtail the inflow of any global information that would cause uncomfortable debates inside China.
- To enhance government and Party decisiveness, the leadership has centralized all the political and military titles, and all the small leading groups, in Xi's office, but this has begun to lead to slow decisions in some areas and to hasty decisions that do not always reflect the considered expertise of the bureaucracies in others. Foreign ministries say they can't get decisions out of anyone except the President. Financial experts find themselves circumvented on the big decisions.

- The government needs to enhance efficiency through competition, but it has embarked on a campaign to consolidate huge businesses, some of which are quite inefficient, into national champions.
- China has made itself the best place in the world to make money, but, because of its legal system, one of the most risky places to keep it. High proportions of its most successful business leaders in all sectors are determined to move their assets and their families abroad.
- In the interest of stability the government has imposed a wave of repression, but this repression has itself become a destabilizing factor, creating a sense of risk among the middle class, which has responded with widespread efforts to move assets and family abroad.

In response to this set of dilemmas, there has been no clearly articulated political strategy analogous to the economic strategy. Xi Jinping's administration has cracked down hard on a wide variety of groups: internet users, Christian churches, Tibetans, Muslims, university students and administrators, feminists, lawyers, political reformers, educational equality advocates, environmental advocates, corruption whistle-blowers, researchers on any of these topics, and nearly every group that receives foreign funding. The National People's Congress Standing Committee passed a law to require State Council approval of any foreign NGO opening an office in China. The government has imposed stringent new security requirements on foreign businesses that seem to them to put their intellectual property at risk or to drive them out in favor of local companies.

In other words, so far the Xi administration's clearly articulated strategy has been that it will accede to the economic pressures of the complexity revolution by relying on the market to aggregate and adjudicate interests. (So far, the theory is better than the practice.) On the political side it has sought to suppress the forces of complexity. So far, there is no publicly articulated political strategy for aggregating and adjudicating these myriad powerful, conflicting interests. To the extent that broader political strategy is being discussed, all this writer has gleaned is a decision by certain advisors to study the Japanese system for clues as to how to maintain a dominant-party system with a lighter touch. The search for a more sophisticated political solution which is being carried out by leading Chinese thinkers has been repressed and rendered almost invisible to outsiders, but it continues vigorously just beneath the surface.

The Two Dynamics

There are two fundamental dynamics driving China's politics – almost like two different gearings on a bicycle. Different circumstances cause one dynamic or the other to kick in.

One dynamic is the sense that China is prosperous and peaceful when it has powerful and assertive leadership. In the eyes of much of the Chinese population, including much of the thought leadership and much of the youth, all of Chinese history points to this view. The times when it has been great to be Chinese have been times when dynasties had powerful leaders imposing unity at home and projecting power abroad, albeit often at the cost of repression at home and struggle with neighbors. When China's leaders are soft and ambivalent, when they are looking inward, China becomes vulnerable to challenges from the north (most of Chinese history) or from the sea (mainly from the middle of the nineteenth century to the middle of the twentieth century). When China seems to be at risk, from economic or geopolitical problems, and when a strong leader is offering a persuasive strategy for overcoming the problems, this dynamic kicks in. That is the situation today, as China faces an unprecedented economic transition and increasing tensions with the United States.

The other dynamic is quite different, focused on families, localities, personal well-being, and concepts of democracy and freedom. China is a very family-oriented society, held together neither by an ideology as in the United States nor by gigantic institutions as in Japan. People want to focus on their families. When the whole country is suffering from disunity, there is a yearning for unity – as there was during the first half of the last century – and that empowers the first dynamic. But there is also strong centrifugal force – pride in local culture, local dialect, local cuisine, local business practices, all affirmed by the slogan "The mountains are high and the emperor is far away." There are powerful movements for human rights, for academic integrity, for feminism, for law, for the right to speak out, for justice, and for religious freedom, all sometimes subsumed under the umbrella of democracy (in various definitions and with many contradictions). This dynamic kicks in under different circumstances, especially when the country does not feel threatened and also when the leadership doesn't quite seem to have its act together or when some of the leadership is advocating change in some of these directions.

The two dynamics do not necessarily lead to a decisive outcome for one or the other. Some combination of indecision, leadership conflict, popular dissent, and Japanese-style economic mismanagement and stagnation could lead to a (possibly long) period of repressive stagnation. But it is important to understand that the gears can change very quickly.

The Transformation of the Party's Role

This book has highlighted a crucial change in the Party's relationship to society. In the Deng Xiaoping and Jiang Zemin eras, the Party stepped back from detailed control of people's lives, both in the rural areas when it dismantled the communes and in the urban areas when it reduced direct control of the SOEs, let most of the SOEs (the smaller ones) move out of central government control, and freed people to choose their own jobs, locations, spouses, and much else. As I have emphasized, for Party leaders looking forward, this entailed a frightening loss of Party control over vast areas of social life. But the benefits to the larger society were so great that these decisions actually strengthened Party leadership. People were grateful.

Now, as I have also emphasized, the next layer of broad economic gains requires the Party to step back further from direct control of the banks, the SOEs, and the courts. The Party's own goals require this. For instance, the renminbi (RMB) will never become an important reserve currency as long as the Party controls the relevant courts. More importantly, interest group conflicts and resentment will boil over into protest more and more if there is no widely trusted judicial and political adjudication and interest aggregation system. And Party leaders recognize much of this; that is why, for instance, they have called for stock market listings to occur based on market criteria rather than on Party priorities enforced by the China Securities Regulatory Commission licensing requirements.

There is a vast struggle, focused on the SOEs, over whether the "market allocation of resources" emphasized in the economic plans will take priority or whether the Party's efforts to strengthen its detailed control over enterprise decisions and other allocation decisions will prove victorious. Xi Jinping's own statements, that market allocation of resources and SOE reform will be enforced and that Party control over enterprises will be strengthened, embody this struggle. These contradictory goals can be compromised, but the leadership cannot have its cake and eat it too. This is a defining moment, and the question at hand needs to be specified very precisely: will the Communist Party seek to strengthen its role by continuing to seek the broadest social and economic benefits, at the cost of abandoning many crucial levers of direct power, or will it seek to retain direct controls at the cost of slower economic growth? At the time of writing, those who take a narrow, maintain-the-detailed-tools-of-Party-control strategy dominate Beijing. But there are numerous advocates, including at high levels, of providing the broadest social benefits at the cost of abandoning many of the Party's detailed levers of control, particularly over the judicial system.

Stock market controls provide an indicator of the tension between the two viewpoints. The government has decided that the stock market listing system must change from one where a Party-designated regulator chooses which companies will list and when to a system where any company can list if it meets appropriate criteria. But insiders believe that resistance will delay the shift for five years.

Of course, the Party leaders assert that the Party's interests coincide with those of the broader society. That is what political leaders in all countries say. But the reality of all leaders in all countries is that leaders' and parties' interests are not coterminous with those of society. If the Chinese Communist Party continues on the path toward being an interest group rather than a vanguard, it will maximize its control in the short run but grievously impair it in the long run.

The Reality of Change

Chinese are much more conscious than Westerners that, like their economy, their polity is still developing. China under Xi has a very different political dynamic from China under Hu, and China under Hu had a very different dynamic from China under Jiang. The ideology changes. The structure of the leadership changes. The relationship between the center and the periphery changes. Americans think that the difference between Bush 43 and Obama is important, and on some scale it certainly is, but the basic structure remains the same. Compared with those occurring in emerging countries, US debates actually take place within a very narrow consensus. The consensus in China is that political development is not yet at an advanced stage, that as with the economy there is a long path upward. But there is no consensus about the end state either of the economy or of the polity. This is not Leonid Brezhnev's ossified Soviet Union. However, the gradual transformation of the Communist Party's role from a national vanguard into an interest group is the central political tendency of the Hu Jintao and Xi Jinping eras. The tension between the vanguard role and the interest group role is exhibited dramatically in the tensions over China's response to the complexity revolution. There is a clear plan to respond to the economic aspects of the complexity revolution but no comparable plan to respond to equally compelling political aspects. And the clear economic plan is obstructed by a powerful effort to maintain political controls that are inconsistent with it.

Overview

The Communist Party has rebuilt and created a society with considerable resilience. Chinese society today faces huge economic and social problems, but the leadership has addressed them forthrightly and forcefully. The degree to which it has created an inclusive society, managed the shape-shifting problem of inequality, tackled corruption, helped displaced SOE workers find new jobs, and begun to tackle environmental degradation contrasts sharply with neighboring countries like India and the Philippines. The contrast with US politicians' refusal to address the technology-driven job crisis forthrightly, and indeed to blame it on China, is equally sharp.

Likewise, the Party's ability to conceptualize China's current economic situation and to formulate detailed conclusions from the general premise of market allocation of resources is a historic achievement.

However, implementation of impressive plans is a political issue. A political strategy that infringes the interests of every major power group in Chinese society simultaneously is highly risky. For the first time in the reform era the regime's ability to implement vital changes decisively is unclear. Xi Jinping's second term will be crucial. If all the accumulation of power in the first term is put to decisive use in the second term, he and the system will both be vindicated. If not, China's economic progress and political morale will be seriously degraded.

The centralization of power under Xi Jinping had a valid, and widely accepted, collective purpose: to reverse the dangerous devolution of authority that had begun under Hu Jintao, to suppress widespread corruption in very powerful quarters, and to ram through painful economic reforms against fierce opposition. But the results so far have not been decisive reform; rather, the decision process has slowed, officials have become fearful to act, and the safety valve of the top leader's being able to blame and fire powerful subordinates has been lost.

For all its accumulation of centralized power, the Xi administration has so far proved strategically indecisive. What I have called the ten great paradoxes are monuments to strategic indecision. The tensions can be resolved, but they have not yet been resolved. Of course, that resolution need not always be achieved by tilting entirely in one direction. The debate over how they should be resolved has been less forthright than the purely economic analysis, and the lack of movement has so far sacrificed many of the principal benefits expected from economic reform.

The anti-corruption campaign, like the economic reforms, is a vital necessity for continuation of the regime. Unlike the economic reforms, it has proceeded with gusto. But its methods and outcome remain in doubt. It has not employed the successful methods of Jiang Zemin and Zhu Rongji: cutting back the bureaucracy, enhancing competition, and limiting the military's role in economic life. Its efforts to reduce bribe-opportunity regulations, unlike Zhu's, appear to be ineffectual. The risk is that the campaign could push back the tide here and there, but be gradually submerged in the longer run. Moreover, the end-game in the other Asian miracle economies, all of which have drastically curtailed although not completely eliminated corruption, has always required independent courts supported by an engaged citizenry and outspoken media. Establishing permanent anti-corruption commissions throughout China, as seems to be the current plan, runs three risks as long as they are controlled by a political party. They could become instruments of local political conflict, they could become *perceived* as instruments of local political conflict, and they could deaden the entrepreneurial initiative of local governments that is so crucial to China's rapid growth. The anti-corruption campaign is the principal source of legitimacy of the Xi administration; it is difficult to overstate the potential negative consequences if it is seen, a few years from now, as having failed to institutionalize positive results.

While Party policies seek broad social benefits historically associated with the term "socialism," the effort to enhance legitimacy by appeal to a more primitive form of Marxism, and by suppressing the history of Mao's errors, will achieve little and may do harm. Nationalism has more appeal as a source of legitimacy, but can turn easily against the administration or lead to dangerous conflicts.

The Party itself is behaving less like an arbiter of the greater social good and more like an interest group. The Party that surrendered detailed control over farms, many companies, and individuals' life choices (jobs, location, marriage) in service of greater prosperity for the whole society is now hoarding its detailed controls over SOEs, courts, and capital markets. In Taiwan this kind of shift by the Guomindang presaged diluted legitimacy and future weakness.

While the conceptual response to the economics of the complexity revolution has been a triumph, the political response to the complexity revolution has been crude: a wave of repression, often gratuitous repression such as the measures against religious and feminist groups, that betokens fear[20] rather than incisive analysis and confident leadership.

Fearful repression can lead to explosive consequences, as the fate of Park Chung Hee shows, particularly if economic progress seems curtailed. In China this could mean sudden displacement of a leadership team or a split in the Party.

---

[20] This is not the shared social fear that underlies an Asian miracle, a fear that inspires leaders to take great risks and achieve great things, supported by a people whose shared fear leads them to accept extraordinary disruption. This is a paralyzing fear experienced by officials fearful for their individual jobs, and by a Party that is fearful of losing its power and its emoluments if it surrenders any of its levers of control.

6 | *What Will Happen?*

The flux in China today is too rapid, and the opacity of political strategy too great, to forecast with great confidence the exact outcome. When I wrote *The Rise of China: How Economic Reform Is Creating the Next Superpower*, I could see that Deng Xiaoping and his immediate successors were learning from South Korea, Taiwan, Singapore, and to some extent Japan, and were implementing a model that should therefore work. It was a model that Western commentators have always hated, but the cat caught mice. The only question was whether they could scale it up creatively to the continental and billion-person scale of China. They have answered that question, vigorously and affirmatively. But there is no evidence whatsoever that Xi Jinping is a student of the earlier Asian miracles in the way that Deng Xiaoping and Zhu Rongji were. And there is no successful precedent among the Asian miracles for a strategy that accedes to the complexity revolution economically but tries to repress it politically.

The Chinese system, and the position of the Communist Party there, have enormous strengths. China has, in a little more than one generation, lifted a society of 1.4 billion people largely out of poverty, an achievement unique in world history. It has lifted all major social groups – not equally but with huge economic gains to every social group, including minorities. Beyond income, the government has given most of the population a substantial stake in society, particularly through jobs and housing policies, and therefore a stake in stability of the system. The Chinese people are aware of this, and most are profoundly grateful for it. According to valid polls conducted by Western standards, the overwhelming majority of the population sees the central government as having benevolent intentions and, notwithstanding serious mistakes, as having largely fulfilled those intentions. There are ethnic minorities, notably in Tibet and Xinjiang, with severe political discontents, but they are too small to shake the overall stability of the system. Although China has diverse dialects, cuisines, and

256

customs, well over 90 percent of the people identify themselves as Han Chinese and have a patriotic attachment to China. This is a society with a solid foundation. The common Western media image of a people feeling terribly oppressed by their government is a fiction. The idea, popular through the turn of the century in some Western academic and think tank circles, that mainland China is vulnerable to fragmentation was always a fantasy, a fantasy that became prominent in part because of generous funding by Taiwan's President Lee Deng-hui. The trend of recent generations has been a reunification of China and a strengthening of its foundations after an interlude of weakness and disunity.

In China as in the other Asian miracle economies, a performance-oriented government administration provides a solid stable core that will survive any foreseeable circumstances, including potential structural changes in the political system. There will not be another Cultural Revolution. There will not be an uprising that will destroy this governmental core – unless it destroys itself.

A strong role for the Communist Party is likewise deeply entrenched. The Chinese people have benefited sufficiently that they are prepared to put aside resentments over the catastrophic, bloody mistakes of the Mao era. Likewise, each of the Asian miracle societies (except Singapore) and the near-miracle Asian societies, like Indonesia and Thailand, has suffered some analogue of June 4, 1989, in most cases proportionately worse ones, and their peoples have let larger successes overshadow the massacres. (History does show, however, that ultimately people put these disasters behind them more easily if the regime faces up to them rather than trying to hide them as current Chinese leaders are doing.) What happened around Tiananmen Square on June 4, 1989, was morally repugnant and gratuitously violent, but the idea that it is uniquely awful is a Western ideological fiction that can't withstand any comparative look at the numbers or processes involved.

What dominates in the minds of the overwhelming majority of the Chinese people is that Communist Party leadership has achieved and preserved national unity and peace and brought a degree of prosperity that seemed unimaginable four decades ago. Taiwan's Guomindang, Singapore's People's Action Party, and Japan's Liberal Democratic Party display how the benefits of economic success perpetuate themselves in public support of parties with authoritarian legacies of varying degrees. Dominant parties can fritter away these benefits, as

Taiwan's Guomindang has done in part, but it would take an extraordinary degree of economic and political mismanagement to dislodge the Chinese Communist Party from a central, although not necessarily exclusive, role in China's future politics.

Having said that, the political side of the complexity revolution must be faced eventually, and failing to face it for too long could risk all of the favorable legacy. The era when fear simplified politics is long past. The diversification of the economy and the emergence of huge interest groups creates an era when politics can no more be managed in detail by a central bureaucracy than the economy can. Just as the complexity of the economy means that the government must cede more and more control to the market, the complexity of the polity requires some kind of "automated" method for aggregating and adjudicating the myriad conflicting interests. Some of the wisest, most successful, and (very importantly) toughest leaders in the modern world – Lee Kwan Yew, Jiang Jingguo, South Korea's Korean CIA chief, South Korea's subsequent military leaders – have concluded that it is just as necessary to make "market adjustments" to the political side as it is to the economic side. All concluded that one can sit on the lid of the boiling pot only so long. Deng Xiaoping accepted that lesson and as a general point repeatedly called for political reform – while vigorously reacting against leaders like Zhao Ziyang who seemed to him to be going too fast or potentially letting uncontrollable forces gain momentum. None of China's communist leaders has defined the desired end-state of Chinese politics; unlike the ossified USSR leadership they have all, to varying degrees, acknowledged that China's politics is just as much a work in progress as its economy.

The complexity revolution, and the revolution in popular expectations (moving up the Maslow hierarchy) are facts – important, incontrovertible facts. After one clears the cobwebs of Washington's ideology that US-style institutions work everywhere, and of resurgent efforts by some Chinese leaders to put everything in an obsolete Marxist-Leninist framework, the facts of the complexity revolution and of people's rising expectations about personal dignity remain. They are the political face of the economic and social facts. They require as thoughtful and clear-headed a strategy as the economic strategy. Attempting to deal with them by forcing them into the mold of what worked in a simpler era, or by reviving old ideological formulae, will impose social costs at least as expensive as would ignoring the economic facts.

Unwillingness to accept the political implications of the complexity revolution has led to what I termed the ten great paradoxes.

In economics, the administration has faced a choice of either intensive reform accompanied by much slower short-term growth (because the reforms require restructuring and deleveraging) with a dividend of higher growth later or, alternatively, debt-fueled higher growth and slower reform followed by years of much slower growth. So far, unwilling to resolve the ten great paradoxes, it has chosen the latter. This is not the choice Deng or Jiang would have made.

Likewise, in politics the Xi administration faces a choice between two strategies. One would be a sequel to the reforms of Deng Xiaoping and Zhu Rongji: step back from direct political controls over the lives of farmers (through the communes) and the factories (through detailed management of the SOEs) and strengthen support for the Party through the positive reaction of the people to the ensuing economic growth. Today such a strategy would entail stepping back from direct Party control of the legal system, the capital markets, and SOE strategies by the Party committees. So far, the Xi administration has chosen a fearful insistence on retaining direct controls over legal decisions and SOE strategies, and it has stalled on its promise to remove political controls over capital markets (such as stock market listings). This is a repudiation of the approach that created such success under previous leaders.

Given China's enormous strengths under Communist Party rule, the potentially overwhelming force of the complexity revolution, and the current administration's seemingly gratuitous alienation of key sectors, we face the old question, what happens when an irresistible force meets an immovable object? Anyone who has a precise answer probably hasn't thought sufficiently about the question, but a first approximation to the answer is: something different.

Economic failure, due to possible failure to implement reforms, would force changes in the political structure, because, for all the legacy of popular gratitude, the Communist Party has built its legitimacy on economic performance. It must either continue to perform or it must amend the basis of legitimacy. Performance does not mean indefinite continuation of 10 percent growth. That rate always fades with the passing of the early economic and political simplicities and with the exhaustion of opportunities for easy catch-up in technology and management. Indefinite continuation of 6 percent growth would be a spectacular success, but even that is difficult and unlikely without drastic alteration of current policies.

Paradoxically, economic success would also force political change. With success, the complexity revolution will only become more complex. The expectations of people for more personal and group dignity will only increase. The availability of information that stimulates critical views, and the increase of education that inculcates complex thinking, will only increase regardless of careful textbook editing and technological marvels of internet control.

Given this context, based on the experience of the other Asian miracle economies, there are several ways that China can evolve. The future will undoubtedly merge and mix and match combinations of these scenarios, but they are likely to provide the main themes.

Consolidation First Term, Economic Reform Second Term, Political Reform Later

It has become customary, although not constitutionally required, that Chinese top leaders get two five-year terms. The scenario that many Chinese are hoping for is that Xi Jinping spends his first five-year term consolidating power and his second term using that power to ram through decisive economic reforms. While there is already extensive disappointment that reform has not moved faster, China is so large and complex that it can indeed take five years to consolidate power. (It takes 18 months for a US president to consolidate a new administration, and China is proportionately bigger and more complex.) The center of gravity of Chinese opinion is to give him great leeway to consolidate power and then decisively enact reform in the period 2018–2022. If he were to follow this scenario, popular support for the anti-corruption campaign would carry him through his first term and then a critical mass of top elite support plus some popular support for economic reform would carry him through his second term. Then anxiety about the economy would pass and his successor would have to come up with a clear plan for managing the new era of political complexity.

A successfully reforming, confident China would have the domestic authority to clean up the environment, deleverage the country's debt, and undertake the great tax/fiscal reform that is required. Such a China would be a steadier negotiating partner on difficult international issues.

Domestic politics would be less likely to force the leadership to act tough on key international issues because of domestic vulnerability, as with Hu Jintao, or because of desperate need for military support of reform, as in Xi Jinping's first term. That does not mean it would back off easily from issues where it disagrees with the United States, but it would be a predictable force in international affairs with a strong interest in the overall stability of the international system. Note that this conclusion is the opposite of the widespread assumption, particularly in military circles and among political science advocates of inexorable conflict between rising powers and established powers, that a more successful China will be a more difficult China.

A reform success would enable China to become a global leader, in the mode of Japan and (post-Trump) probably well ahead of the United States, in addressing climate change and environmental problems. This is in China's self-interest to do, because China itself is so much more vulnerable than the United States both to climate change and to further deterioration in the sea, the air, and the soil. Likewise a reform success would make the Belt and Road Initiative feasible and begin to curtail the economic woes that have made Central Asia, the Middle East, and North Africa the most unstable parts of the world. China would then be an acknowledged leader of globalization and a force for stability in what are currently the world's most unstable areas.

Successful economic reform does not make subsequent political reform inevitable, but political issues will eventually have to be on the agenda. They will either get much better or much worse. As we have seen with Taiwan and South Korea, this kind of economic success creates the social prerequisites to make a more liberal society work – without in any way guaranteeing that a liberal option will be tried. Xi Jinping is sitting on the lid of a boiling kettle. If economic progress seems good in the face of severe problems, the boiling kettle will not explode in the short term. But if the political repression does not seem to be buying successful economic reform, then the mood will shift, possibly quite suddenly. Similarly, if, later, the debt crisis and the transition to a new model of growth seem to have been largely resolved, then pressures will grow to address the political structure. As noted above, the paradox of repressive reform is that *either economic failure or economic success will eventually bring political modernization to the top of the agenda.*

Again it is useful to emphasize that most leaders of the Chinese Communist Party acknowledge their political structure to be a developing story. Every reform administration has been drastically different from its predecessor. The Western public and commentariat generally do not understand this, except as technical details, because so many in the West see political structures in Manichean terms: good democracies and bad dictatorships, with communist dictatorships being the worst kind. But I write these words a day after attending a brilliant lecture by planners reporting to the State Council, who passed out a chart of developments between 2017 and 2050, with a goal of (undefined) democracy by 2050. The previous month a leading administrator from Peking University gave an impassioned lecture at Harvard about the need for democracy and the rule of law; the Party leaders know his views and he keeps his job. Future progress is in no way guaranteed, but neither is continued regression locked in.

As of 2017, the prospects for the positive scenario of successful consolidation of power, then successful economic reform followed by political reform later (under Xi or someone else) are both dimmer and more urgent than they seemed at the beginning of Xi Jinping's tenure. The pushback against reform from most power elites is strong. The trend of increased political repression is even stronger.

Xi was allocated great powers in order to implement great reforms, but his personal political base was never strong. What the Party gives, the Party can take away. Xi Jinping has so far been far more effective at eliminating competitors than at implementing decisive reforms. Moreover, Prime Minister Li Keqiang has been severely weakened, first by Xi Jinping's overriding decisions but also by the failure to move decisively on SOE reforms and the mishandling of stock market volatility. The administration has the full panoply of titles and positions and propaganda, but it is at risk if it does not deliver decisively in 2018–2019 on reforms and growth.

Reform Failure/Japan Scenario

Economic reform success is not assured. Resistance is widespread, and each quarter that passes enables resistance to become more and more organized behind the scenes. It is therefore conceivable for Xi Jinping to maintain power and stability throughout his first term, while propping up the economy with fiscal and monetary stimulus, but rather than consolidating reformist power he could prove unable to move his reform agenda forward decisively. This scenario delivers higher growth in the short run, but much lower growth in the longer term. This China would be slow-growing for the same reason that Japan grows slowly – reactionary interest groups controlling the political system and inhibiting competitive change in the economic structure. The shift to a consumer- and services-driven economy would slow, the great infrastructure-building programs would slow, and the resources available to the Belt and Road Initiative and the military would decline at the margin. In this scenario, unlike Japan, interest group power would inhibit or block critical environmental reforms.

In such a scenario China's growth would not be as slow as Japan's, but the slowing would come at a time when China remains much poorer than Japan and has just begun the immense task of funding its pension, medical insurance, unemployment, and other social programs. Thus the burden of caring for an aging population would weigh more heavily than it does in Japan. Because Chinese are so aware of conditions in the rest of the world, the expectations for improvement in standards of living would be much higher than in already-wealthy Japan. Political discontent at the decline of great hopes would not be as easily assuaged, so movements would emerge demanding a different economic and political model.

In this scenario, Chinese leaders would be more vulnerable to criticism for failure of the great international ambitions that have been announced in the early Xi Jinping years, and they would be under even more pressure to show their toughness. Since the beginning of the twentieth century, whenever they were discontented with their own leaders, Chinese students have expressed discontent by mounting demonstrations against Japan, because it is safer than demonstrating against their own leaders. A pattern of increasingly vigorous anti-Japanese and anti-American movements, muted during the 1994–2014 period of university-based support for the leadership, would likely arise in this scenario. Chinese leaders fear these movements, and would react in part by acting toughly toward the United States and particularly Japan.

A scenario of economic reform failure combined with highly repressive politics of the kind that has emerged under Xi Jinping might well lead to earlier domestic political unrest. That in turn could lead to increasing use of the military to ensure domestic stability and to a much bigger role for the military in China's governance. Military units could well start taking dangerous initiatives without clear mandates from civilian authority, or with support from particular Party factions, or with the acquiescence of intimidated Party leaders. This is one of two particularly dangerous scenarios for regional peace. As Susan Shirk has educated us in *China: Fragile Superpower*,[1] contrary to conventional wisdom, the dangers of a confrontational China come more from leadership weakness than from strength.

Leadership Fracture

If Xi Jinping imposes the high degree of repression that has already occurred, without being able to implement decisive economic reforms, sustain belief in a long-term rapid rise of living standards, and institutionalize the anti-corruption campaign, he will lose the support of the "masses," which currently give him overwhelming popular support. If he frightens, and damages the economic interests of, every major interest group in China in the name of reform and anti-corruption, without actually making rapid progress on economic reform in the early years of his second term, the leadership could fracture, and that fracture would coincide with a shift in popular sentiment to what I called above the second dynamic, a dynamic focused on the family, on comfort, on freedom. If under these conditions he attempts to remain the top leader even after serving the conventional two terms, both popular and leadership support would likely dwindle.

China could then return to the kind of split it saw between conservative leaders like Li Peng and reformist leaders like Zhao Ziyang in the late 1980s. Under Jiang Zemin in the 1990s, the Party leader kept the peace between Zhu Rongji, who was undertaking stressful market reforms, and Li Peng, who remained more of a traditional bureaucratic socialist. Under Xi Jinping nobody is performing such a balancing faction. One force, Xi Jinping, is in charge, holding most of the key titles and taking all the initiatives, while others ponder their resentments and quietly organize resistance – very strong albeit not public resistance. In this situation, a credible allegation of failure could bring powerful antagonisms into the open. An early indicator will be the negotiations over who will be promoted to the Politburo Standing

---

[1] Susan Shirk, *China: Fragile Superpower. How China's Internal Politics Could Derail Its Peaceful Rise* (Oxford: Oxford University Press, 2007).

Committee for Xi's second term, but the open split could come later, if the new team does not seem to be making rapid progress.

Signs of potential leadership fracture abound, in relatively mild protests at the annual National People's Congress (NPC) meeting, in accounts of the intense hostility and fear that is endemic in Beijing, and even in high-level rumors about assassination attempts. In 2017 the political atmosphere in Beijing is extraordinarily tense. Investment outside the housing sector is collapsing. As previously noted, the rate of increase of private investment has collapsed. China's wealthy and much of the middle class want their money and their children relocated outside of China. The strong popular support that the administration received as a result of its anti-corruption campaign could reverse very quickly if the economic reform seems permanently stalled, if spending to keep the economy growing fast creates a severe financial problem, or if the anti-corruption campaign comes to be seen as largely self-serving. Opposition to Xi is dispersed, fearful, and offset by widespread hopes that his implementation of policies will prove as impressive as his destruction of adversaries. But it is intense among groups that are well-organized, well-funded, articulate and respected. If Xi disappoints, opposition could suddenly coalesce.

An open leadership fracture would likely be particularly intense for several reasons. The groups whose interests have been hurt are exceptionally numerous and powerful. The individuals whose careers have been destroyed are exceptionally powerful and still have powerful backers. National security issues would quickly come to the forefront. One consequence of repressive domestic politics is that negative feelings toward Beijing's leadership have broadened and consolidated in Taiwan and Hong Kong. For the foreseeable future peaceful rapprochement with Taiwan under a single flag has become impossible, meaning that there is no chance of unification short of war. Moreover, because of the way China has handled the maritime disputes, countries that once were sympathetic to China's claims over Taiwan now are likely to see any kind of unification as a security threat to themselves. So the question "Who lost Taiwan?" will be at the forefront of domestic politics, and the question of whether to use force against Taiwan will emerge at the forefront of national security debates.

Such an open split would be dangerous for China and might well make foreign policy even more of a domestic political football than it has been. If internecine elite conflict persisted indefinitely, it could slow the economy even more than in the Japan scenario, and it could begin to erode the legitimacy of the Communist Party.

This scenario would be the worst for China and the worst for the rest of the world. Aside from the negative economic impact on the rest of the world, Chinese foreign and security policies would become unpredictable and foreign powers might get drawn into the domestic Chinese conflicts.

At the same time it could lead to the kind of deep reflections about China's political response to its new social structure that parallel the brilliant economic plans developed in response to that same new social structure. That is what happened in South Korea in 1979 and afterward: a political and economic crisis led to President Park's downfall and inaugurated a process – a very bumpy process that included years of dictatorship – toward a more responsive political system.

Gradual Democratization, Likely a Variant of the Japan Political Model

The new political complexity of China must eventually be faced. If there is an indefinitely long effort to sit on the boiling pot, trying to use force to repress the emergence of a new politics, then some combination of instability, leadership fracture, and military rule seems virtually inevitable. All Asian miracle economies have had to confront the political consequences of a more complex, more mobilized society by undertaking transformative evolution of their political system. The social changes are objectively enormous; they demand a response.

That response need not necessarily be detailed emulation of US- or EU-style democracy. China has shown that it can transcend many Western economic shibboleths on the way to economic success. Perhaps it can do so on the political side too. Anyway, the detailed institutions of Western representative government are increasingly stressed. In polls the US Congress barely attracts double-digit levels of support, and in 2016 US candidates for the presidency were without exception regarded with net public disdain. Citizens increasingly express their concerns in the street, not by writing to their Congressmen. Both in the United States and in Europe the representativeness of existing forms of representative democracy is widely questioned. Nobody has a good alternative, but Americans don't think their Congressmen really represent them, British people reject the representativeness of Europoliticians and Eurocrats, and Scottish people doubt the representativeness of the UK parliament. In Europe as a whole, antipathy to the EU is becoming a majority view, and anti-elitist movements are disturbing individual countries. In the United States, of all the major national institutions, only the military is held in high regard. Anyone with a sense of history recognizes that as an ominous development in a democracy. Change is afoot; history has not ended. China's challenges are an order of magnitude greater – hence far more threatening but also perhaps a greater inspiration to creativity.

Everywhere, including China, the ideal of "democracy" – outside the West a vague term signifying some degree of popular input and governance in the common good – remains preeminent. To Chinese, the idea of "democratization" at some very abstract level has always been a goal and remains attractive. But within China the case for Western-style democracy has weakened. The social and economic failings of poor-country democracies like the Philippines, Thailand, and India are much more vivid for Chinese than they are for Washington and Brussels. The great Western financial crisis of 2008 has weakened admiration for the Western model in general. The United Kingdom's Brexit, the election of Trump in the United States, and the EU's ongoing economic and populist crisis diminish respect for Western democracy. The catastrophic results of post-Soviet Russia's effort at shock therapy democratization and marketization frighten many Chinese who might otherwise advocate Western-style democracy. Above all, US military efforts to encircle and contain China, along with the constant pillorying and subversion of China by two anti-China Congressional commissions, Radio Free Asia, the National Endowment for Democracy, and much else, and fear of Western-inspired color revolutions, mean that adoption of a Western political model would come across as a humiliating national defeat in the eyes of most Chinese. Ironically, few things support autocratic forces in China more than the constant pro-democracy propaganda and military pressure out of Washington.

Nonetheless, China's dilemma remains. For China any solution must be some analogue of a market for aggregating interests in a way that does not require the leadership or the central bureaucracy to impose decisions on each of a myriad of issues. People want to feel that their voices are heard. Awareness of rights, as defined in Chinese law or in Western ideas, is pervasive in China. The society must come to terms with the contradiction between betting the economic future on globalization and trying to constrict the information link between the Chinese people and the rest of the globe.

The rest of the world has so far found only two reliable mechanisms for managing the complexity revolution. For areas where there is a high degree of stability in beliefs about what is right, and where high stability is needed for economic agreements to prosper, rule under law is the mechanism that provides automatic decision-making without the constant intervention of political leaders. For areas where society's needs change and groups' preferences change, some kind of representative democracy aggregates social demands through a process that leads to widely accepted outcomes without imposition by top leaders or violent strife.

For decades China's leaders and thought leaders have been pondering the need for a more sophisticated way to handle political issues. This is the last phase of China's century-long debate about how to adapt to the challenge of modernization that came from the West in the middle of the nineteenth century. In both China and Japan, that debate began with minimalism: acquire Western weapons while retaining traditional institutions and culture. The subsequent gambit was to acquire Western technology while retaining traditional Chinese institutions and culture.[2] All such limited strategies proved inadequate, so, over the course of more than a century China has adopted and adapted aspects of Western weaponry, civilian technology, government administrative systems, civilian management systems, constitution, monetary and fiscal management, law, finance, competition, innovation systems, university structures, educational curricula, intellectual property, most Western established norms of trade and international investment, and the principal establishment institutions (the WTO, IMF, and World Bank) – along with much else.

Western, particularly US, commentary about China has tended to take the successful adaptations for granted and to focus on relatively marginal continuing frictions. It is easy to forget how ridiculous it would have seemed only a generation ago for someone in Washington to have suggested that China would one day accept enforcement of WTO trade rulings. The extent to which the post-World War II system

---

[2] For a more thorough and sophisticated presentation of the great Chinese debates than this necessarily oversimplified summary, see Orville Schell and John DeLury, *Wealth and Power: China's Long March to the Twenty-First Century* (New York: Random House, 2013).

was able to accommodate China's needs is an extraordinary tribute to the Western, largely US and UK, founders of that system. The extent to which China has been able to dovetail its own needs with that system is an extraordinary tribute to China's post-1979 leadership.

In some cases China's adoption has been partial (the idea of a constitution) or incomplete (the evolving legal system, protection of intellectual property) or a synthesis of traditional and Western (Confucian bureaucracy, Western bureaucracy, the Communist Party as an evolution of the dynastic Censorate). Some of the adaptations have been more efficient than their Western counterparts, most notably the overall economic development strategy, which emulated South Korea and Taiwan while rejecting core Western shibboleths. Some aspects have been uniquely Chinese, most notably the one country, two systems, one sector, two systems, and one company, two systems transition strategies. Overall, this process has so far led to a remarkable, and remarkably successful, synthesis. But there is as yet no political synthesis and nothing like a domestic political consensus. Moreover, the lack of a political synthesis is now interfering with economic reform, with the tension between political control and market efficiency in the ten areas I identified earlier and more.

There is always a debate going on inside China, at high levels, about political reform as well as economic reform. There was rapid political reform during the years 1980–2002, and even under the stasis of the Hu Jintao era there have been efforts to refine the system of elections within the Party and to demand that officials expecting promotion display a "democratic" mentality. Currently most of the debate is repressed and invisible to outsiders, but it continues and cannot be stopped.[3] Xi Jinping has made it risky to express creative thoughts, and the United States' confrontational posture has made advocating Western-style democracy unpatriotic. For the time being, that has put the Taiwan model, of starting elections at the bottom and gradually

---

[3] For a brief and particularly eloquent statement, just as the Xi Jinping administration was beginning, see Yu Keping, "How to Push Forward Orderly Democracy in China," *Beijing News*, July 13, 2013, www.bjnews.com.cn/opinion/2013/07/13/273079.html (in Chinese). Professor Yu has not changed his opinions and has become a dean at Peking University, one of China's two most prestigious universities. Serving under him are numerous professors whose democratic opinions are much stronger than his but who are very cautious in the current environment. That is true throughout China.

moving them up the political ladder, off the table; not so long ago it was very much on the table. Invigoration of the NPC has made significant progress, but it remains a part-time reviewer of legislation and auditor of government performance, not an institution that authoritatively aggregates all the conflicting interests of Chinese society. Elections within the Party have made a great deal of progress, now receding somewhat, but moving toward the Japanese model, where public elections modify the balance of factions within a dominant party, would require open factions within the Communist Party and a mechanism for the public to influence the balance of those factions.

The concept of democracy (as opposed to the specific institutions of Western democracy), which is currently embodied in village elections, accountability reviews and occasional outspokenness in the NPC, and a variety of elections inside the Party, remains legitimate and acceptable in all parts of Chinese society. Some influential political leaders find the Japanese dominant-party system highly attractive and are studying it carefully. Singapore remains the most admired model, but it is very hard to scale up, and Singapore is being forced by internal pressures to evolve in ways (more acceptance of opposition legislators and diverse opinions, less use of imported foreigners even if they have superior expertise) that Xi Jinping seemingly would find unacceptable. Either a crisis or a successful economic reform followed by the advent of a new administration in 2023 could lead to a revival of open advocacy of liberalizing political reform. If that seems ludicrous given the heightening authoritarianism under Xi, one must recall how decisively China has changed each time it has transitioned from one leadership to the next.

Which of these scenarios is more likely? The scenario of a relatively smooth consolidation in the first term and a relatively smooth implementation of economic reforms in Xi's second term remains possible, but it will fade quickly if there seems to be no decisive progress immediately following the choice of a new Politburo Standing Committee in the autumn of 2017.

The other scenarios are not mutually exclusive. We may see them in some sequence. One way to have indicators of direction is to compare today's China with the other Asian miracle economies as they hit the era of complexity revolution. Xi Jinping is definitely not following the pragmatic political adjustments of Jiang Jingguo's Taiwan or the longer-delayed ones of contemporary Singapore. Like

Park Chung Hee in the late 1970s, he is doubling down on the old approach of political repression.

Does this mean that China today is like South Korea in 1979? The simultaneous buildup of financial problems and political repression is certainly analogous. (China's debt is local rather than foreign, and inflation is controlled, but even so the financial risks are rising.) China has a much more inspiring economic plan than Park did, and widespread support for Xi's anti-corruption campaign, but a lot more resistance to implementing a new economic direction than South Korea's government had. Elite questioning of the administration's direction in China in 2017 is perhaps similar to South Korea in 1979, but popular Chinese enthusiasm for Xi's anti-corruption campaign and reformist agenda had no counterpart in South Korea at the end of the Park era. Xi's problem is that, if the anti-corruption campaign and the economic reforms seem to be failing to achieve their results, the popular support could reverse overnight. Already there are early signs of youth restlessness, shown most prominently in the rise of youth populism on the internet. The risks of a Japanese-style stalemate with the interest groups, or of an open split within the leadership, are serious and rising.

If either of those happens, the inclination of most of the leadership would be to leave Xi in place but take the papers off his desk. Although it is dangerous to rule out any scenario in a crisis, the institutionalized Chinese system is not inclined toward military coups, assassinations, or sudden public repudiation of a leader. China is not Thailand or Egypt. But passions are high, and Xi's tough actions toward his opponents have raised the stakes in elite conflict.

Xi Jinping has chosen the most risky political strategy of any leader of a serious country today. If one looks for examples of leaders who have taken on every major interest group simultaneously, one comes up with a very short list: the Shah of Iran in the late 1970s, the Polish leadership at the beginning of 1980, a few others. To escape their fate, he very much needs that economic plan to begin to show fruit visibly and soon. He needs to show that the anti-corruption plan is not a broom pushing back the tide.

Foreign risks magnify the domestic risks. On top of the domestic risks, Xi is simultaneously taking on the foreign business community and challenging the US Navy. His technological plans require high levels of foreign investment from the most sophisticated economies, but US, Japanese, and Taiwanese investments are declining just when they are most needed. The growth of the Chinese military is rapid and impressive, but it remains quite vulnerable and rests on the foundation of the economy's fragile finances. All the big countries are conducting themselves in ways intended to minimize the risks of major international conflict, but the risk of maritime escalation is there. The only likely outcome of an unexpectedly escalating major power conflict would be a humiliating, massively more mutually destructive, analogue of the Opium War. No power wants this, but then no leader in 1914 wanted a big war. No major bank wanted an escalating financial crisis in 2008. Banking leaders took big risks and assumed that, because they deemed themselves wise, the risks would not materialize. Nonetheless World War I happened and the Global Financial Crisis happened.

China is on the cusp of greatness, stagnation or tragedy, and the risks are so high that small, unexpected events could make the difference. That is the defining quality of China's crisis of success.

Index

Printed in the United States
By Bookmasters